Mastering C++ Game Development

Create professional and realistic 3D games using C++ 17

Mickey MacDonald

BIRMINGHAM - MUMBAI

Mastering C++ Game Development

Commissioning Editor: Amarabhab Banerjee
Acquisition Editors: Meeta Rajani
Content Development Editor: Devika Battike
Technical Editor: Mohd Riyan Khan
Copy Editor: Safis Editing, Dipti Mankame
Project Coordinator: Judie Jose
Proofreader: Safis Editing
Indexer: Pratik Shirodkar
Graphics: Tania Dutta
Production Coordinator: Nilesh Mohite

First published: January 2018

Production reference: 1240118

Published by Packt Publishing Ltd.
Livery Place
35 Livery Street
Birmingham
B3 2PB, UK.

ISBN 978-1-78862-922-5

www.packtpub.com

`mapt.io`

Mapt is an online digital library that gives you full access to over 5,000 books and videos, as well as industry leading tools to help you plan your personal development and advance your career. For more information, please visit our website.

Why subscribe?

- Spend less time learning and more time coding with practical eBooks and Videos from over 4,000 industry professionals

- Improve your learning with Skill Plans built especially for you

- Get a free eBook or video every month

- Mapt is fully searchable

- Copy and paste, print, and bookmark content

PacktPub.com

Did you know that Packt offers eBook versions of every book published, with PDF and ePub files available? You can upgrade to the eBook version at `www.PacktPub.com` and as a print book customer, you are entitled to a discount on the eBook copy. Get in touch with us at `service@packtpub.com` for more details.

At `www.PacktPub.com`, you can also read a collection of free technical articles, sign up for a range of free newsletters, and receive exclusive discounts and offers on Packt books and eBooks.

Contributors

About the author

Mickey MacDonald is a professional game designer and developer who has experience in developing both AAA and indie titles for a variety of gaming platforms and devices. Growing up, he always enjoyed playing video games, which inspired him to start creating his own. He is also a technical evangelist at Microsoft with focus on game development. As part of his role, a lot of his time is spent talking to other game developers and sharing the lessons he has learned in his development experiences. In his spare time, he enjoys researching video games and collecting vintage game consoles and computer systems.

*To my family and friends, who have always helped and supported me,
and to my grandfather, who taught me the joy of pursuing knowledge.*

A big thanks to the Packt Publishing team, who have worked tirelessly to bring this book to life. Thank you for the support, patience, and hard work!

About the reviewer

Bryan Griffiths is a software engineer who has worked in the gaming industry for more than 15 years and shipped multiple AAA, AR, VR, indie, mobile, and web games. In his career, he has worked on projects for most of the major publishers, including Microsoft, Apple, Sega, and Activision-Blizzard.

Most days, he can be found instructing the next generation of game developers from triOS College's Kitchener campus. Other days, he's out helping companies iterate on their game prototypes, expanding their teams with qualified individuals, or hunting down the last few bugs in a project before release.

I'd like to thank my parents for setting me on this path by constantly providing the tech and experiences that challenged me and broadened my mind throughout my childhood as well as Krystal and Kaizen for holding down the fort during crunch time.

Packt is searching for authors like you

If you're interested in becoming an author for Packt, please visit authors.packtpub.com and apply today. We have worked with thousands of developers and tech professionals, just like you, to help them share their insight with the global tech community. You can make a general application, apply for a specific hot topic that we are recruiting an author for, or submit your own idea.

Table of Contents

Preface

Although many languages are now being used to develop games, C++ remains the standard for professional development. The vast majority of libraries, engines, and toolchains are still being developed strictly in C++. Known for its performance and reliability, C++ continues to be the best option for true cross-platform compatibility.

By picking up this book, you are beginning your journey to mastering this powerful language. Although the journey will be long, it will be filled with discovery! Even after the countless hours I have spent working with C++, I still find myself filled with joy at finding new techniques and approaches. In this book, I want to give you the tools and understanding that will prepare you for continuing this learning journey. While new and flashy tools and engines will arise and potentially fall, having a strong understanding of how games, their tools, and engines are developed at a low level will provide you with valuable knowledge you can always lean on.

Who this book is for

This book is intended for intermediate to advanced C++ game developers who are looking to take their skills to the next level and learn the deep concepts of 3D game development. The reader will learn the key concepts used in the development of AAA-level games. Advanced topics, such as library creation, artificial intelligence, shader techniques, advanced effects and lighting, tool creation, physics, networking, and other critical game systems, will be covered throughout the journey.

What this book covers

Chapter 1, *C++ for Game Development*, covers some of the more advanced C++ topics used in modern game development. We will look at inheritance and polymorphism, pointers, referencing, and the common STL generic containers. The concept of templating and building generic code with class, function, and variable templates. Type inference and the new language keywords auto and decltype and their uses in combination with the new return value syntax. Finally, we will close out the chapter by looking at some core game patterns used today.

Chapter 2, *Understanding Libraries*, will teach the advanced topic of shareable libraries. We will look at the different types of libraries available. We will walk through the various ways you can create your own shareable libraries.

Chapter 3, *Building a Strong Foundation*, will take a look at the different methods of using object-oriented programming and polymorphism to create a reusable structure for all your game projects. We will walk through the differences in helper, managers, and interfaces classes with examples from real code.

Chapter 4, *Building the Asset Pipeline*, will cover a very important part of development, the handling of assets. We will take a look at the process of importing, processing, and managing content, such as sound, images, and 3D objects. With this groundwork system in place, we can move on to rounding out the rest of the systems needed for game development.

Chapter 5, *Building Gameplay Systems*, will cover a lot of ground and make strong progress in developing the core game systems needed to develop professional-grade projects. By the end of the chapter, we will have our own custom game state system that can be adopted by many of the other components in the game engine itself. We will develop our own custom camera system while building an understanding of how cameras work at a lower level. Finally, we will look at how we can add complete third-party game systems to our projects by adding the Bullet physics engine to our example engine.

Chapter 6, *Creating a Graphical User Interface*, will discuss the different aspects needed to create GUI. We will walk through its implementation, diving deep into the core architecture behind a working GUI. We will develop a panel and an element architecture complete with anchor points for controlling positioning. We will implement a user input structure using the observer design pattern and round it out by coding up the rendering pipe needed to display the GUI elements on the screen.

Chapter 7, *Advanced Rendering*, will cover the basics of working with shaders. We will learn how we can build a compiler and link abstraction layers to save us time. We will gain knowledge about lighting techniques theories and how we can implement them in shader language. Finally, we will close out the chapter by looking at other uses for shaders such as creating particle effects.

Chapter 8, *Advanced Gameplay Systems*, will dive deep into how you can include a scripting language such as Lua in your game projects. Then, we will build on that knowledge to examine ways of implementing dialog and quest systems into our example engine.

Chapter 9, *Artificial Intelligence*, will cover a large field of study in a short period of time. We will develop a basic definition of what game AI really is, and for that matter, what it is not. We will also look at expanding the decision-making functions with the inclusion of AI techniques. We will cover how AI agents' movements can be controlled through the use of steering forces and behavior. Finally, we will cap off the chapter by looking at the use of pathfinding algorithms to create paths from point to point for our AI agents.

Chapter 10, *Multiplayer*, will take big steps in the understanding of how multiplayer is implemented at a low level. You will learn about the TCP/IP stack and the different network topologies in use for game development. We looked at using UDP and TCP protocols in order to pass data to and from a client-server setup. Finally, we will look at some of the issues faced by developers when they start to implement multiplayer features.

Chapter 11, *Virtual Reality*, will be a quick introduction to the world of VR development; it should provide you with a great testing bed for your experience ideas. You will learn how to handle multiple view frusta and various hardware options, and finally look at how we could add VR support to our example engine using the OpenVR SDK.

To get the most out of this book

This book will assume some previous knowledge of C++. Having a basic understanding of game development. In general, will go along way in helping you throughout the book, but should not be considered a prerequisite.

To get the most out of the examples and development experience, it is recommended you to have a relatively newer development device with at least the following things:

- **CPU**: 4 cores
- **Memory**: 8 GB RAM
- **Disk space**: 40 GB

The examples (with a few exceptions) have been designed to run on both macOS and Windows PC devices.

To follow along you should have the following software installed:

- **PC**: Visual Studio 2015 Community or better
- **macOS**: XCode 8.x or better.

Other software needed will be described as required.

Download the example code files

You can download the example code files for this book from your account at
`www.packtpub.com`. If you purchased this book elsewhere, you can visit
`www.packtpub.com/support` and register to have the files emailed directly to you.

You can download the code files by following these steps:

1. Log in or register at `www.packtpub.com`.
2. Select the **SUPPORT** tab.
3. Click on **Code Downloads & Errata**.
4. Enter the name of the book in the **Search** box and follow the on-screen instructions.

Once the file is downloaded, please make sure that you unzip or extract the folder using the latest version of:

- WinRAR/7-Zip for Windows
- Zipeg/iZip/UnRarX for Mac
- 7-Zip/PeaZip for Linux

The code bundle for the book is also hosted on GitHub at `https://github.com/PacktPublishing/Mastering-Cpp-Game-Development`. We also have other code bundles from our rich catalog of books and videos available at `https://github.com/PacktPublishing/`. Check them out!

Download the color images

We also provide a PDF file that has color images of the screenshots/diagrams used in this book. You can download it from `https://www.packtpub.com/sites/default/files/downloads/MasteringCppGameDevelopment_ColorImages.pdf`.

Conventions used

There are a number of text conventions used throughout this book.

`CodeInText`: Indicates code words in text, database table names, folder names, filenames, file extensions, pathnames, dummy URLs, user input, and Twitter handles. Here is an example: "The only problem with this is that it will include all of the `ConsoleHelper` libraries."

A block of code is set as follows:

```
int m_numberOfPlayers;

void RunScripts(){}

class GameObject {};
```

When we wish to draw your attention to a particular part of a code block, the relevant lines or items are set in bold:

```
int m_numberOfPlayers;

void RunScripts(){}

class GameObject {};
```

Any command-line input or output is written as follows:

```
cl /c hello.cpp
```

Bold: Indicates a new term, an important word, or words that you see onscreen. For example, words in menus or dialog boxes appear in the text like this. Here is an example: "Select **Developer Command Prompt for VS2105** when it appears."

Warnings or important notes appear like this.

Tips and tricks appear like this.

Get in touch

Feedback from our readers is always welcome.

General feedback: Email feedback@packtpub.com and mention the book title in the subject of your message. If you have questions about any aspect of this book, please email us at questions@packtpub.com.

Errata: Although we have taken every care to ensure the accuracy of our content, mistakes do happen. If you have found a mistake in this book, we would be grateful if you would report this to us. Please visit www.packtpub.com/submit-errata, selecting your book, clicking on the Errata Submission Form link, and entering the details.

Piracy: If you come across any illegal copies of our works in any form on the Internet, we would be grateful if you would provide us with the location address or website name. Please contact us at copyright@packtpub.com with a link to the material.

If you are interested in becoming an author: If there is a topic that you have expertise in and you are interested in either writing or contributing to a book, please visit authors.packtpub.com.

Reviews

Please leave a review. Once you have read and used this book, why not leave a review on the site that you purchased it from? Potential readers can then see and use your unbiased opinion to make purchase decisions, we at Packt can understand what you think about our products, and our authors can see your feedback on their book. Thank you!

For more information about Packt, please visit packtpub.com.

C++ for Game Development

Ever since I was young, I was told, whether it was the pursuit of perfection in a sport, learning a musical instrument, or even a new technical skill, strong understanding of the fundamentals and practice is what makes the difference. Game development with C++ is no different. Before you can master the process, you have to perfect the fundamentals. That is what the first chapter of this book is all about, covering the foundational concepts that will be used throughout the book. The chapter is broken down into the following sections:

- An overview of advanced C++ concepts
- Working with types and containers
- Game programming patterns

The conventions used in the book

Throughout the book, you will encounter code snippets and examples. To keep the code readable and uniform, I will follow a few basic coding conventions. While the topic of coding standards is a complicated and lengthy discussion, I do think it is important to lay out some guidelines for any advanced project. Having an accessible guide to what is the expected notation and the naming conventions, at the very least, should be considered necessary before any work can begin. If you are interested in knowing more about common code standards used in C++, a great place to start is the coding standards frequently asked question section on the ISO C++ site at `https://isocpp.org/wiki/faq/coding-standards`. There, you will find a wealth of commonly used standards for various situations and a pile of suggested reading links to expand your knowledge even further.

The standards and conventions used in this book are based on some of the core C++ guidelines, industry best practices, and my own personal experience. We will be using the latest ISO C++ standard, C++14 throughout the book. However, at times, we may make use of some of the functionality in the latest proposed revision, C++17, also known as C++1y. When this occurs, a note will be made explaining why.

Classes and function names will follow the *MixedCase* style, while variables will follow a *camelCase* style. Some examples would look like the following:

```
int m_numberOfPlayers;

void RunScripts(){}

class GameObject {};
```

Another important convention used in this book that you should be aware of is the use of scope prefixes. Scope prefixes are a quick way of improving readability for other developers, and yourself when you enviably forget what scope a variable belongs to. The following is a list of the prefixes used:

- m_: This is used for class member variables. These are `private` and by using the prefix, tells anyone using the variable that it is available plainly in the class or through getters or setters if external, for example, `m_numberOfPlayers`.
- s_: This is used for static class members. This tells anyone using this variable that only one copy exists across all instances of the class and that it is static, for example, `s_objDesc`.
- g_: This is used for global variables. This tells anyone using this variable that it is available everywhere. We will not see many of these in the book, for example, `g_playerInfo`.

An overview of advanced C++ concepts

Before we jump into building our tools, libraries, and other game components, it is probably a good idea to run over some of the more common concepts that will show up often as we continue throughout the book. In this section, we will take a quick look at some of the advanced topics. This is not meant to be a complete list, and the goal is not to be a comprehensive overview of each subject instead the object is more of a review and explanation of the concepts when it comes to game development.

We will take a look at some simple examples and highlight some of the issues that could arise when working with these concepts. Some of the more seasoned C++ developers might be able to skip this section, but since these topics will play an influential role in the rest of the book, it is important to have a firm understanding of each of them. If you are looking for a broader review or a deeper explanation of the topics, check out some of the suggested reading in the *Summary* section at the end of the chapter.

Working with namespaces

Namespaces might not seem like a very advanced topic when compared to, say, smart pointers, but as you advance in your C++ game development adventure, namespaces will become an important part of your development toolkit. For a quick review, a namespace is a declaration that provides scope for all the variables, types, and functions inside of its encapsulation. This is important because it gives us a way of organizing our code into logical groups. By breaking our code up into these groups, we not only make it easier to read but also prevent what is known as **name collisions**. Name collisions occur when you have more than one class, function, or type with the same name. This becomes a big problem when you start to work with multiple libraries. Using namespaces prevents this through its use of scope. For example, say we had an implementation for a specialized string class for a certain platform. To keep this specialized version from interfering and colliding with the standard library implementation, we can wrap our type in a namespace like this:

```
namespace ConsoleHelper
{
  class string
  {
    friend bool operator == (const string &string1,
    const string &string2);
    friend bool operator < (const string &string1,
    const string &string2);
    //other operators ...
    public:
    string ();
    string(const char* input);
    ~string() ;
    //more functions ...
  }
}
```

Then we can call our particular string implementation like this:

```
ConsoleHelper::string name = new ConsoleHelper::string("Player Name");
```

Of course, if we did not want to keep typing the `ConsoleHelper` part over and over again, we could add a `using` statement that will tell the compiler to use a particular namespace to find the functions, types, and variables we are using. You can do that for our namespace with the following line of code:

```
using namespace ConsoleHelper;
```

The only problem with this is that it will include all of the `ConsoleHelper` libraries. If we only wanted to include a specific member of the namespace, we can do that with the following syntax:

```
using namespace ConsoleHelper::string;
```

This would include just the string member and not the whole namespace.

Inheritance and polymorphism

Inheritance and polymorphism are topics that could easily fill their own chapters. They are complex and very powerful components of C++. My goal in this section is not to cover the entire ins and outs of inheritance and polymorphism. Instead, I want to take a quick look at how these concepts can be used to help you build your code structure. We will cover the highlights, but I am going to assume that you have a basic understanding of object-oriented development concepts and are familiar with topics such as access modifiers and friendship.

To begin with, we will focus on inheritance. The concept of inheritance is an important part of modern object-oriented design and development. While the ability of inheritance to save keystrokes is a huge plus, inheritance really shows its power when allowing a programmer to develop complex hierarchies of derived classes. Let's take a look at the use of inheritance through a simple example. In this example, we have created a simple `Enemy` class. This class will handle things like the entity's health, weapons, damage to deal, AI scripts, and so on:

```
class Enemy
{
  public:
    void RunAIScripts();
    void Update(double deltaTime);
  private:
    int m_health;
    int m_damage;
};
```

As we start to implement more enemies to the game, we will probably start adding some different conditional statements to allow for some more variation in our enemies. Adding more and more if statements, maybe even a couple cases in a switch inserted here and there. This quickly becomes a tangled, hard-to-read, mess of code. What happens if we decide to add a slightly different enemy-one that has its own possible conditionals, for our example, a boss enemy type. This new boss enemy type has a similar structure as the original Enemy class and shares many of the same types and functions. We could just copy the overlapping code into our new Boss class. This would work, but it is not the ideal solution. We would have a lot of code duplication, and with this needless duplication comes more chances for bugs. Then if you do have to fix a bug, you now have to make the fix in multiple places. This is an unnecessary maintenance headache. Instead, we can use inheritance. If our new boss enemy type inherits from the original enemy type, this means we can use the types and functions that the original class has available to us. What makes inheritance even more powerful is the fact that we not only can adopt the functions of the inherited class, we can override them with our own implementations. The new Boss class can then be written something like this:

```
class Boss : public Enemy
{
  public:
    void Update(double deltaTime);
    //more functions...
};
```

This type of structure is commonly referred to as a **parent** and **child** hierarchy where the Boss class is a child of the Enemy class. This means that Boss will now have all the required structure from the Enemy class. I should point out that we only inherited the functions and variables that are declared public. That is because when using inheritance, the public methods and variables of the class are exposed to everyone using the class. The protected methods and variables are only available to the class itself and any classes derived. The private methods and variables are only available to that class, no one else has access, even derived clas

ve overwritten the implementation of the Update() function with a special version for the new Boss class. Now, in our code, we could write something like the following:

```
//Somewhere in game or level manager
void UpdateObjects (double deltaTime)
{
  enemy.Update(deltaTime);
  boss.Update(deltaTime);
}
```

When this code is run, it will call each of the separate implementations of the Update() function for the object. On the flip side of this, consider that we have the following code:

```
//Somewhere in game or level manager
void UpdateAI ()
{
  enemy.RunAIScripts();
  boss.RunAIScripts ();
}
```

Here we have not overwritten the RunAIScripts() function, as it does not inherit the original class's implementation of the function. While this is a very basic example, it does demonstrate the abilities of single inheritance, which brings me to my next topic-multiple inheritance.

Suppose we continue with the previous example, and we decide we want to add a new enemy type, a boss that can fly. We have a Boss class, an Enemy class, and even a FlyingEnemy class that inherits from the Enemy class, which looks like this:

```
class FlyingEnemy : public Enemy
{
  public:
    void Update(double deltaTime);
    void FlightAI();
    //many more functions...
}
```

The problem is we want the functionality of FlyingEnemy, but we also want some of the functionalities of Boss. Again, we could just copy the code chunks we want into a new class, but C++ provides us with an even better solution, **multiple inheritance**. As the name suggests, multiple inheritance allows us to derive our class from multiple sources. We can then build classes that have two or more parent classes leading to complex hierarchies, but as we will see, this can also lead to some problematic situations.

To continue with our example, our new FlyingBoss class would look something like the following:

```
class FlyingBoss : public Boss, public FlyingEnemy
{
  public:
    void Update(double deltaTime);
    //other functions...
}
```

At first glance, this looks like the perfect class, we have inherited the functions and variables we needed from both of the parent classes. However, there are a few issues that can start to come into play when working with multiple inheritance. First is the issue of ambiguity. Ambiguity happens when two or more of the classes that are being inherited from have functions or variables with the same name. For instance, in our example, if we did not override the Update() function, and we called Update() on the object, the compiler would look at the classes we inherited from for the implementation. Since they both have an implementation of the same name, the compiler throws a compiler time error complaining of ambiguity in the call. To solve this problem, we have to use a prefix on the function call to identify the class with the implementation we want to use. To do this, we use the scope operator (::) in our code to call the implementation from the FlyingEnemy class, which would look like this:

```
FlyingEnemy::Update(deltaTime);
```

The second issue might be a little less obvious; it has to deal with the way the class inheritance tree is structured in our example. On the surface, everything looks good; the FlyingBoss class inherits from the Boss class and the FlyingEnemy class. The problem lies one step up the inheritance tree, both the Boss and FlyingEnemy classes inherit from the Enemy class. This creates the dreaded diamond of death pattern in the class hierarchy. This might not seem like a big deal, but having this pattern causes some unfortunate issues. First is again the issue of ambiguity. Every time you try and access any member variable or function of the Enemy class from the FlyingBoss class, it is ambiguous. This is because there are multiple paths to each variable and function. To solve this, we can specify which path we want to follow by again using the scope operator (::). Another issue that the diamond of death pattern causes is the problem of duplication. When we create a FlyingBoss object, it will have two copies of everything it inherits from the Boss class. This is because both FlyingEnemy and Boss classes have copies from the Enemy class that they have inherited. As you can see, this is messy and can lead to all kinds of headaches. Fortunately, C++ provides us with a solution, the concept of **virtual inheritance**. With virtual inheritance, we can make sure that a parent class only appears in any children classes once. To implement virtual inheritance, we simply use the virtual keyword when declaring the class we want to inherit from. In our example, the class declaration would then look something like this:

```
class Boss : public virtual Enemy
{
  public:
    //functions...
};

class FlyingEnemy : public virtual Enemy
```

```
{
  public:
    //functions...
}
class FlyingBoss : public Boss, public FlyingEnemy
{
  public:
    //other functions...
}
```

Now the `FlyingBoss` class only has one instance of anything gained through inheritance.

 While this does solve the issue of the diamond of death and other possible hierarchy issues, these issues are usually a sign of the underlying design issues. I would suggest researching all other options before automatically jumping to virtual inheritance as a solution.

Finally, I want to quickly mention two important topics that work hand in hand to make inheritance the incredible tool it is, polymorphism and virtual functions. Boiling it down to the basics, polymorphism is the ability to use an object of a class as if it was part of another class. To make this simple, let's examine the following:

```
FlyingBoss* FlyBoss = new FlyingBoss();
```

This line of code creates a pointer to a new `FlyingBoss` object, nothing new here. However, we can also create a new pointer like so:

```
Boss* FlyBoss = new FlyingBoss();
```

This works thanks to inheritance and polymorphism. We are able to refer to the `FlyBoss` object as if it was a `Boss` class object. It might seem simple now, but as you progress in your understanding of C++, you will start to see just how powerful this concept can be. It also leads us to the last topic I want to touch on with inheritance, virtual functions. Since we can create pointers to objects like this, what happens if we call the `Update()` function on `Boss*` of the `FlyingBoss` object? This is where virtual functions come in. If a function is marked with the `virtual` keyword like so:

```
virtual void Update(double deltaTime);
```

This tells the compiler to use the type of object calling the function to determine which implementation should be used in that situation. So in our example if we were to use a virtual function in the `FlyingBoss` implementation, it would use that implementation when called from the `Boss*` of the `FlyingBoss` object.

Pointers and referencing

One of the most misunderstood and feared concepts in C++ is the concepts of pointers and references. It is often the reason new developers shy away from continuing their study of C++. There have been many books and tutorials written, trying to demystify the topic and to be quite honest I could easily write a chapter or even a separate book on the ins and outs of pointers and referencing. By now I am hoping you have come to peace with the topic of pointers and references in the classical sense and have built a healthy appreciation for their power and flexibility. So, in this section, we are not going to cover the core principles, but instead, look at the more important uses of, the older, or classical pointers and references and briefly cover the new pointers designed to help remove some of the mysticism and memory management concerns.

We will start out with the classical pointers and references. While you will quickly see the benefits of using the newer pointers, I still believe, as do a lot of C++ game developers, that the older versions still have their place. One of these places is when dealing with the passing of data to functions. When calling a function, it is often quite tempting to write something like the following:

```
void MyFunction(GameObject myObj)
{
  //do some object stuff
}
```

While this code is totally legal, if the object is more than a negligible size, it can pose a serious performance concern. When passing an object like this, the compiler automatically creates a copy of the object in memory. In most cases, this is not what we want. To prevent the compiler from creating a copy in memory, we can pass the object using a classic pointer or reference. The previous code would then look something like this:

```
void MyFunction (GameObject& myObj)
{
  //do some object stuff
}
```

Alternatively, it would look like the following:

```
void MyFunction (GameObject* myObj)
{
  //do some object stuff
}
```

Now the object is not copied into memory and allows us to operate on the actual object through dereferencing. This is one of the more common, continued uses of the classical pointers and references. Another common use of the classical pointers and references is when working with string literals and when moving objects. This type of application is still seen in many game development libraries. As such you should be comfortable with seeing code like:

```
const char* pixelShader;
```

With the move to modern C++ and the C++11 standards, came a new set of managed pointers to help simplify the understanding and use of pointers. These new pointers are much like the classic pointers except for one crucial difference; they are managed. What this really boils down to is that these new pointers will handle their own memory allocation and deletion. Since one of the major issues with the classic pointer was the necessary manual memory and the problem of ownership, as in who is going to delete it and when this makes the use of pointers a little more welcoming and a lot more flexible. These managed pointers (unique_ptr and shared_ptr) are commonly used in the more modern game development libraries.

unique_ptr and shared_ptr

The unique_ptr or unique pointer, is considered a smart pointer. The reason it is called unique is because this type of object holds sole ownership of its pointer. This means that no two unique_ptr pointers can manage the same object, it is unique. One of the biggest advantages of unique_ptr is that it manages its own lifetime. What this means is that when the pointer goes out of scope, it automatically destroys itself and deallocates its memory. This solves the dreaded dangling pointer issues and avoids memory leaks. This also removes the issue of ownership since now it is explicit who deletes the pointer.

Since the C++14 standard, we can now use a handy little function to create a unique pointer, make_unique. The make_unique function creates an object of type T and then wraps it in a unique pointer. The syntax for creating the unique_ptr pointer with make_unique would look something like the following:

```
std::unique_ptr<T> p = new std::make_unique<T>();
```

Once created, you can use the pointer much like a classic pointer. The dereference operators, * and ->, work just like they normally would. Again the big difference here is that the pointer is automatically destroyed when it goes out of scope, freeing us from having to track every exit point manually to avoid any memory leak issues.

The shared_ptr or shared pointer is a lot like the unique pointer. It is considered a smart pointer, it handles deletion and deallocation of memory automatically. The difference is that the shared pointer *shares* ownership of the object. This means that, unlike the unique pointer, a shared pointer can be one of many shared pointers, pointing to a single object. This means that if a shared pointer goes out of scope or is pointed to another object, through reset() or the = operator, the object still remains. It is only destroyed and its memory deallocated when all the shared_ptr objects owning the object are either destroyed, go out of scope, or are reassigned to another pointer.

Again, like the unique pointer, the shared pointer also has a handy function for creation. The make_shared function creates an object of type T and then wraps it in a shared pointer. The syntax for creating the shared_ptr function using the make_shared function would look like the following:

```
std::shared_ptr<T> p = new std::make_shared<T>();
```

Also, like the unique pointer, the shared pointer has the typical dereference operators, * and ->.

const correctness

The topic of const correctness can be a contentious one in the C++ community. The instructor of my first C++ course went as far as to say that the const keyword was one of the most important keywords in the language. Of course, I have also heard the other side, with developers telling me how they never use const and it is a complete waste of keystrokes. I like to think I fall somewhere in the middle on const; I believe that it has important uses, but it can be overused just like any other feature. In this section, I want to show some of the better uses for const.

As a quick review, the `const` keyword is used as a type qualifier to let the compiler know that this value or object cannot change, it is constant. When first starting out with C++ game development, your first exposure to `const` will probably come early on. Most commonly, the introduction to using *const-ness* has been in the defining of important values that we want to have easy access to, say something like this:

```
const int MAX_BULLETS = 100;
```

This then gives us a named value that we can easily use many times in other parts of our code. The big advantage of doing this is that if we then decided to change the value, in this case, the maximum amount of bullets, we can just change this constant value instead of having to change numerous amounts of hardcoded values scattered throughout the codebase.

As you get deeper into C++ development, the `const` keyword will become a more familiar site. It is used heavily in libraries and engine code in a variety of ways. It is also utilized in the definition of parameters for functions or used as a modifier for a function definition. Let's briefly take a look at these.

First, when used in the definition of parameters, it becomes an insurance that the function we are giving the value to is not going to modify it in any way. Take the following code, for example:

```
void ObjFunction(GameObject &myObject)
{
  //do stuff
  If(*myObject.value == 0)
  {
    //run some logic
    Game.changeState(newState);
    //possible unknown modifier function
    *myObject.value = 1;
  }
}
```

Okay, this is a very simple example, but if you did call a function like this, unaware of the fact that it could modify the object, you would end up with results you might not have been expecting. There are two ways that the `const` keyword helps solve this possible issue. One is by using the `const` keyword when passing the value:

```
void ObjFunction(const GameObject &myObject)
{
  //do stuff
  If(*myObject.value == 0)
  {
```

```
      //run some logic
      Game.ChangeState(newState);
      //possible unknown modifier function
      *myObject.value = 1; //now will throw a compile error
   }
}
```

This now makes it impossible to modify the value passed in anywhere in the function, keeping it constant.

The other way is by creating functions that are const safe. When you define a function as being a const function, it then allows const objects to call it. By default, const objects cannot call non const functions. However, non const objects can still call const functions. To define a function as being a const function, we can add the const keyword to modify the function definition itself. You simply add const to the end of the function signature, like so:

```
void ObjFunction(const GameObject &myObject) const
{
  //do stuff
  If(*myObject.value == 0)
  {
    //run some logic
    Game.ChangeState(newState);
    //possible unknown modifier function
    *myObject.value = 1; //now will throw a compile error
  }
}
```

This is my preferred method of writing any function that is not going to modify any objects or values. It allows some flexibility in ensuring that it can be called from const objects in the future, and it also allows other developers using the function in their code to easily identify that the function will not modify any object or value used in combination with it.

Memory management

The idea of **memory management** in C++ is often the topic of nightmares for beginners. I have commonly heard developers make statements like *I don't use C++ because of its manual memory management*. The truth is manual memory management is very rare in the vast majority of projects. These days with modern concepts like managed smart pointers, hand built memory management systems is of little importance for day-to-day development. It is only when you get to high-performance computing, such as game development, does the idea of controlling memory allocation and deallocation become a concern. When it comes to game development, the overall memory availability and speed on consoles continue to be a concern for developers, which is also true for most mobile devices, despite the rapid growth of affordable high memory devices. Over this next section, we will take a refresher look at the stack and heap, and the differences in how to handle memory allocation. This will lay the groundwork for the next chapter where we will see an example of a custom memory manager system.

Let's start with the stack, the appropriately named, **memory construct**, which you can think of much like a stack of plates or dishes. When you create an object or variable on the stack, it is placed on the top of the pile. When the object or variable goes out of scope, this is analogous to the plate or dish being removed from the stack. An allocation on the stack would look something like this in the code:

```
int number = 10;
Player plr = Player();
```

The first line creates an integer value, and assigns it the value of 10. The memory needed to store the integer is allocated on the stack. The second line has exactly the same idea, just for a Player object instead.

A good thing about using the stack is that any memory we allocate will be cleaned up for us when the object or variable goes out of scope. This can, however, be a double-edged sword; a lot of newer developers run into issues where they look for or make calls to objects after they have gone out of scope because they used the stack to store them. The other issue with the stack is that it is limited in size, which depends on the platform and compiler settings. This can become an issue if you have a lot of objects being created and held for an extended period of time. Trying to allocate more memory than available on the stack will throw a runtime error.

The alternative is the heap, which you can think of as being a large blob or container of memory. Unlike the stack, this heap of memory is unordered and can easily become fragmented. The good news is modern memory, and operating system implementations offer a low-level mechanism for dealing with this fragmentation, commonly known as **memory virtualization**. Another bonus of this virtualization is that it provides access to more heap storage than the physical memory provides, by swapping memory out to the hard drive when needed. To allocate and destroy memory on the heap, you use the keywords new and delete, and new[] and delete[] for containers of objects. The code will look something like so:

```
Player* plr = new Player();
char* name = new char[10];
delete plr;
delete[] name;
```

The first two lines create a Player object and a character array on the heap. The next two lines delete these objects, respectively. It is important to remember for every chunk of memory you create on the heap, you must call delete to destroy or release that chunk of memory. Failure to do so can cause memory leaks, where your application continues to consume more and more memory until the device runs out and crashes. This is a common issue and can be hard to track out and debug. Memory leaks are one of the reasons new developers tend to think C++ memory management is hard.

So what should you use, the stack or the heap? Well, it really depends on the implementation and the object or value being stored. A good rule of thumb I recommend is that if you can get away with using the stack for your allocation, that should be your default. If you do find yourself needing to use the heap, try and use a manager system to handle the creation and deletion. This will cut down on the chances of memory leaks and other issues that arise from handling your own memory management. We will look at how to build your own memory manager as part of your core libraries in the next chapter.

Dealing with errors

I wish I could say that every line of code I write works flawlessly the first time. The reality is that I am human and prone to making errors. Dealing with these mistakes and tracking down the bugs can be where most development time is spent. Having a good way to catch and deal with these any other issues that occur during the running time of your game is crucial. This section covers some of the C++ techniques used for finding and handling errors.

One technique that you can use when you hit an issue is to gracefully let the program crash. Meaning that instead of having the computer crash on its own, we tell the computer to stop the execution of our code and exit immediately. To do this in C++, we can use the assert() method. An example would look something like the following code:

```
#include <assert.h>
...
void MyFunction(int number)
{
    ...
    assert(number != NULL);
    ...
}
```

When the computer hits the line of code assert (number != NULL); it checks to see whether the integer number is NULL, whether this evaluates to true, in this case, it will cause an assertion failure that immediately stops execution and exits the program. This allows us, at least, some control. We can use the opportunity provided by the assert() function to capture more information to create a crash report. We can print out the file, line, and even a description of the error as a custom message. While this does work, it leaves a lot to be desired.

Another technique that handles errors which can provide a little more flexibility is exceptions. Exceptions work like this; when the program runs into an issue, it can throw an exception that halts the execution. The program then looks for the nearest exception handling block. If it is unable to find that block in the function that threw the exception, it then looks to the parent function for a handling block. This process unwinds the stack, meaning that all objects created on the stack will be destroyed in the order they were passed in. This process will continue until the program finds a handling block or hits the top of the stack at which point the default exception handler will be called, and the program will quit. The overall the syntax used to handle exceptions in C++ is pretty straightforward. To throw an exception, you use the keyword throw. This will trigger the program to look for a handling block, denoted with the keyword Catch. A Catch block must be located right after a Try block, which encapsulates the code that might throw the exception. A simple example of this would be:

```
Void ErroringFunction()
{
    ...// do something that causes error
    throw;
}
Void MyFunction()
{
    ...
```

```
Try //the try block
{
   ...
   ErroringFunction();
   ...
}
Catch(...)//catch *all exceptions block
{
   ... //handle the exception
}
}
```

You can also catch and handle specific errors by passing the exception type as an argument to the Catch block, as shown in the following code:

```
...
Throw MyExeception("Error! Occurred in Myfunction()");
...
Catch(MyException e)
{
   ...//handle exception
}
```

The advantage of using exceptions is that we have the flexibility to handle the error any way we want. We could, if the situation allows, correct this issue that caused the error and continue on, or we could simply dump some information to a log file and exit the program. The choice is ours.

Which solution you implement to handle errors is completely up to you and the project you are working on. Some developers do, in fact, choose just to ignore handling errors all together. I, however, highly recommend using some sort of error handling system. In the example code used for the demos throughout the book, I implement an exception handling system. I recommend looking at that implementation as a starting reference. The suggested reading section at the end of this chapter also contains some great references on handling errors.

Working with types and containers

C++ is a strongly-typed unsafe language. It provides an incredible amount of control, but it ultimately expects the programmer to know what they are doing. Understanding how to work with types at an advanced level is paramount to mastering game library and core system programming. Game development relies heavily on the flexibility of types in C++, it also relies on the advanced libraries available like the **Standard Template Library** (**STL**). Over the next few sections, we will look at some of the more common containers used in game development and their STL implementations. We will also cover how to create generic code through use templating. Finally, we will wrap up the topic of types and containers with a look at type inference and its more often seen use cases.

STL generic containers

The C++ STL is a collection of container classes that allow storage of data in different structures, with iterators that provide access to elements of the container, and algorithms that can perform operations on the containers and the elements they hold. These structures, iterators, and algorithms are extremely optimized and in most cases use the latest implementations of the C++ language standard. The STL makes extensive use of the templating feature in C++ to allow easy adaptation for use with our own types. We will take a look at templating in the next section. The STL is a huge topic, with many books written on the concepts and implementation. If you have had little experience with the STL, I highly recommend reading some of the amazing books that have been written on the subject. I have listed a few in the *Summary* section at the end of this chapter. This section will concentrate on highlighting some of the STL containers that are more commonly used in game development. I am going to assume that you have a basic understanding of containers and that you have had some experience using iterators to traverse elements in a container.

Let's start with two sequence containers, vector and list. The reason they are referred to as **sequence containers** is because they store their elements in a specific order. This allows elements to be added or removed anywhere in that order, or sequence. Vector and list are some of the most popular STL sequence containers you will come across. Knowing some key facts will help you decide which one is the best for a particular task. I have included a few suggestions to help guide you.

Vector

Vector is one of the most basic containers offered in the STL. While it is comparatively simple, it is highly flexible and is one of the most widely used containers in game development. The place you are most likely to see it is in replacement of a C array. One of the bigger drawbacks that comes with using arrays is that you have to define the size of the array at declaration. This means, in most cases, you will need to know the maximum amount of elements needed, or you need to allocate more than you will ever need. Luckily for us vectors do not have this, predefined size, drawback; a vector will grow to accommodate new elements that are added. To create a vector of integers, we can use the following syntax:

```
std::vector<int> playerID ;
```

You probably noticed `std::` before `vector`, that is because the `vector` class is part of the `std` namespace, so we need to identify that we wish to use that implementation. See the *Working with namespaces* section earlier in the chapter for a review. We can avoid having to type this by adding a `using namespace std;` statement at the beginning of the code file. I prefer to add `std::` to my standard library calls, or any other specific namespace call. Since game development uses so many libraries having a lot of `using` statements can become messy and error prone. Although it takes a few extra keystrokes, it can save a pile of headaches.

I personally use vectors in place of arrays in most cases, and would suggest you do too. Before you go changing all of your arrays to vectors, though, it is important to note one aspect of vectors that could potentially cause issues. When you create a vector, one contiguous block of memory is allocated for it. The amount of memory depends on the amount of elements in the vector. There will always be room for all the elements currently in the vector plus a little extra to allow for the addition of new elements. This is the trick of a vector, as you add more elements, and ultimately start to run out of space, the vector will grab more memory so that it always has room for new elements. It does this by first creating a new block of memory, copying all the contents of the first block of memory and then deleting it. This is where the issues can creep in. To prevent constant allocation, copy, and deletion, when a vector allocates new memory, it generally doubles the previous size. Since a vector can never shrink, if we have used a vector in a way that creates large additions and subtractions of elements, this can easily become a memory issue, especially for lower memory devices. Knowing this should not prevent you from using vectors, when implemented in the right situations this should rarely become a problem and can be easily mitigated through refactoring if it does arise.

Some perfect examples of when to use a vector would be in cases like; a list of players, character animation lists, player weapons, really any list that you might add to and remove from infrequently. This will avoid the possible memory issues while giving you access to vector's iterators, algorithms, and other benefits.

List

A **list** is another type of sequence container you are likely to see when developing games with C++. To create a list container of integer values the syntax would look something like:

```
std::list<int> objValues;
```

The list container is quite different from the vector in its implementation and general usage in development. The key difference is that unlike a vector, the list container does not store all its elements in one large contiguous block of memory. Instead, it stores its elements as nodes in a doubly linked list. Where each of these nodes holds a pointer to the next and previous nodes. This, of course, makes the extra memory allocation issues of the vector disappear since only the memory for each element in the list is allocated beforehand. When a new element is added only memory for the new node is created, saving the wasted memory you might see in a vector implementation. This also allows elements to be added anywhere in the list with far better performance compared to a vector container. There are some drawbacks, though. Due to this setup of individual nodes in memory, each operation on the list will more than likely end up causing a memory allocation. With each node possibly scattered around memory in no guaranteed ordered, this constant memory allocation might be a potential issue on systems with slower dynamic memory. This also means that a list is slower to traverse through its elements than a vector is. Again this is not meant to discourage you from using lists in your projects. I would give the advice to use a list wherever you have a group of objects or elements that you plan on adding to or deleting from frequently. A good example would be of a list game objects or meshes to render in each frame. A list should not be thought of as a replacement for a vector. Each has its own advantages and disadvantages, finding the best choice for a solution is often the hardest part.

Finally, the last container we will take a look at is a commonly used **associative container**. Unlike sequence containers, associative containers do not preserve the relative positions of the elements in them. Instead associative containers are built for speed, more specifically element lookup speed. Without getting into **Big O notation**, these associative containers, and their corresponding algorithms far outperformed vector and list when it comes to looking up specific elements. The reason they are referred to as associative containers is that they usually provide a key/data pair that facilitates this faster lookup. It should be noted that sometimes the key in the container is the data itself. The one we will be focusing on here is the map container.

Map

Maps are very handy containers for a multiple of uses in game development. What makes maps unique compared to vectors or list, is that each map is made up of two pieces of data. The first piece of data is a key and the second is the actual element stored. This is what makes maps so performant at looking up elements. An easy way of thinking of this is that maps are like arrays, but instead of using integer values to index elements, maps use keys, that can be of any type, to index its elements. Maps even have a specialized [] operator that allows you to access elements using the familiar array syntax.

To create a map with an integer as the key and strings as the element type or value, our code would look something like the following:

```
std::map<int,string> gameObjects;
```

When it comes to memory usage, maps are different from both the list and vector containers. Maps do not store their data in contiguous blocks like vectors, instead they hold their elements in nodes, much like a list. The difference in how the list and map handle their allocation is in the way the nodes are structured. The nodes in a map have pointers to the next node and previous node, like the list, but these nodes are arranged in a tree pattern. This tree pattern autobalances itself with the addition and deletion of nodes. The good news is that this balancing act does not add any new allocations. The performance of a map is very similar to a list, since the memory management is similar, the only time you might see a difference is in the very slight overhead of the automatic balancing of the node tree.

One way maps are often used is in the form of a dictionary. They provide very fast lookup of unique values through their key; because of this, some good example maps in game development are: a list of game elements with unique IDs, a list of multiplayer clients with unique IDs for keys, and for almost any situation in which you have a group of elements that you want to store with some sort of key-value pair.

Templating

Templates are a newer concept in the C++ language. Templates help solve the all too common issue of having to rewrite the same code when different datatypes or classes are being used. This allows us to write what is referred to as generic code. We can then use this generic code in other parts of our project. As of the C++14 standard, there are now three types of templates that can be used: **class templates**, **function templates**, and **variable templates**. Let's take a closer look at each of them in the upcoming sections.

Class templates

Using class templates, we can create abstract classes that can be defined without specifying what datatype will be handled by the functions of the class. This becomes very useful when building libraries and containers. In fact, the C++ Standard library makes extensive use of class templates, including the `vector` class we saw earlier in the chapter. Let's take a look at a simple implementation of a `Rectangle` class. This could be a useful class for finding screen coordinates, buttons and other GUI pieces, and even simple 2D collision detection.

A basic implementation without using class templates will look something like this:

```
class Rectangle
{
  public:
    Rectangle(int topLeft, int topRight, int bottomLeft,
    int bottomRight) :
    m_topLeft (topLeft), m_topRight(topRight),
    m_bottomLeft(bottomLeft), m_bottomRight(bottomRight){}
    int GetWidth() { return m_topRight - m_topLeft; }
  private:
    int m_topLeft;
    int m_topRight;
    int m_bottomLeft;
    int m_bottomRight;
};
```

This works fine in most cases, but if we want to use this rectangle in a different coordinate system that uses values of say 0.0 to 1.0, we will have to make some changes. We could just copy the code and change the integer datatypes to float, that would work just fine, but using class templates we can avoid this code duplication.

Using templates, the new `Rectangle` class will look something like this:

```
template <class T>
class Rectangle
{
  public:
    Rectangle(T topLeft, T topRight, T bottomLeft,
    T bottomRight) :
    m_topLeft(topLeft), m_topRight (topRight),
    m_bottomLeft(bottomLeft), m_bottomRight(bottomRight){}
    T GetWidth() { return m_topRight - m_topLeft; }
    T GetHeight() { return m_bottomLeft - m_topLeft;}
  private:
    T m_topLeft;
    T m_topRight;
    T m_bottomLeft;
    T m_bottomRight;
};
```

The first change you will notice is the inclusion of `template<class T>` right before our class definition. This tells the compiler that this class is a template. The `T` is a placeholder for a datatype. The second change is that all the integer datatypes have been replaced with this placeholder. So now we can create a rectangle using the `int` datatype like so:

```
Rectangle(10,20,1,2);
```

When the compiler comes across this line of code, it goes through the template class and replaces all the instances of the placeholder with `int`, and then compiles the new class on-the-fly. To create a rectangle using float values, we could then use the following code:

```
Rectangle (1,1,0.5,0.5);
```

We can do this for any datatype we like; the only restriction is that the types must be supported in the operations of the class. If they are not, a runtime error will be thrown. An example of this would be a class template that has the multiplication function and is trying to use that template with a string.

Function templates

The concept of function templates is very similar to class templates; the big difference is that function templates do not need to be explicitly instantiated. They are created automatically based on the datatypes passed in. The following will swap two values, but it is not specific to any class type:

```
template<class T>
void Swap (T &a, T &b)
{
    T temp = a;
    a = b;
    b = temp;
}
```

You can then pass integer values:

```
Swap(23,42);
or float values;
Swap(12.5, 5.2);
```

In fact, you can use this function with any type that supports assignment operators and a copy constructor. The restriction here is that both datatypes must be of the same type. This is true even if the datatype has an implicit conversion.

```
Swap(1.8, 22); // Results in a compile time error
```

Variable templates

The last type of template I want to mention quickly is the variable template, not to be confused with **variadic templates**. Introduced in C++14, the variable template allows the wrapping of a variable within a templated struct or class. The conical example often used is for the mathematic construct of pi:

```
template<class T>
constexpr T pi = T(3.1415926535897932385);
```

This then means you can refer to pi as a float, int, or double variable and use it in generic functions, for example, to compute the area of a circle with a given radius:

```
template<typename T>
T area_of_circle_with_radius(T r)
{
    return pi<T> * r * r;
}
```

And again this templated function can be used with various datatypes, so you can return an area as an integer, a floating point value, or any other supported datatype. You may not see variable templates used that often, yet. They are still considered a new idea in C++, but it is important to be aware of their existence. They do have some unique cases and may one day help you solve a difficult problem.

As you can see, templates do have their benefits, and I encourage you to use them where it makes sense. However, it is important to note some of the possible drawbacks when implementing templates. The first potential drawback is that all templates must have their entire implementation in the same file, usually the header. The export keyword corrects this, but not all commercial compilers support it. Another drawback of templates is that they are notorious for being hard to debug. Compilers tend to give cryptic errors when the issue resides inside of the templated code. My biggest advice is to use them with caution, just like every other feature. Just because a feature is advanced does not mean it's a good fit. Finally, check your compiler for exact details on implementation.

Type inference and when to use it

With the C++11 standard came some very useful **type interference** capabilities. These new capabilities give programmers, even more, tools to create generic, flexible code. In this section, we will look at these new capabilities in more depth.

We will begin with a new, powerful keyword. The auto keyword allows you to have the compiler infer the variable type, if possible, at the time of declaration. This means that instead of defining a variable like so:

```
int value = 10;
```

You can now just use auto:

```
auto value = 10;
```

However, this is not the best use of the auto keyword, in fact, this is a perfect example of what you should not do. As tempting as it might be to use auto when declaring any variable, this not only adds completely unnecessary overhead to compiles, it makes your code harder to read and follow. That's what you should not do with auto, so what should you do with auto? Well, where auto really shows its helpfulness, is when it is used in concert with templates. When coupled with the auto keyword, templates can become extremely flexible and powerful. Let's take a look at a quick example.

In this example, we have a simple templated function that creates some game objects for us, something like the following:

```
template <typename ObjectType, typename ObjectFactory>
void CreateObject (const ObjectFactory &objFactory)
{
  ObjectType obj = objFactory.makeObject();
  // do stuff with obj
}
```

To call this code, we will use the following code:

```
MyObjFactory objFactory;
CreateObject<PreDefinedObj>(objFactory);
```

This code works fine, but it could be a little more flexible and easier to read with the use of the auto keyword. Our code will now look something like the following:

```
template <typename ObjectFactory >
void CreateObject (const ObjectFactory &objFactory)
{
  auto obj = objFactory.MakeObject();
  // do stuff with obj
}
```

And then our code to call this function will be:

```
MyObjFactory objFactory;
CreateObject (objFactory);
```

While this is an oversimplification, it should allow you to see the possibilities that auto can provide. By not defining what type the object factory will return, we allow the factory more freedom in its implementation, which in return allows for greater uses of the factory in our code base.

One of the places you will tend to see the `auto` keyword in action, outside of templates, is in the declaration of iterators in for loops. This has become the common practice in a lot of the more modern libraries. You will often see for loops written like so:

```
for (auto it = v.begin(); it != v.end(); ++it)
{
   //do stuff
}
```

The `auto` keyword has a helper keyword, `decltype`, which extracts the type from a variable. So where `auto` is used to let the compiler infer what the variable type is, the `decltype` is utilized to determine what a variable's type is. This becomes very useful when you add in the last part of the `auto` keywords functionality, as a `return` value. Before C++11 and the `auto` keyword, `return` values had to be declared before the function name, like so:

```
TreeObject CreateObject (const ObjectFactory &objFactory)
{
   auto obj = objFactory.MakeObject();
   return obj;
}
```

This means that the `CreateObject` function must return a `TreeObject` type, but as mentioned earlier, letting the compiler infer what `objFactory.MakeObject();` returns allows greater flexibility. In order to infer the type of object returned from a function, we can use the concept of `auto`, `decltype`, and the new `return` syntax. Our new function will now look like this:

```
template <typename ObjectFactory >
auto CreateObject(const ObjectFactory &objFactory) -> decltype
(objFactory.makeObject())
{
   auto obj = objFactory.MakeObject();
   return obj;
}
```

Also note that `auto` and `decltype` do add some overhead to our compile time. In most cases this will be insignificant, but in certain circumstances it could become an issue, so be conscious of this when incorporating these new keywords in your codebase.

As you continue to build more libraries and toolsets, having the ability to build more generic, flexible code will become crucial. Tricks like using `auto`, `decltype`, and the new `return` syntax are just some of the ways to accomplish this. In the next sections and chapters, we will see more of these useful concepts.

Game programming patterns

A programming pattern or development pattern, simply put, is a solution to a commonly faced or reoccurring problem. It is a description or template that provides a solution that can be used in many different situations. These patterns are formalized best practices, often developed through years of iterations. By using patterns in your project, you can make your code more performant, stronger, and more adaptable. They allow you to build structured code that is decoupled by nature. Having this decoupling is what makes your code more generic and easier to work with. You no longer have to cram the entire program into your mind to understand what a particular section of code is trying to accomplish. Instead, you can focus on smaller chunks that function independently. This is the true power of object-oriented design. This decoupling will also make it easier to track down bugs during testing by isolating the issue or issues to a certain segment of code.

Having a solid understanding of, at the least, the most fundamental patterns will be critical as you start to build your own libraries and engine structure. In the next few sections, we will look at some of these basic patterns.

Working with loops

Arguably, one of the most important concepts in game development is the concept of loops. If you have ever built a game before, I can almost guarantee that you have used some sort of loop. Even though loops are common, the particular implementation of a loop is often not. Patterns give developers guidelines and structure to build performant, flexible loops.

One of the most common loop patterns is the **game loop pattern**. The intent of the game loop pattern is to provide a mechanism to decouple the passage of game time from the user input and other events, regardless of the processor's clock speed. An easy way to explain it is: a game loop runs continuously during the operation of the game, or during a specific state, see state machines in a later section. During this continuous looping, each tick or turn of the loop, we have a chance to update parts of the game. This usually includes updating the current game state, checking and updating any user input, without blocking, and a call to draw or render any game objects. Many platforms and almost all engines have their own implementation. It is important to note whether the platform or engine you are using does have their own game loop. If it does, you will then have to hook your code and loop structure into the provided mechanism.

As an example, the Unity game engine abstracts the looping process, they expose connectivity to the internal game loop through the Update() function inherited by all game objects. This Unity structure is an excellent example of how the game loop pattern can be combined with other patterns like the update pattern to build a cascading loop system that allows the main game loop to drive the internal looping mechanism of each object. We won't build a complete example right now, but as we continue through the book, we will see more of how structures like this are built. The next few sections will continue this idea of combining patterns to build a complete game system flow.

To help picture how a game loop is constructed, let's take a look at a typical, slightly simple example:

```
double lastTime = getSystemTime();
while (!gameOver)
{
   double currentTime = getSystemTime ();
   double deltaTime = currentTime - lastTime;
   CheckInput();
   Update(deltaTime);
   Draw();
   lastTime = currentTime;
}
```

The first line of code, `double lastTime = getSystemTime();`, stores the time before the first run of the loop. Next we have a simple `while` loop, in this situation, the loop will continue to run while the variable `gameOver` is not true. Inside the `while` loop, first we get the current time. Next we create a `deltaTime` variable, which is the amount of time that has passed since the last step of the loop. We then make calls to run the other components of the game: `Input`, `Update`, and `Draw`. This is the key to the game loop pattern; we use this standard running loop to drive the game forward. You might notice that we pass `deltaTime` through to the `Update` method. This is another important component of the loop, without getting too deep into the update pattern, by passing along the time that has elapsed between loops we are able to modify things like the game object physics using proper time slices, which is important to keep everything in sink and looking smooth. This style of the game loop pattern implementation is called a **variable time step** pattern since the loop steps are based on the amount of time the update takes. The longer the update code takes, the longer the time between the steps will be. This means each step of the loop will determine how much real time has passed. Using this method means that the game will run at a consistent rate on different hardware, it also means users with powerful machines will be rewarded with smoother gameplay. This implementation is far from perfect though. It doesn't optimize the rendering or deal with lag that can occur between steps, but it's a good start. Understanding what is happening under the hood is a significant step. In the next section, we will look at a pattern that allows us to create code paths based on events, this coupled with loops is the natural evolution of the game system flow.

State machines

The next pattern we will examine is the **state pattern**; more specifically, we will look at finite state machines. State machines are an extremely powerful engineering concept. While not a common pattern in most programming disciplines, except maybe AI development, finite state machines play a significant role in building branching code. It might be surprising to know that many mechanical logic circuits found in our day-to-day life are constructed from forms of finite state machines.

A real-world example would be a set of traffic lights, which changes state based on cars waiting (maybe not fast enough sometimes). A finite state machine can be boiled down to an abstract system where the machine can be in one, and only one, of a limited number of states. The machine will stay in this state, referred to as the current state, until an event or triggered condition causes a transition. Let's look at an example that demonstrates this concept:

```
//simple enum to define our states
Enum GameState
{
  Waiting,
  Playing,
  GameOver
}

GameState currentGameState = GameState.Waiting;

//Other game class functions...

void Update(double deltaTime)
{
  //switch case that acts as our machine
  switch(currentGameState)
  {
    case Waiting:
      //do things while in waiting state
      //Transition to the next state
      currentGameState = Playing;
    break;
    case Playing:
      //do things while in playing state
      CheckInput();
      UpdateObjects(deltaTime);
      Draw();
      //Transition to the next state
      currentGameState = Gameover;
    break;
    case Gameover:
      //do things while in waiting state
      UploadHighScore();
      ResetGame();
      //Transition to the next state
      currentGameState = Waiting;
    break;
  }
```

To begin with, we have an `enum` structure that houses our game states. Next, we create a `GameState` variable type to hold the current game state that the machine is in. Then in an `Update` loop, we implement a `switch case` construct that controls the flow of transitions from state to state. The key to this implementation is that each state of the machine has a transition state to the next. This keeps the machine running and allows us to perform different actions depending on the current state the machine is in. While this is probably one of the most basic forms of a game state machine, it does demonstrate the usefulness of the finite state pattern. As you move on to the creation of libraries and other components, you will start to see more and more uses for these incredible tools. There are many other, more complicated implementations and, even more, patterns to help describe them. Some of these will be seen in the later chapters of this book.

Event listeners

Very often in the game development process, you will find cases where you have a need for certain code to execute based on some user input, or from a condition fired from another chunk of code. Maybe you just need a solid way for game object communicate. This is where the idea of using an event or message passing system comes in. Numerous patterns have been created to help solve this problem, including **Overseer**, **Model View Controller**, and others. Each of these patterns implements a different mechanic for handling events; many actually build off of each other. However, before we jump into using one of these patterns, I believe it is important to understand the foundation of what is happening under the hood to power all these solutions. By building our own solution, we will gain a better understanding of the problem, and more appreciation for the patterns that solve it. In our example, we will use the concepts we have learned throughout the chapter to build a simple, but reusable event systems that could be used in your own projects.

The first approach we could take uses the simple version of the state machine we just looked at. In this approach, we use a `switch case` construct to branch the code based on the type of event passed in. To save space and time, some basic structure code has been omitted:

```cpp
//Event could be an enum or struct that houses the different event types
void GameObject::HandleEvent(Event* event)
{
  switch(event)
  {
    case Collision:
      HandleCollision();
      //Do other things...
    break;
    Case Explosion:
```

```
      HandleExplosion()
      //More things...
    break;
  }
}
```

This is a quick and dirty implementation, and will work in some very basic situations. If we use a struct or union for our event type, we could add some simple message capability which would make it even more useful. Unfortunately, this approach ultimately has too many significant issues. First is the fact that we need to have a single source of event types. We then have to edit this source every time we want to add a new event type. Second is the switch case construct, again every time we wish to add a new event type we have to append and modify this section. All this is very tedious, prone to errors, and is bad design in an OOP-enabled language.

A second approach we can take relies on the capabilities of **Run-time type information (RTTI)**, which is the concept of determining the type of a variable at runtime. Using RTTI gives us the ability to use dynamic_cast to determine the event type in our solution. I should point out that not all RTTI implementations are the same, and may not be turned on by default in all compilers. Check your compiler's documentation for exact information.

To start off with, we create a simple base class for all of the specific events we will create:

```
class Event
{
  protected:
    virtual ~event() {};
};
```

Now it is simply a matter of using dynamic_cast to determine the type of event and passing along the message info to the object's own handling function:

```
void onEvent(Event* event)
{
  if (Collision* collision = dynamic_cast<Collision*>(event))
  {
    onCollision(collision);
  }
  else if (Explosion* explosion = dynamic_cast< Explosion *>(event))
  {
    onExplosion(explosion);
  }
  //etc...
}
```

This is a more elegant solution than the first one we saw. It provides more flexibility and is easier to maintain. However, we can refactor this code to make it even simpler. Using the concept of templates we learned earlier, and good old fashion overloading, our new code can be structured like so:

```
Template <class T>
bool TryHandleEvent(const Event* event)
{
  If(cosnt T* event = dynamic_cast<const T*> (event))
  {
    Return HandleEvent(event);
  }
  Return false;
}

void OnEvent( const Event* event)
{
  If(TryHandleEvent<Collision>(event)) return;
  Else if(TryHandleEvent<Explosion>(event)) return;
}
```

Like the other examples in this chapter, this example is meant to be basic. While it is true that this new approach is cleaner and more adaptable than the first, it does have some drawbacks of its own. This includes the overhead of dynamic_cast, which is entirely dependent on the structure of the class hierarchy. The problem of maintenance and error-prone code still exists with the if...else chain. Plus, we also have the bigger, much more important issue of improper type detection. For example, with this approach, if we have a type that is inherited from another, say a LargeExplosion class from the Explosion class. If the queries to the object's type are out of order, the event pointer is cast to the Explosion class first, when in actuality it is pointing to the LargeExplosion class, the compiler will improperly detect the type and call the wrong version of the function. A somewhat more ideal solution would be to have an EventHandler class that would handle the registration, storage, and polymorphic functions for all events. You could then have member function handlers that would implement specific event types, which could, in turn, inherit from a handler function base class. This would solve many of the issues we have seen with the other two approaches while giving us a more generic, reusable implementation.

We'll stop our implementation here, though. Since event handling systems play such a strong role in many different parts of game systems, from the toolchain to user input and networking, we will see a lot more of these patterns and techniques used throughout the rest of the book.

Summary

We covered a lot in this chapter. We discussed some of the more advanced C++ topics used in modern game development. We looked at inheritance and polymorphism, pointers, referencing and the common STL generic containers. The concept of templating and building generic code with class, function, and variable templates. Type inference and the new language keywords `auto` and `decltype` and their uses in combination with the new `return` value syntax. Finally, we closed out the chapter looking at some core game patterns used today.

In the next chapter, we will look at how we can use these key concepts to create core libraries that can be used and reused in our game development projects.

2
Understanding Libraries

Understanding how libraries work is extremely important to mastering C++ game development. Gaining knowledge of how libraries work in C++ will allow you to build more robust games and tools. Often the most fundamental ingredients to create the core of game engines can be found in easy-to-use, *Redistributable* libraries. In this chapter, we will explore the key differences between library types and how you can create, build, and consume them. For this chapter, I am going to assume you have read through `Chapter 1`, *C++ for Game Development*, and you have a general understanding of the compiling and linking process. This chapter consists of the following sections:

- Library build types
- Building a custom shareable library

Why do we use libraries?

Libraries are a key concept in C++ and they are the mechanism that allows the language to build modular designs and portable code. By using libraries, we are able to create reusable code that we can easily share among multiple programs, and with other developers. It allows developers to save time by not having to constantly rewrite a particular code chunk over and over again. It also saves the developers time by allowing the use of other developers solutions for commonly occurring problems. The **Standard Template Library (STL)** is a great example of this. STL has solutions for a large amount of problems commonly found in C++. These solutions include the implementation of data types such as string, containers such as vector, and algorithms such as sort. These standard implementations come from years of refinement and development. As such they tend to be incredibly performant and highly optimized, I would suggest defaulting to using an STD implementation over a handwritten implementation where applicable as a general rule. There are literally thousands and thousands of libraries available for C++ development.

Library build types

There are a few different ways to create library files. You can use the different tools such as an **Integrated Development Environment (IDE)**. Development environment tools such as Visual Studio and XCode, often have templates or starter projects included to create library files for various platforms and situations. Another somewhat simpler way and the way we will use here is via the command line. More specifically the Developer Command Prompt that comes with Visual Studio 2015 and the terminal program that comes with macOS X. You can obtain a copy of Visual Studio 2015 Community edition, a free version for teams of five or fewer developers, at the Visual Studio website.

To open the Developer Command Prompt on Windows 8 or higher, hit the windows key and start typing `developer command prompt`, and select **Developer Command Prompt for VS2105** when it appears:

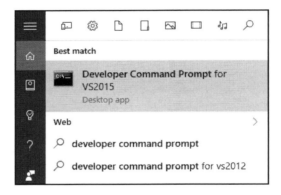

To open the Terminal on OS X, open the application launcher and type `Terminal` in the search bar at the top of the screen:

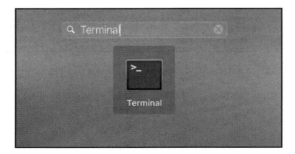

To start with, let's create a basic library that we will then be able to consume from other programs. In this example, we will just write a simple function that will print out the time-honored line `Hello World`. It wouldn't be a book on programming without at least one hello world program. Here is the file we will use, I saved mine as `hello.cpp`.

```
#include <iostream>
void Hello()
{
  std::cout<< "Hello World!"<<std::endl;
}
```

Statically linked libraries

A static library is a library that is compiled as part of the application itself. What this means is that all the code relating to the library is contained in a single file, `.lib` on Windows and `.a` on Linux/OS X systems, and it is directly linked into the program. A program that incorporates a static library creates copies of the code that it requires from the library and places that copy in the program where the library implementation was called. It does this for every call to the library. This leads to one of the larger drawbacks of using a static library, it increases the overall size of the executable. On the other hand, the advantage of using a static library is that there are no external dependencies that the user requires to run the program. This helps to avoid the issue of the libraries on the user's system being the wrong version or having to distribute it with the program, which can create a whole pile of problems. You will often hear this common issue referred to *Dll Hell*. Another advantage to static libraries are since they are linked as part of the build process, this will allow compilers and build tools more opportunities to optimize the implementations. A good rule of thumb to follow is, for common or standard libraries, ones that most users will have (OpenGL or DirectX) use dynamic or shared libraries. For less common libraries (GLFW or SDL) you are more likely to use a static library.

To turn our `hello.cpp` file into a static library from the Developer Command Prompt, we follow the following steps:

On Windows

Follow these steps:

1. For Windows, you need to type the following command:

   ```
   cl /c hello.cpp
   ```

cl is the command to compile and link. The /c tells the compiler we only want to compile and not link our file. Finally, we pass in the file we want to compile. This will create an object file, hello.obj, that we can then use to create our static library file.

2. Now that we have our object file created, we can use a library building tool to create our static library. We use the following command to generate a .lib file:

   lib /out:MyLib.lib hello.obj

   lib is the command to launch the build tool. The /out:MyLib.lib tells the compiler to name the library build MyLib.lib.

3. If we list the contents of the directory, you will see we now have our static library MyLib.lib:

```
    120 hello.cpp
 75,882 hello.obj
     50 main.cpp
111,210 MyLib.lib
```

4. We can now consume our newly created library in other projects. Let's create a very simple program that will use our library:

```
void Hello(); //Forward declaration of our Hello function
void main()
{
  Hello();
}
```

I saved the file as main.cpp.

This program will call the Hello function which the compiler we then look for an implementation in our linked libraries.

5. To compile this program and link our static library, we can use the following command:

   cl main.cpp /link MyLib.lib

6. Once the compile has finished, we will now have a `main.exe` on Windows in our directory:

```
      120 hello.cpp
   75,882 hello.obj
       50 main.cpp
  168,448 main.exe
      622 main.exp
    1,684 main.lib
      527 main.obj
  111,210 MyLib.lib
```

On macOS X

Follow these steps:

1. For macOS X, you need to type the following command:

   g++ -c hello.cpp

   g++ is the open source compiler we are using. The flag −c tells g++ to output an object file. After the flag, we state which cpp file to use when building the object file. This command will produce the file `hello.o`.

2. On the macOS X platform, we use the following command to generate an .a file:

   arvsMylib.ahello.o

   ar, short for archiver, is the library building tool that we use to create our static library. First we set a few flags, rvs, which tell the ar tool how to set up the library archive. We then tell the tool the name of the library we are creating, followed by the object file(s) that make up the library.

   If we list the contents of the directory, you will see we now have our static library `Mylib.a`:

```
7.9K Mylib.a
334B hello.cpp
7.2K hello.o
 62B main.cpp
```

3. We can now consume our newly created library in other projects. Let's create a very simple program that will use our library:

```
void Hello(); //Forward declaration of our Hello function
void main()
{
   Hello();
}
```

I saved the file as main.cpp.

This program will call the Hello function which the compiler we then look for an implementation in our linked libraries.

4. We compile the program and link our static library with the following command:

g++ main.cpp MyLib.a -o Main

Once the compile has finished, we will now have a main.exe on Windows, or a main executable file on macOS X, in our directory.

```
8.2K Main
7.9K Mylib.a
334B hello.cpp
7.2K hello.o
62B main.cpp
```

Notice the size of this executable file for Windows and macOS X. Again, since we are statically linking our library, we actually include the necessary parts of the library in the executable itself. This eliminates the need to package the library with the program separately, which stops the library mismatches. In fact, now that the library, .lib file, has been compiled into the executable we no longer need it and can delete it. Our program will still run, but if we want to make any changes to the library, we would have to repeat the preceding steps to recompile the library, link it, and add it to our program's build.

Dynamically linked libraries

Dynamic or shared libraries are libraries that have their code implementations linked at runtime. What this means is that a dynamic library, .dll on Windows, .so on Linux, and .dylib on OS X, are the libraries that can be referenced in the source code of a program. When a compiler sees these references it looks for links in the library implementation. The referenced code is included through these created links when the program is launched. When a program uses a dynamic library, it only creates references to the code, not any copies of the code. This is one of the biggest advantages of using dynamic libraries, since they are only referenced hence they do not add to the overall size of the executable like a static library does. Another big advantage of using a dynamic library is maintainable or modification. Since the library is included at runtime, you can make updates or modifications without having to recompile the whole program. This is great for *patch* style updates and for allowing the modifications by the user themselves. The biggest disadvantage, is the one I mentioned earlier. Using dynamic libraries usually requires you to include the library with the program in some sort of package or installer. This of course could lead to mismatches and the dreaded Dll Hell.

For dynamic or shared libraries, we have to make a few modifications and follow slightly different steps for compilation and linking. To begin with, we will have to change our library file to let the compiler know that we would like to share certain parts with other programs. We do this, on the Microsoft platform, with __declspec or declaration specification. Passing the dllexport parameter to __declspec lets the compiler know that this function or even classes should be exported as part of the dynamic linked library. On the OS X platform, we also use a type of declaration to let the compiler know that the classes or functions are to be exported. Here we use __attribute__((visibility("default"))) in place of __declspec.

Compiling and linking dynamic libraries on Windows

Following are the step for compiling and linking dynamic libraries on Windows:

1. The hello.cpp file would now look like:

```cpp
#include <iostream>
__declspec(dllexport) void Hello()
{
    std::cout<< "Hello World Dynamically" <<std::endl;
}
```

Now that we have the function specified for export, we can compile the file into a dynamically shared library.

2. On Windows, we can create a `.dll` from the developer console prompt with the following command:

```
cl /LD /FeMyDynamicLib.dll hello.cpp
```

Again `cl` is the command to launch the compiler and linker. The `/LD` tells the compiler that we want to create a dynamically linked library. The `/FeMyDynamicLib.dll` sets the name of the library `/Fe` being the compiler option and `MyDynamicLib.dll` being the name. Finally, again, we pass in the file(s) we want to use to create the library.

3. When the compiler is finished, and we list the directory, we will now have both `MyDynamicLib.lib` and `MyDynamicLib.dll`:

```
    121 hello.cpp
 75,882 hello.obj
     50 main.cpp
161,280 MyDynamicLib.dll
    638 MyDynamicLib.exp
  1,858 MyDynamicLib.lib
```

The first thing you may have noticed is that this version of the `.lib` file is much smaller than in the previous static library example. This is because the implementation is not stored in this file. Instead, it acts as a pointer to the actual implementation in the `.dll` file.

4. Next, we can link and build our program with our newly created library exactly like the previous example with the following commands (on Windows):

```
cl main.cpp /link MyDynamicLib.lib
```

5. So now if we run the program and will see the line `Hello World Dynamically!` displayed:

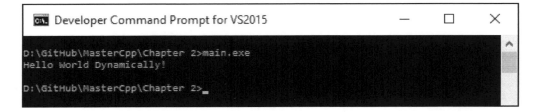

If we do a listing of the directory now, we will notice that the new main executable, like the .lib file from this example, is much smaller than the previous version that used the static library. This, again, is because we do not include the needed parts from the library at build time. Instead, we are loading them as needed at runtime, dynamically:

```
    128  hello.cpp
 75,889  hello.obj
     50  main.cpp
 77,312  main.exe
    527  main.obj
161,280  MyDynamicLib.dll
    638  MyDynamicLib.exp
  1,858  MyDynamicLib.lib
```

6. One of the bonuses I mentioned earlier is the fact that when you make changes to a dynamically linked library, you do not have to recompile the entire program; we only have to recompile the library. To see this in action, let's make a small change to the hello.cpp file:

```cpp
#include <iostream>
__declspec(dllexport) void Hello()
{
    std::cout<< "Hello World Dynamically!"<<std::endl;
    std::cout<< "Version 2" <<std::endl;
}
```

7. Next, we can recompile our library with the same command as before:

```
cl /LD /FeMyDynamicLib.dll hello.cpp
```

8. This will add our new changes, and we can see them take effect without recompiling main.exe, and simply running it instead. The output will now be the two lines: Hello World Dynamically! and Version 2:

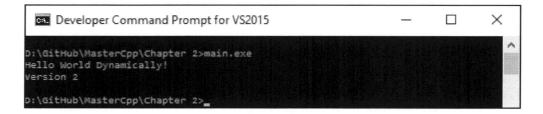

This makes upgrading very easy, but can also quickly lead Dll mismatching on machines without the updated library, often referred to as Dll Hell.

Compiling and linking dynamic libraries On macOS X

The `hello.cpp` file would now look like:

```
#include <iostream>
__attribute__((visibility("default"))) void Hello()
{
  std::cout<< "Hello World Dynamically" <<std::endl;
}
```

We can create a `.dylib` from the terminal shell with the following command:

g++ -dynamiclib -o MyDynamicLib.dylib hello.cpp

Here we use the `g++` compiler and set a flag to create a dynamic library file, `-dynamiclib`. The next flag `-o MyDynamicLib.dylib`, tells the compiler what to name the outputted file. Finally, we specify the file(s) to use when creating the library. If you list the directory now, you will see the newly created `MyDynamicLib.dylib` file:

```
 8440  Main
15148  MyDynamicLib.dylib
  334  hello.cpp
   48  hello.h
 7324  hello.o
   62  main.cpp
```

Next, we can link and build our program with our newly created library exactly like the previous example with the following commands:

g++ main.cpp MyDynamicLib.dylib -o Main

So now if we run the program and will see the line `Hello World Dynamically!` displayed:

```
● ● ●              Chapter2 — -bash — 80×24
[Michaels-MacBook-Air:chapter2 Mickey$ ./Main
Hello World Dynamically!
Michaels-MacBook-Air:chapter2 Mickey$ 
```

If we do a listing of the directory now, you will notice that the new main executable, like the .lib file from this example, is much smaller than the previous version that used the static library. This, again, is because we do not include the needed parts from the library at build time. Instead, we are loading them as needed at runtime, dynamically:

```
 8440  Main
15148  MyDynamicLib.dylib
  334  hello.cpp
   48  hello.h
 7324  hello.o
   62  main.cpp
```

One of the bonuses I mentioned earlier is the fact that when you make changes to a dynamically linked library, you do not have to recompile the entire program; we only have to recompile the library. To see this in action, let's make a small change to the hello.cpp file:

```
#include <iostream>
__attribute__((visibility("default"))) void Hello()
{
  std::cout<< "Hello World Dynamically!"<<std::endl;
  std::cout<< "Version 2" <<std::endl;
}
```

Next, we can recompile our library with the same command as before:

```
g++ -dynamiclib -o MyDynamicLib.dylib hello.cpp
```

Output from the preceding command will be like this:

```
● ● ●              Chapter2 — -bash — 80×24
[Michaels-MacBook-Air:chapter2 Mickey$ ./Main
Hello World Dynamically!
Version 2
Michaels-MacBook-Air:chapter2 Mickey$ 
```

This makes upgrading very easy, but can also quickly lead Dll mismatching on machines without the updated library, often referred to as Dll Hell.

Header only or source libraries

There is one last way to share libraries that I want to mention, and that is simply sharing the source or header implementation. This is an entirely legitimate way to share libraries and is very common among open source and smaller projects. It has the clear bonus of providing the source for modification and can easily allow the consuming developer to pick and choose which parts they would like to implement in their project. This can also be seen as a drawback, though, as now your source code is available publicly. By offering your code openly and freely, you give up a lot of control over its use and depending on the licensing could have little or no proprietary claims to the solution it implements.

To change our little example to a header only implementation, we would simply change the `hello.cpp` file into a header file, `hello.h`, and do all the function's implementation inside. Our new `hello.h` file will now look like the following:

```
#pragma once
#include <iostream>
void Hello()
{
  std::cout<< "Hello World Header!"<<std::endl;
}
```

Then to consume the header library, we will include it in the `main.cpp` file just like any other header file:

```
#include "hello.h"
void main()
{
  Hello();
}
```

Since we are using the header only implementation, we don't have the worry of linking the library during the build process. We can compile the program from the developer console prompt with the following command.

On Windows:

```
cl main.cpp
```

Once compiled, you can run the main executable and see similar a hello world message, Hello World Header!:

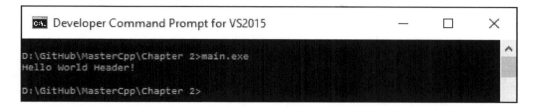

On macOS X:

```
g++ main.cpp -o Main
```

Once compiled, you can run the main executable and see similar a hello world message, Hello World Header!:

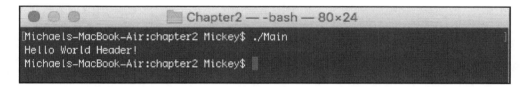

Building a custom shareable library

Having the ability to create your own custom library is an extremely valuable skill. Building a strong understanding of the steps needed to create, build, and consume libraries will allow you to create more capable systems and solutions. In the next section, we dive a little deeper and take a look at how you can create then build and consume a shareable library project in a managed development environment.

Setup and structure

For this example, I am going to stick with using Visual Studio for Windows, and XCode for macOS X. While some of the exact details will be different in each development environment, it should not be too difficult to extrapolate the steps. You can find the full source for this example in the Chapter02 folder of the code repository.

To start we will create a new project.

Creating a new project on Windows

On Windows, we can do this by going to **File | New | Project**, then expanding the **Visual C++** drop down and finally selecting **Win32 Console Application**. I named my new project `MemoryMgr`:

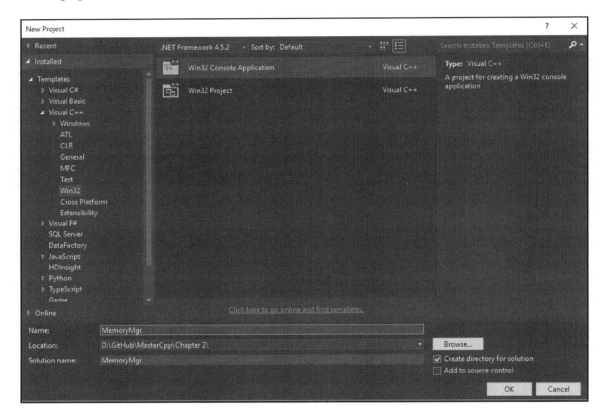

Once you select **OK**, the **Win32 Application Wizard** dialog will pop up. Click on **Next** to move the dialog to the next page:

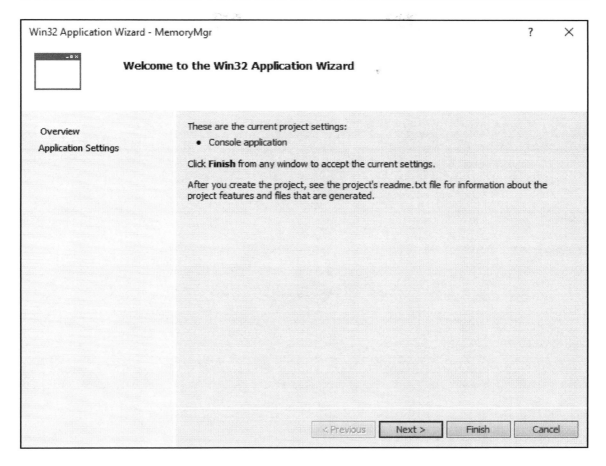

On this dialog page, we are presented a few different application settings. For our **Application type**, we are going to select **DLL**. This will create a .dll and accompanying .lib file that we can then share and consume. The reason we are picking a dynamic or shared library as opposed to a static library is because I can demonstrate how to build and compile a shareable library. This is a simplistic memory manager library that in most cases would be included in a suite of other utility libraries. We could easily modify this library to be static, see the previous section for an explanation on how.

Select the option for **Empty project**, this will give us a completely blank project from which we can build our library. This will also gray out most of the other options, such as the **Precompiled header** in the **Additional options**. This is a commonly used option to help speed up the compilation of large projects by calling all or most needed header files in a single header file, which you then add as a single header to other implementation files. You can leave **Security Development Lifecycle (SDL) checks** selected as it will not cause any issues. Click on **Finish** to exit the dialog and open the new project:

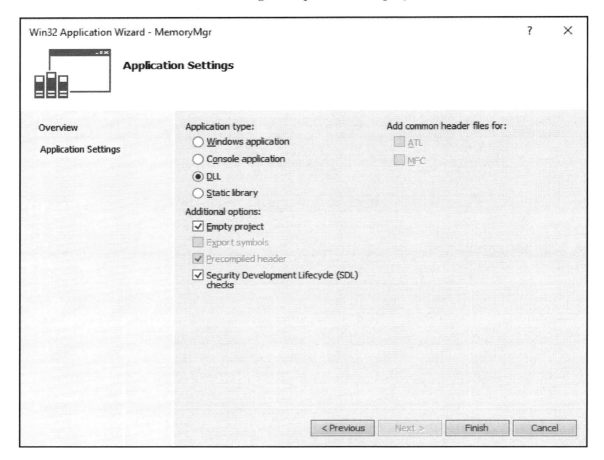

Once the project is loaded, we are greeted with a blank editor window and empty solution explorer.

Creating a new project on macOS X

We create a new project by going to **File | New | Project**, then selecting **OS X** from the platform list, and then **Library** from the template choices:

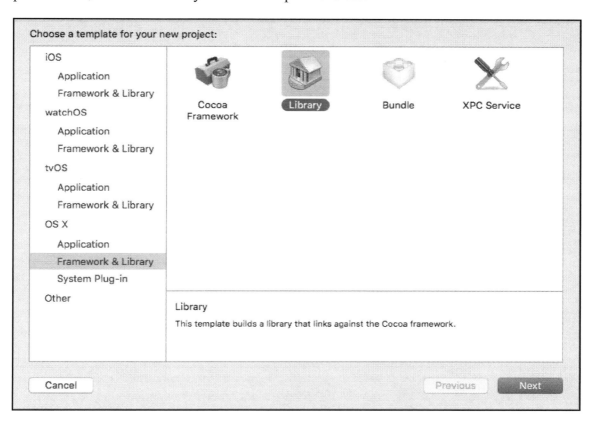

Once you click on **Next**, a dialog with project setting options will appear. These options include the **Product Name**, which I chose `MemoryMgr` for, **Organization Name** and **Organization Identifier**, which I left as the default choices. In a production setting, you would want to adjust these to match your project. The last two options are **Framework** and **Type**. For the **Framework**, select **STL (C++ Library)** this is the template used when working with a library that will include access to the STL. For **Type** select **Dynamic**, there is also the option for a static library project:

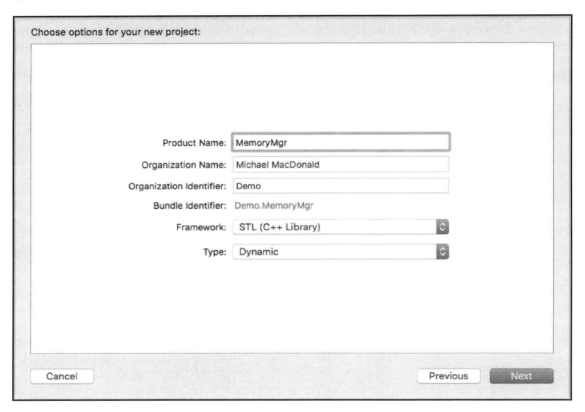

Our next step is to create the source files that we will need for the library. In this example, we will only be creating one class consisting of a single header, `.h`, and implementation file, `.cpp`.

Creating source files on Windows

We can add this class quickly in Visual Studio using the **Add** | **Class...** dialog.

Right-click on the **MemoryMgr** project in the **Solution Explorer**; navigate to **Add | Class** from the menu list:

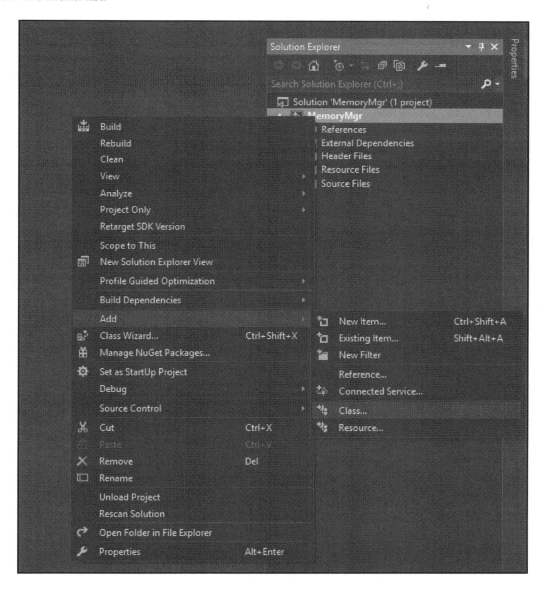

A new screen will pop up with a few options for creating new classes; we are just going to use the default generic **C++ Class** option.

Select **Add** to advance to the next dialog screen. We are now on the **Generic C++ Class Wizard** screen. In the **Class name** section, add the name of the new class you are creating, in my case I called it MemoryMgr. When you enter the class name, the wizard will auto populate the **.h file** and **.cpp file** for you. Since this is not a class that is inheriting, we can leave the **Base class** section empty. We will leave **Access** at the default setting of **public**, and finally we will leave the **Virtual destructor** and **Inline** options unchecked.

Click on **Finish** to add the class to our project:

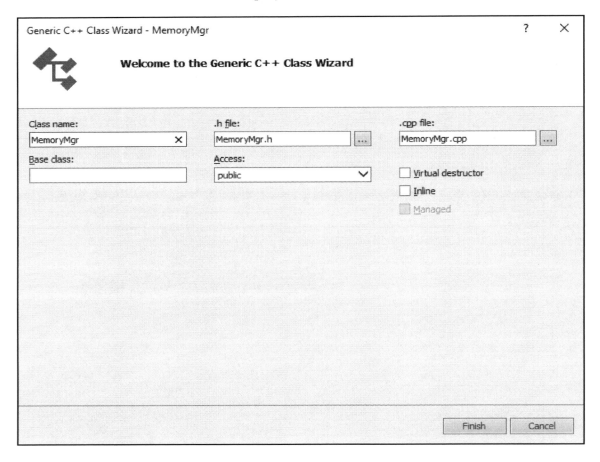

Of course, this would be the exact same as if we simply typed out the full export specifier like so:

```
__declspec(dllexport) int n; //Exporting a variable
__declspec(dllexport) intfnMemoryMgr(void); //Exporting a function
```

Creating source files on macOS X

This step is already done for us by default. The project creation wizard automatically includes an implementation file, `.cpp` and a **Header File**, but in this case the header file's extension is `.hpp`. The automatically created files also have a bunch of stubbed code to help get things started. In our example case, to make things more coherent, we are going to delete this stubbed code and remove both `.hpp` files. Instead we are going to create a new `.h` file and insert our own code. To create a new `.h` file is quite simple, navigate to **File | New | File**. In the new file dialog, select **OS X** from the platform list on the left and **Header File** from the type selection window:

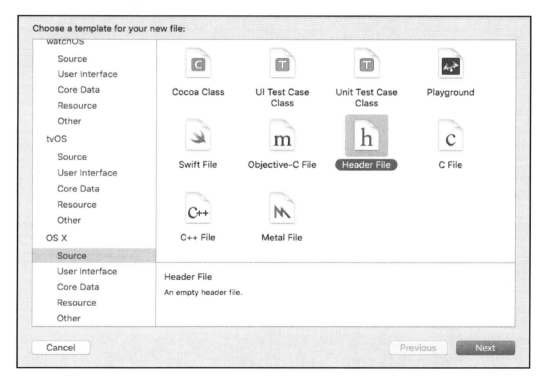

Clicking on the **Next** button will bring up the file save dialog. Save the file as `MemoryMgr.h`, notice I specified `.h` as the extension. If you do not specify the extension, the wizard will default to `.hpp`. Also of note, make sure the target project is selected at the bottom of the dialog, this will make sure it is counted as part of the XCode project solution.

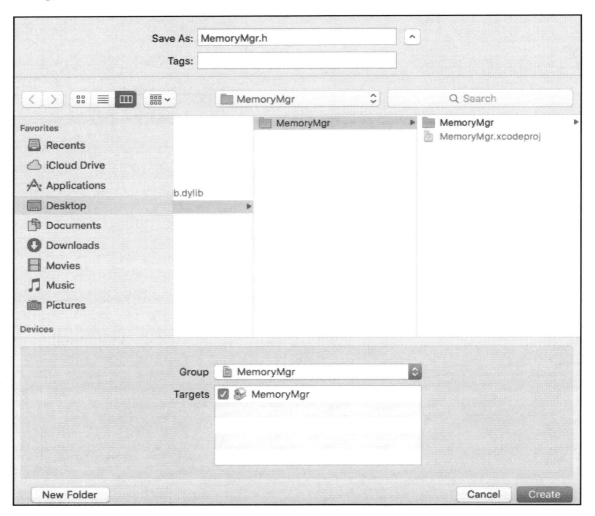

You project layout should now look like the following:

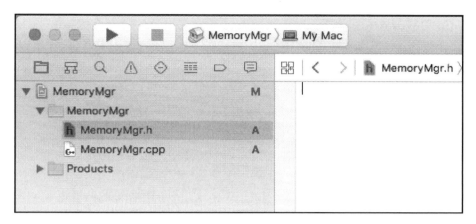

Now it's time for the code. We will start with the MemoryMgr header file, MemoryMgr.h. In this file, we will declare all the functions and variables we will be using along with the definitions that will provide access to our dynamic library. Here is MemoryMgr.h with the comments removed for brevity:

```
#ifdef MEMORYMGR_EXPORTS
#ifdef _WIN32
#define EXPORT __declspec(dllexport)
#else
#define EXPORT __declspec(dllimport)
#elif __APPLE__
#define EXPORT __attribute__((visibility("default")))
#endif
#endif
```

 The full file contents are available in the code repository in the Chapter02 folder.

The first step we take when creating the new dynamic library is a helpful shortcut that allows us to save a few keystrokes and simply the creation of exported classes, functions, or variables. Using `ifdef` directives, we can first create an identifier for our memory manager, `MEMORYMGR_EXPORTS`, then for the target platforms, `_WIN32` for Windows and `__APPLE__` for macOS X. Inside the `ifdef` directives for each platform, we can then add defines for the macro `EXPORT`, on Windows these are for `dllexport` and `dllimport`. This is a standard way of using macros to make the process of exporting and importing easier. With these macros in place, any project that includes this file will see the exposed functions as being imported whereas the dynamic library will see anything defined with this macro as being exported. This means we can now simply use `EXPORT` in place of `_declspec(dllexport)` or `__attribute__((visibility("default")))` when specifying what should be made available to others in the dynamic library.

The next step for creating our memory manager is to create a couple of `struct` for our `Block` and `Heap` objects. A block is a slice or block of memory where we will store individual objects. The `Heap` is a collection of these `Block` contained in a contiguous container of the memory. The `Block` struct simply holds a pointer to the next `Block` pointer; this creates a single linked list for the `Block` objects in each `Heap`. The `Heap` struct also holds a pointer to the next `Heap` in memory, which again creates a single linked list for the `Heap` objects. The `Heap` struct also contains a little helper function that returns the next block in the `Heap`:

```
struct Block
{
  Block* next;
};

struct Heap
{
  Heap* next;
  Block* block()
  {
    return reinterpret_cast<Block*>(this + 1);
  }
};
```

Now that we have our `Heap` and `Block` structs in place, we can move on to defining the actual memory manager class, `CMemoryMgr`. This is where the define we created earlier comes in handy. In this case, we use `EXPORT` to specify that we want the entire class to be exported in our dynamic library. When we export the class this way, the class access is exactly like any other class. That means that all the `private`, `protected`, and `public` objects continue to have the same access.

```
class EXPORT CMemoryMgr
```

While in our simple example, it makes sense to export the entire class, that might not always be the case. If we want to export just a function or variable, we could do that with our created `EXPORT` macro like so:

```
EXPORT int n; //Exporting a variable
EXPORT void fnMemoryMgr(void); //Exporting a function
```

Of course, this would be the exact same as if we simply typed out the full export specifier like so (on macOS X):

```
__attribute__((visibility("default"))) int n; //Exporting a
variable__attribute__((visibility("default"))) intfnMemoryMgr(void);
//Exporting a function
```

More about the `MemoryMgr` file:

Now that we know how to export class, functions, and variables, let's continue on with a quick look at the rest of the `MemoryMgr` header file. To begin with, we define our public methods that will be available when calling our library. These include the constructor, which takes three parameters; `dataSize`, the size of the objects for each block, `heapSize`, the size of each memory heap, and `memoryAlignmentSize`, this is the variable we use to shift the objects in memory.

Shifting the objects in memory means that we will always use a set amount memory to hold an object no matter the size. We do this so that the objects are aligned in such a way that we can reduce the amount of calls to the actual memory hardware which of course will increase performance. This is often the main reason developers will use a custom memory manager.

Next, we have the destructor which takes no parameters, followed by the `Allocate`, `Deallocate`, and `DeallocateAll`, which do exactly what their names imply. The only function that takes a parameter is the `Deallocate` function, which takes a pointer to the memory that you wish to delete:

```
class EXPORT CMemoryMgr
{
public:
    CMemoryMgr(unsigned int dataSize, unsigned int heapSize, unsigned int
            memoryAlignmentSize);
    ~CMemoryMgr();
    void* Allocate();
    void Deallocate(void* pointerToMemory);
    void DeallocateAll();
```

These functions are the only ones exposed through our library, and, in this simple example, can be considered a basic implementation interface for this library.

After the public declarations come, of course, the private declarations are needed for our library. They begin with three static constants that hold simple hexadecimal patterns we will use. This will help us identify each memory segment while debugging and provide a simple mechanism to check that we are working on the right segment at the right time:

```
private:
    static const unsigned char ALLOCATION_PATTERN = 0xBEEF;
    static const unsigned char ALIGNMENT_PATTERN = 0xBADD;
    static const unsigned char FREE_MEMORY_PATTERN = 0xF00D;
```

Then we have the `private` methods we use to do the heavy lifting in our library. The helper function `GetNextBlock` will return the next linked `block` in the `Heap`. The `OverWriteHeap` function takes a pointer to heap that will write to that specific `Heap`. An `OverWriteBlock` takes a pointer to a block to write to, and an `OverWriteAllocated` again takes a `Block` pointer that is allocated to write over:

```
    Block* GetNextBlock(Block* block);
    void OverWriteHeap(Heap* heapPointer);
    void OverWriteBlock(Block* blockPointer);
    void OverWriteAllocatedBlock(Block* blockPointer);
```

After the `private` methods, we have the member variables that will store the various types of data needed for our memory manager library. The first two are lists of pointers that we use to hold the heaps we have created and the free blocks available:

```
    Heap* m_heapList = nullptr;
    Block* m_freeBlockList = nullptr;
```

Finally, we have a group of unsigned integers that hold various pieces of data. Since the names of the variables are pretty self-explanatory, I won't go through each one:

```
unsigned int m_dataSize;
unsigned int m_heapSize;
unsigned int m_memoryAlignment;
unsigned int m_blockSize;
unsigned int m_blocksPerHeap;
unsigned int m_numOfHeaps;
unsigned int m_numOfBlocks;
unsigned int m_numOfBlocksFree;
};
```

Now, in our implementation file (MemoryMgr.cpp), since in this example we are exporting the entire class we do not have to include anything special, all of the publicly access contents will be available to any projects using our library. If we instead decided to export only selected functions and variables, instead of the whole class, we would have to use the EXPORT macro we created to specify that they should be exported in our library. To do that, you would simply add EXPORT in front of the implementation like so:

```
// This is an example of an exported variable
EXPORT int nMemoryMgr=0;
// This is an example of an exported function.
EXPORT int fnMemoryMgr(void)
{
   return 42;
}
```

To save time and space here, I am not going to go through each line of the MemoryMgr.cpp implementation. The file is well documented and should explain the simple mechanics of the memory manager well enough. Although it is simple, this library is a great starting point for building a more robust memory manager system to suit any project's particular needs.

Building a custom library

Before you or anyone else can use your custom library, you need to build it. There are a few different ways we can accomplish this.

On Windows

In our example from the preceding section, we used Visual Studio 2015, and in this case building the library is quite simple. For example, to build the MemoryMgr library, you can right-click on the **Solution 'MemoryMgr'** in **Solution Explorer** and select **Build Solution**, or use the keyboard shortcut *Ctrl + Shift + B*:

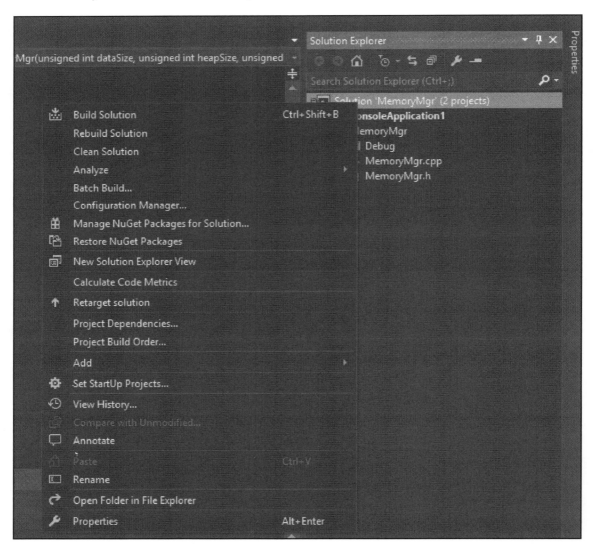

This will create the needed `MemoryMgr.dll` and `MemoryMgr.lib` files in the project's output folder under either **Debug** or **Release**, depending on the build setting selected. Another way we can build our library is with the developer command-line tools that we discussed in the first part of this chapter. In this case, we could simply change directories to the project file and run the `cl` command with the library name and input files included:

```
cl /LD /FeMemoryMgr.dll MemoryMgr.cpp
```

Again this will create the `MemoryMgr.dll` and `MemoryMgr.lib` files that are needed to use our library in other projects.

On macOS X

To build an XCode library project is quite easy. You can simply select **Product** from the toolbar and the click on **Build** or use the keyboard shortcut Command + *B*:

This will create the `MemoryMgr.dylib` file that we will need when including the library in other projects. Another way we can build the library is with the terminal shell the we looked at earlier in the chapter. In this case, we could simply change directories to the project file and run `g++` with the library name and input files included:

```
g++ –dynamiclib –o MemoryMgr.dylib MemoryMgr.cpp
```

Building dynamic library on Windows using .def file

We will explore the options of building the dynamic library using either only `.def` file or by using linker options as well.

Using only .def file

There is one more way that I want to mention that we can use to build our dynamic library, and that is with the use of a `.def` file. A module-definition or `.def` file is a text file that contains module statements that describe the exported attributes of the dynamic library. With a `.def` file, you do not need to create any macros or use the `__declspec(dllexport)` specifier to export the DLL's functions. For our `MemoryMgr` example, we can create a `.def` file by opening a text editor and adding the following:

```
LIBRARY MEMORYMGR
EXPORTS
   Allocate      @1
   Deallocate    @2
   DeallocateAll @3
```

This will tell the compiler that we wish to export these three functions: `Allocate`, `Deallocate`, and `DeallocateAll`. Save the file as a `.def` file; I called mine `MemoryMgr.def`.

Before we can recompile the library using the module definition file, we have to make a few changes to the source code of `MemoryMgr`. First, we can remove the macros we created and remove the `EXPORT` before the `CMemoryMgr` class definition. Instead of needing the macro or `_declspec(dllexport)` specifier, the `.def` file we created earlier will handle telling the compiler what should be exported.

To compile a dynamic library using a module definition file on the Windows platform, we have a couple of options. We could compile the library using the developer console, much like we did earlier, but with an extra option to specify the `.def` file. The command to compile the `MemoryMgr` library from the console would look something like this:

```
cl /LD /DEF:MemoryMgr.def /FeMemoryMgr2.dll MemoryMgr.cpp
```

The /DEF:filename is the flag that tells the compiler to use the specified module definition file to build the library. This command will produce a dynamic library called MemoryMgr2.dll.

Setting linker options

The second option we have to build the dynamic library using a .def file is by setting linker options in the Visual Studio development environment. It's fairly straightforward to do this.

First, we open the **Property Pages** dialog box by right-clicking on the project's name in **Solution Explorer** or by using the keyboard shortcut *Alt + Enter* with the project highlighted. With the **Property Pages** dialog open, select **Linker**, click on the **Input** property page, and finally, enter the name of the .def file in the **Module Definition File** property. The end result should look something like the following:

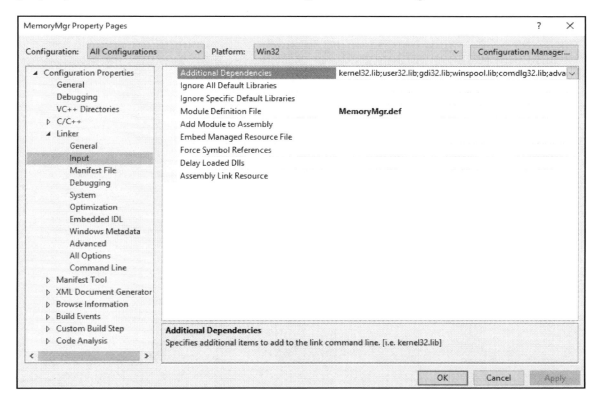

Now when you build your dynamic library project, the compiler will use the `MemoryMgr.def` file to determine which attributes should be exported.

Next, we will look at how we can consume this and other libraries when working with Visual Studio and XCode projects.

Sharing and consuming libraries

Now that we have our custom library built, we can start to use it in other projects. As we saw earlier in the chapter, we can link the dynamic and static libraries using the command-line compiler tools. This is OK if you have just a few libraries or have maybe created a custom build script, but in most cases when working with an IDE like Visual Studio, there are simpler ways to manage. In fact, adding libraries to a project in Visual Studio can be quite easy. To add the library first, we open the **Property Pages** dialog again, right-click and go to **Properties** or *Alt + Enter* with the project selected in the **Solution Explorer**. Next, expand **Linker** and select **Input**. At the top of the dialog on the **Additional Dependencies** property, click on the drop down and select **Edit**. This will bring up a dialog like the one shown here:

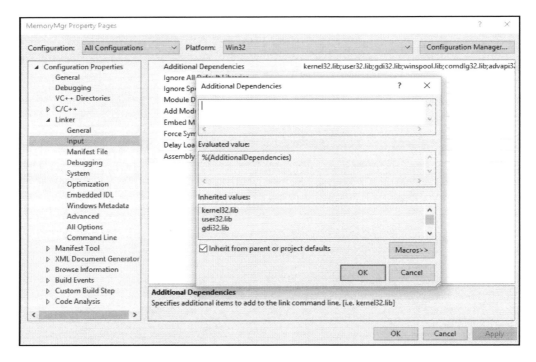

In this dialog's property window, we can specify the libraries we wish to include at compile time. We include the .lib file regardless of whether it is a dynamic library or a static library. If you have set up your library directories in the **VC++ Directories** folder under **Configuration Properties**, you can simply use the library name like this: MemoryMgr.lib. You can also include the libraries by specifying the path to the library such as C:\project\lib\MemoryMgr.lib. This property also accepts macros, which are important to use since moving the project to another directory would break the include otherwise. Some of the macros you can use are:

- $(SolutionDir): This is the top solution directory
- $(SourceDir): This is the directory of the source for the project
- $(Platform): This is the platform that is selected (Win32, x64, or ARM)
- $(Configuration): This is the configuration that is selected (**Debug** or **Release**)

This means if I have a few libraries for each platform and configuration in a folder called lib located in the solution directory, I can save myself a bunch of work by using a macro like this:

$(SolutionDir)/lib/$(Platform)/$(Configuration)/MemoryMgr.lib

Now if I switch platforms or configurations, I don't have to go back into the property pages and make changes each time.

That takes care of linking the library, but there is one more piece needed when consuming or sharing a library. In the first set of examples of this chapter, you must have noticed that when creating the little console program to demonstrate the use of the library, I used a forward declaration to specify the implementation of the Hello function from the library.

```
void Hello(); //Forward declaration of our Hello function
```

While this works in small examples like this one, if you are using libraries with multiple attributes, forward declarations will become quite tedious. In order to make use of libraries in your project, you will often have to include the definition files, the headers. This is why when you see libraries shared they will usually have an Include folder that has all the header files needed to work with that library. In the case of our MemoryMgr library, that would mean if I wanted to use it in a new project or share it with another developer I would include three files. The MemoryMgr.dll library, is actually a dynamic library. The MemoryMgr.lib library, is the library file used for linking. Lastly, I would also need to include the MemoryMgr.h file, the file that includes all the attribute definitions for my library.

Since most libraries you will work with have more than one header file, simply copying them into your project can get messy. The good news is, like most IDEs, Visual Studio has configuration settings that allow you to specify which folders house the files you wish to include in your project. Setting these configuration options is again quite simple. First, open the **Property Page** dialog, *Alt + Enter* with the project highlighted in the **Solution Explorer**.

Next, click on the **C/C++** folder to expand it. Then select the **General** section. In this property window at the top, you will see **Additional Include Directories**, select the drop down from this property and click on **Edit**. This will bring up a dialog like the one shown here:

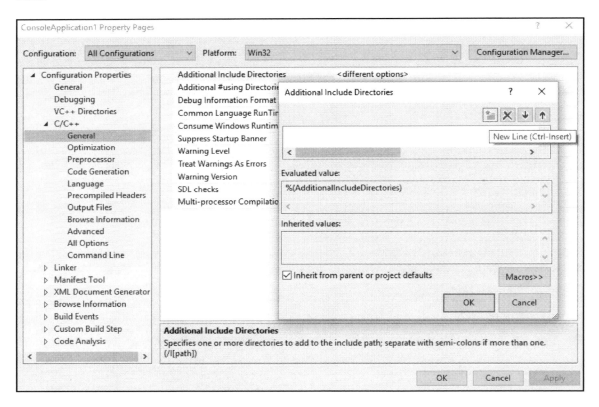

In this dialog window, we can add a new line by clicking on the add folder icon, or by using the keyboard shortcut *Ctrl + Insert*. You can use the folder explorer dialog to find and select the folders you need to include, but this property also supports macros, so a much better way to specify the needed include folders would be by using macros. If we had a folder in the main solution directory called Include that had a folder inside it called `MemoryMgr`, we could include that folder using the following macro:

```
$(SolutionDir)Include\MemoryMgr\
```

Once you select **OK** and **Apply** to close the **Property Pages** dialog, you can include the header files just like any other header file in your project. In the case of our `MemoryMgr` folder we would use the following code:

```
#include<MemoryMgr\MemoryMgr.h>;
```

Notice that the filesystem hierarchy is respected.

Summary

In this chapter, we covered the advanced topic of shareable libraries. We looked at the different types of libraries available. We walked through the various ways you can create your own sharable libraries.

In the next chapter, we are going to use this advanced library knowledge to build an asset management pipeline.

3
Building a Strong Foundation

While building your own libraries from scratch can be a rewarding process, it can also quickly become a time consuming one. This is why most professional game developers rely on some common libraries to speed up development times, and more importantly, provide a specialized, performant implementation. By connecting these common libraries and building helper and manager classes that abstract these libraries, you are in fact building the structure that will ultimately power your tools and gameplay engine.

In the next few sections, we will cover how these libraries can work together and build some of the libraries needed to round out the structure and give us a strong foundation to expand on the demos throughout the rest of the book.

To get started, we will focus on, arguably one of the most important aspects of any game project, the rendering system. Proper, performant implementations not only takes a significant amount of time, but it also takes specialized knowledge of video driver implementations and mathematics for computer graphics. Having said that, it is not, in fact, impossible to create a custom low-level graphics library yourself, it's just not overly recommended if your end goal is just to make video games. So instead of creating a low-level implementation themselves, most developers turn to a few different libraries to provide them abstracted access to the bare metal of the graphics device.

For the examples found throughout this book, we will be using a few different graphic APIs to help speed up the process and help provide coherence across platforms. These APIs include the following:

- **OpenGL** (`https://www.opengl.org/`): The **Open Graphics Library (OGL)** is an open cross-language, cross-platform application programming interface, or API, used for rendering 2D and 3D graphics. The API provides low-level access to the **Graphics Processing Unit (GPU)**.
- **SDL** (`https://www.libsdl.org/`): The **Simple DirectMedia Layer (SDL)** is a cross-platform software development library designed to deliver a low-level hardware abstraction layer to multimedia hardware components. While it does provide its own mechanism for rendering, SDL can use OGL to provide full 3D rendering support.

While these APIs save us time and effort by providing us some abstraction when working with the graphics hardware, it will quickly become apparent that the level of abstraction will not be high enough.

You will need another layer of abstraction to create an efficient way of reusing these APIs in multiple projects. This is where the helper and manager classes come in. These classes will provide the needed structure and abstraction for us and other coders. They will wrap all the common code needed to set up and initialize the libraries and hardware. The code that is required by any project regardless of gameplay or genre can be encapsulated in these classes and will become part of the engine.

In this chapter, we will cover the following topics:

- Building helper classes
- Encapsulation with managers
- Creating interfaces

Building helper classes

In object-oriented programming, a helper class is used to assist in providing some functionality, which is not, directly the main goal of the application in which it is used. Helper classes come in many forms and are often a catch-all term for classes that provide functionality outside of the current scope of a method or class. Many different programming patterns make use of helper classes. In our examples, we too will make heavy use of helper classes. Here is just one example.

Let's take a look at the very common set of steps used to create a Window. It's safe to say that most of the games you will create will have some sort of display and will generally be typical across different targets, in our case Windows and the macOS. Having to retype the same instructions constantly over and over for each new project seems like kind of a waste. That sort of situation is perfect for abstracting away in a helper class that will eventually become part of the engine itself. The following code is the header for the Window class included in the demo code examples, you can find the full source under the Chapter03 folder of the GitHub repository.

To start, we have a few necessary includes, SDL, glew which is a window creation helper library, and lastly, the standard string class is included:

```
#pragma once
#include <SDL/SDL.h>
#include <GL/glew.h>
#include <string>
```

Next, we have an enum WindowFlags. We use this for setting some bitwise operations to change the way the window will be displayed; invisible, full screen, or borderless. You will notice that I have wrapped the code in the namespace BookEngine, as I mentioned in the previous chapter this is essential for keeping naming conflicts from happening and will be very helpful once we start importing our engine into projects:

```
namespace BookEngine
{
  enum WindowFlags //Used for bitwise passing
  {
    INVISIBLE = 0x1,
    FULLSCREEN = 0x2,
    BORDERLESS = 0x4
  };
```

Now we have the Window class itself. We have a few public methods in this class. First the default constructor and destructor. It is a good idea to include a default constructor and destructor even if they are empty, as shown here, despite the compiler, including its own, these specified ones are needed if you plan on creating intelligent or managed pointers, such as unique_ptr, of the class:

```
class Window
  {
  public:
    Window();
    ~Window();
```

Next we have the `Create` function, this function will be the one that builds or creates the window. It takes a few arguments for the creation of the window such as the name of the window, screen width and height, and any flags we want to set, see the previously mentioned `enum`:

```
int Create(std::string windowName, int screenWidth, int
screenHeight, unsigned int currentFlags);
```

Then we have two `Get` functions. These functions will just return the width and height respectively:

```
int GetScreenWidth() { return m_screenWidth; }
int GetScreenHeight() { return m_screenHeight; }
```

The last public function is the `SwapBuffer` function; this is an important function that we will take a look at in more depth shortly.

```
void SwapBuffer();
```

To close out the class definition, we have a few private variables. The first is a pointer to a `SDL_Window*` type, named appropriate enough `m_SDL_Window`. Then we have two holder variables to store the width and height of our screen. This takes care of the definition of the new `Window` class, and as you can see it is pretty simple on face value. It provides easy access to the creation of the Window without the developer calling it having to know the exact details of the implementation, which is one aspect that makes object-orientated programming and this method is so powerful:

```
private:
    SDL_Window* m_SDL_Window;
    int m_screenWidth;
    int m_screenHeight;
};
}
```

To get a real sense of the abstraction, let's walk through the implementation of the `Window` class and really see all the pieces it takes to create the window itself:

```
#include ""Window.h""
#include ""Exception.h""
#include ""Logger.h""
namespace BookEngine
{
  Window::Window()
  {
  }
  Window::~Window()
```

```
    {
    }
```

The `Window.cpp` files starts out with the need includes, of course, we need to include `Window.h`, but you will also note we need to include the `Exception.h` and `Logger.h` header files also. These are two other helper files created to abstract their own processes. The `Exception.h` file is a helper class that provides an easy-to-use exception handling system. The `Logger.h` file is a helper class that as its name says, provides an easy-to-use logging system. Feel free to dig through each one; the code is located in the `Chapter03` folder of the GitHub code repository.

After the includes, we again wrap the code in the `BookEngine` namespace and provide the empty constructor and destructor for the class.

The `Create` function is the first to be implemented. In this function are the steps needed to create the actual window. It starts out setting the window display `flags` using a series of `if` statements to create a bitwise representation of the options for the window. We use the `enum` we created before to make this easier to read for us humans.

```
    int Window::Create(std::string windowName, int screenWidth, int
    screenHeight, unsigned int currentFlags)
    {
      Uint32 flags = SDL_WINDOW_OPENGL;
      if (currentFlags & INVISIBLE)
      {
        flags |= SDL_WINDOW_HIDDEN;
      }
      if (currentFlags & FULLSCREEN)
      {
        flags |= SDL_WINDOW_FULLSCREEN_DESKTOP;
      }
      if (currentFlags & BORDERLESS)
      {
        flags |= SDL_WINDOW_BORDERLESS;
      }
```

After we set the window's display options, we move on to using the SDL library to create the window. As I mentioned before, we use libraries such as SDL to help us ease the creation of such structures. We start out wrapping these function calls in a `try` statement; this will allow us to catch any issues and pass it along to our `Exception` class as we will see soon:

```
    try {
        //Open an SDL window
        m_SDL_Window = SDL_CreateWindow(windowName.c_str(),
```

```
SDL_WINDOWPOS_CENTERED,
SDL_WINDOWPOS_CENTERED,
screenWidth,
screenHeight,
flags);
```

The first line sets the private member variable m_SDL_Window to a newly created window using the passed in variables, for the name, width, height, and any flags. We also set the default window's spawn point to the screen center by passing the SDL_WINDOWPOS_CENTERED define to the function:

```
if (m_SDL_Window == nullptr)
    throw Exception(""SDL Window could not be created!"");
```

After we have attempted to create the window, it is a good idea to check and see if the process did succeed. We do this with a simple if statement and check to see if the variable m_SDL_Window is set to a nullptr; if it is, we throw an Exception. We pass the Exception the string ""SDL Window could not be created!"". This is the error message that we can then print out in a catch statement. Later on, we will see an example of this. Using this method, we provide ourselves some simple error checking.

Once we have created our window and have done some error checking, we can move on to setting up a few other components. One of these components is the OGL library which requires what is referred to as a context to be set. An OGL context can be thought of as a set of states that describes all the details related to the rendering of the application. The OGL context must be set before any drawing can be done.

One problem is that creating a window and an OGL context is not part of the OGL specification itself. What this means is that every platform can handle this differently. Luckily for us, the SDL API again abstracts the heavy lifting for us and allows us to do this all in one line of code. We create a SDL_GLContext variable named glContext. We then assign glContext to the return value of the SDL_GL_CreateContext function that takes one argument, the SDL_Window we created earlier. After this we, of course, do a simple check to make sure everything worked as intended, just like we did earlier with the window creation:

```
//Set up our OpenGL context
SDL_GLContext glContext = SDL_GL_CreateContext(m_SDL_Window);
    if (glContext == nullptr)
      throw Exception(""SDL_GL context could not be created!"");
```

The next component we need to initialize is GLEW. Again this is abstracted for us to one simple command, glewInit(). This function takes no arguments but does return an error status code. We can use this status code to perform a similar error check like we did with the window and OGL. This time instead checking it against the defined GLEW_OK. If it evaluates to anything other than GLEW_OK, we throw an Exception to be caught later on.

```
//Set up GLEW (optional)
GLenum error = glewInit();
  if (error != GLEW_OK)
    throw Exception(""Could not initialize glew!"");
```

Now that the needed components are initialized, now is a good time to log some information about the device running the application. You can log all kinds of data about the device which can provide valuable insights when trying to track down obscure issues. In this case, I am polling the system for the version of OGL that is running the application and then using the Logger helper class printing this out to a runtime text file:

```
//print some log info
std::string versionNumber = (const
char*)glGetString(GL_VERSION);
WriteLog(LogType::RUN, ""*** OpenGL Version: "" +
versionNumber + ""***"");
```

Now we set the clear color or the color that will be used to refresh the graphics card. In this case, it will be the background color of our application. The glClearColor function takes four float values that represent the red, green, blue, and alpha values in a range of 0.0 to 1.0. Alpha is the transparency value where 1.0f is opaque, and 0.0f is completely transparent:

```
//Set the background color to blue
glClearColor(0.0f, 0.0f, 1.0f, 1.0f);
```

The next line sets the VSYNC value, which is a mechanism that will attempt to match the application's framerate to that of the physical display. The SDL_GL_SetSwapInterval function takes one argument, an integer that can be 1 for on or 0 for off:

```
//Enable VSYNC
SDL_GL_SetSwapInterval(1);
```

The last two lines that make up the `try` statement block, enable blending and set the method used when performing alpha blending. For more information on these specific functions, check out the OGL development documents:

```
//Enable alpha blend
glEnable(GL_BLEND);
glBlendFunc(GL_SRC_ALPHA, GL_ONE_MINUS_SRC_ALPHA);
}
```

After our `try` block, we now have to include the `catch` block or blocks. This is where we will capture any of the thrown errors that have occurred. In our case, we are just going to grab all the exceptions. We use the `WriteLog` function from the `Logger` helper class to add the exception message, `e.reason` to the error log text file. This is a very basic case, but of course, we could do more here, possibly even recover from an error if possible:

```
catch (Exception e)
  {
     //Write Log
     WriteLog(LogType::ERROR, e.reason);
  }
  }
```

Finally, the last function in the `Window.cpp` file is the `SwapBuffer` function. Without going too deep on the implementation, what swapping buffers does is exchange the front and back buffers of the GPU. This in a nutshell allows smoother drawing to the screen. It is a complicated process that again has been abstracted by the SDL library. Our `SwapBuffer` function, abstracts this process again so that when we want to swap the buffers we simply call `SwapBuffer` instead of having to call the SDL function and specify the window, which is what is exactly done in the function:

```
void Window::SwapBuffer()
  {
     SDL_GL_SwapWindow(m_SDL_Window);
  }
}
```

So as you can see, building up these helper functions can go a long way in making the process of development and iteration much quicker and simpler. Next, we will look at another programming method that again abstracts the heavy lifting from the developer's hands and provides a form of control over the process, a management system.

Encapsulation with managers

When working with complex systems such as input and audio systems, it can easily become tedious and unwieldy to control and check each state and other internals of the system directly. This is where the idea of the manager programming pattern comes in. Using abstraction and polymorphism we can create classes that allow us to modularize and simplify the interaction with these systems. Manager classes can be found in many different use cases. Essentially if you see a need to have structured control over a certain system, this could be a candidate for a manager class. Next is an example of a manager class I have created for the example code in this book. You will see much more as we continue throughout.

Stepping away from the rendering system for a second, let's take a look at a very common task that any game will need to perform, handling input. Since every game needs some form of input, it only makes sense to move the code that handles this to a class that we can use over and over again. Let's take a look at the `InputManager` class, starting with the header file:

```
#pragma once
#include <unordered_map>
#include <glm/glm.hpp>
namespace BookEngine {
  class InputManager
  {
  public:
    InputManager();
    ~InputManager();
```

The `InputManager` class starts just like the others, we have the includes needed and again we wrap the class in the `BookEngine` namespace for convince and safety. The standard constructor and destructor are also defined.

Next, we have a few more public functions. First the `Update` function, which will not surprisingly update the input system. Then we have the `KeyPress` and `KeyReleased` functions, these functions both take an integer value corresponding to a keyboard key. The following functions fire off when the `key` is pressed or released respectively:

```
void Update();
void KeyPress(unsigned int keyID);
void KeyRelease(unsigned int keyID);
```

After the `KeyPress` and `KeyRelease` functions, we have two more key related functions the `isKeyDown` and `isKeyPressed`. Like the `KeyPress` and `KeyRelease` functions the `isKeyDown` and `isKeyPressed` functions take integer values that correspond to keyboard keys. The noticeable difference is that these functions return a Boolean value based on the status of the key. We will see more about this in the implementation file coming up:

```
bool isKeyDown(unsigned int keyID); //Returns true if key is
held    bool isKeyPressed(unsigned int keyID); //Returns true if key
was pressed this update
```

The last two public functions in the `InputManager` class are `SetMouseCoords` and `GetMouseCoords` which do exactly as the names suggest and set or get the mouse coordinates respectively.

```
void SetMouseCoords(float x, float y);
glm::vec2 GetMouseCoords() const { return m_mouseCoords; };
```

Moving on to the private members and functions, we have a few variables declared to store some information about the keys and mouse. First, we have a Boolean value that stores the state of the key being pressed down or not. Next, we have two unordered maps that will store the current `keymap` and previous key maps. The last value we store is the mouse coordinates. We us a `vec2` construct from another helper library the **OpenGL Mathematics (GLM)**. We use this `vec2`, which is just a two-dimensional vector, to store the *x* and *y* coordinate values of the mouse cursor since it is on a 2D plane, the screen. If you are looking for a refresher on vectors and the Cartesian coordinate system, I highly recommend the *Beginning Math Concepts for Game Developers book* by *Dr. John P Flynt*:

```
private:
    bool WasKeyDown(unsigned int keyID);
std::unordered_map<unsigned int, bool> m_keyMap;
    std::unordered_map<unsigned int, bool> m_previousKeyMap;
    glm::vec2 m_mouseCoords;
};
```

Now let's look at the implementation, the `InputManager.cpp` file.

Again we start out with the includes and the namespace wrapper. Then we have the constructor and destructor. The highlight to note here is the setting of the `m_mouseCoords` to `0.0f` in the constructor:

```
namespace BookEngine
{
  InputManager::InputManager() : m_mouseCoords(0.0f)
  {
  }
}
```

```
InputManager::~InputManager()
{
}
```

Next is the `Update` function. This is a simple update where we are stepping through each key in the `keyMap` and copying it over to the previous `keyMap` holder

`m_previousKeyMap`:

```
void InputManager::Update()
{
    for (auto& iter : m_keyMap)
    {
        m_previousKeyMap[iter.first] = iter.second;
    }
}
```

The next function is the `KeyPress` function. In this function, we use the trick of an associative array to test and insert the key pressed which matches the ID passed in. The trick is that if the item located at the index of the `keyID` index does not exist, it will automatically be created:

```
void InputManager::KeyPress(unsigned int keyID)
{
    m_keyMap[keyID] = true;
}
. We do the same for the KeyRelease function below.
 void InputManager::KeyRelease(unsigned int keyID)
{
    m_keyMap[keyID] = false;
}
```

The `KeyRelease` function is the same setup as the `KeyPressed` function, except that we are setting the `keyMap` item at the `keyID` index to false:

```
bool InputManager::isKeyDown(unsigned int keyID)
{
    auto key = m_keyMap.find(keyID);
    if (key != m_keyMap.end())
        return key->second;    // Found the key
    return false;
}
```

After the `KeyPress` and `KeyRelease` functions, we implement the `isKeyDown` and `isKeyPressed` functions. First the `isKeydown` function; here we want to test if a key is already pressed down. In this case, we take a different approach to testing the key than in the `KeyPress` and `KeyRelease` functions and avoid the associative array trick. This is because we don't want to create a key if it does not already exist, so instead, we do it manually:

```cpp
bool InputManager::isKeyPressed(unsigned int keyID)
  {
    if(isKeyDown(keyID) && !m_wasKeyDown(keyID))
    {
      return true;
    }
    return false;
  }
```

The `isKeyPressed` function is quite simple. Here we test to see if the key that matches the passed in ID is pressed down, by using the `isKeyDown` function, and that it was not already pressed down by also passing the ID to `m_wasKeyDown`. If both of these conditions are met, we return true, or else we return false. Next, we have the `WasKeyDown` function, much like the `isKeyDown` function, we do a manual lookup to avoid accidentally creating the object using the associative array trick:

```cpp
bool InputManager::WasKeyDown(unsigned int keyID)
  {
    auto key = m_previousKeyMap.find(keyID);
    if (key != m_previousKeyMap.end())
      return key->second;   // Found the key
    return false;
  }
```

The final function in the `InputManager` is `SetMouseCoords`. This is a very simple `Set` function that takes the passed in floats and assigns them to the x and y members of the two-dimensional vector, `m_mouseCoords`:

```cpp
void InputManager::SetMouseCoords(float x, float y)
  {
    m_mouseCoords.x = x;
    m_mouseCoords.y = y;
  }
}
```

Creating interfaces

Sometimes you are faced with a situation where you need to describe capabilities and provide access to general behaviors of a class without committing to a particular implementation. This is where the idea of interfaces or abstract classes comes into play. Using interfaces provides a simple base class that other classes can then inherit from without having to worry about the intrinsic details. Building strong interfaces can enable rapid development by providing a standard class to interact with. While interfaces could, in theory, be created of any class, it is more common to see them used in situations where the code is commonly being reused. The following is an example interface created for the book's example code that creates an interface to the main class for the game.

Let's take a look at an interface from the example code in the repository. This interface will provide access to the core components of the game. I have named this class `IGame`, using the prefix `I` to identify this class as an interface. The following is the implementation beginning with the definition file `IGame.h`.

To begin with, we have the needed includes and the namespace wrapper. You will notice that the files we are including are some of the ones we just created. This is a prime example of the continuation of the abstraction. We use these building blocks to continue to build the structure that will allow this seamless abstraction:

```
#pragma once
#include <memory>
#include ""BookEngine.h""
#include ""Window.h""
#include ""InputManager.h""
#include ""ScreenList.h""
namespace BookEngine
{
```

Next, we have a forward declaration. This declaration is for another interface that has been created for screens. The full source code to this interface and its supporting helper classes are available in the code repository. Class `IScreen`; using forward declarations like this is a common practice in C++.

 If the definition file only requires the simple definition of a class, not adding the header for that class will speed up compile times.

Moving onto the public members and functions, we start off the constructor and destructor. You will notice that this destructor in this case is virtual. We are setting the destructor as virtual to allow us to call delete on the instance of the derived class through a pointer. This is handy when we want our interface to handle some of the cleanup directly as well:

```
class IGame
  {
  public:
    IGame();
    virtual ~IGame();
```

Next we have declarations for the `Run` function and the `ExitGame` function.

```
    void Run();
    void ExitGame();
```

We then have some pure virtual functions, `OnInit`, `OnExit`, and `AddScreens`. Pure virtual functions are functions that must be overridden by the inheriting class. By adding the `=0;` to the end of the definition, we are telling the compiler that these functions are purely virtual.

When designing your interfaces, it is important to be cautious when defining what functions must be overridden. It's also very important to note that having pure virtual function implicitly makes the class it is defined for abstract. Abstract classes cannot be instantiated directly because of this and any derived classes need to implement all inherited pure virtual functions. If they do not, they too will become abstract:

```
    virtual void OnInit() = 0;
    virtual void OnExit() = 0;
    virtual void AddScreens() = 0;
```

After our pure virtual function declarations, we have a function `OnSDLEvent` which we use to hook into the SDL event system. This provides us support for our input and other event-driven systems:

```
    void OnSDLEvent(SDL_Event& event);
```

The public function in the `IGame` interface class is a simple helper function `GetFPS` that returns the current `fps`. Notice the `const` modifiers, they identify quickly that this function will not modify the variable's value in any way:

```
const float GetFPS() const { return m_fps; }
```

In our protected space, we start with a few function declarations. First is the `Init` or initialization function. This will be the function that handles a good portion of the setup. Then we have two virtual functions `Update` and `Draw`.

Like pure virtual functions, a virtual function is a function that can be overridden by a derived class's implementation. Unlike a pure virtual function, the virtual function does not make the class abstract by default and does not have to be overridden. Virtual and pure virtual functions are keystones of polymorphic design. You will quickly see their benefits as you continue your development journey:

```
protected:
    bool Init();
    virtual void Update();
    virtual void Draw();
```

To close out the `IGame` definition file, we have a few members to house different objects and values. I am not going to go through these line by line since I feel they are pretty self-explanatory:

```
        std::unique_ptr<ScreenList> m_screenList = nullptr;
        IGameScreen* m_currentScreen = nullptr;
        Window m_window;
        InputManager m_inputManager;
        bool m_isRunning = false;
        float m_fps = 0.0f;
    };
}
```

Now that we have taken a look at the definition of our interface class, let's quickly walk through the implementation. The following is the `IGame.cpp` file. To save time and space, I am going to highlight the key points. For the most part, the code is self-explanatory, and the source located in the repository is well commented for more clarity:

```
#include ""IGame.h""
#include ""IScreen.h""
#include ""ScreenList.h""
#include ""Timing.h""
namespace BookEngine
{
```

```
IGame::IGame()
{
  m_screenList = std::make_unique<ScreenList>(this);
}

IGame::~IGame()
{
}
```

Our implementation starts out with the constructor and destructor. The constructor is simple, its only job is to add a unique pointer of a new screen using this `IGame` object as the argument to pass in. See the `IScreen` class for more information on screen creation. Next, we have the implementation of the `Run` function. This function, when called will set the engine in motion. Inside the function, we do a quick check to make sure we have already initialized our object. We then use yet another helper class, `fpsLimiter`, to `SetMaxFPS` that our game can run. After that, we set the `isRunning` Boolean value to `true`, which we then use to control the game loop:

```
void IGame::Run()
  {
    if (!Init())
      return;
    FPSLimiter fpsLimiter;
    fpsLimiter.SetMaxFPS(60.0f);
    m_isRunning = true;
```

Next is the game loop. In the game loop, we do a few simple calls. First, we start the `fpsLimiter`. We then call the update function on our `InputManager`.

It is a good idea always to check input before doing other updates or drawing since their calculations are sure to use the new input values.

After we update the `InputManager`, we recursively call our `Update` and `Draw` class, which we will see shortly. We close out the loop by ending the `fpsLimiter` function and calling `SwapBuffer` on the `Window` object:

```
///Game Loop
    while (m_isRunning)
    {
      fpsLimiter.Begin();
      m_inputManager.Update();
      Update();
      Draw();
```

```
    m_fps = fpsLimiter.End();
    m_window.SwapBuffer();
  }
}
```

The next function we implement is the `ExitGame` function. Ultimately, this will be the function that will be called on the final exit of the game. We close out, destroy, and free up any memory that the screen list has created and set the `isRunning` Boolean to `false`, which will put an end to the loop:

```
void IGame::ExitGame()
{
  m_currentScreen->OnExit();
  if (m_screenList)
  {
    m_screenList->Destroy();
    m_screenList.reset(); //Free memory
  }
  m_isRunning = false;
}
```

Next up is the `Init` function. This function will initialize all the internal object settings and call the initialization on the connected systems. Again, this is an excellent example of OOP or object-orientated programming and polymorphism. Handling initialization in this manner allows the cascading effect, keeping the code modular, and easier to modify:

```
bool IGame::Init()
{
  BookEngine::Init();
  SDL_GL_SetAttribute(SDL_GL_ACCELERATED_VISUAL, 1);
  m_window.Create(""BookEngine"", 1024, 780, 0);
  OnInit();
  AddScreens();
  m_currentScreen = m_screenList->GetCurrentScreen();
  m_currentScreen->OnEntry();
  m_currentScreen->Run();
  return true;
}
```

Next, we have the Update function. In this Update function, we create a structure to allow us to execute certain code based on a state that the current screen is in. We accomplish this using a simple switch case method with the enumerated elements of the ScreenState type as the cases. This setup is considered a simple finite state machine and is a very powerful design method used throughout game development. You can be certain to see this pop up again throughout the book's examples:

```cpp
void IGame::Update()
{
  if (m_currentScreen)
  {
    switch (m_currentScreen->GetScreenState())
    {
    case ScreenState::RUNNING:
      m_currentScreen->Update();
      break;
    case ScreenState::CHANGE_NEXT:
      m_currentScreen->OnExit();
      m_currentScreen = m_screenList->MoveToNextScreen();
      if (m_currentScreen)
      {
        m_currentScreen->Run();
        m_currentScreen->OnEntry();
      }
      break;
    case ScreenState::CHANGE_PREVIOUS:
      m_currentScreen->OnExit();
      m_currentScreen = m_screenList->MoveToPreviousScreen();
      if (m_currentScreen)
      {
        m_currentScreen->Run();
        m_currentScreen->OnEntry();
      }
      break;
    case ScreenState::EXIT_APP:
        ExitGame();
        break;
    default:
        break;
    }
  }
  else
  {
    //we have no screen so exit
    ExitGame();
  }
}
```

After our `Update`, we implement the `Draw` function. In our function, we only do a couple of things. First, we reset `Viewport` as a simple safety check, then if the current screen's state matches the enumerated value `RUNNING`, we again use polymorphism to pass the `Draw` call down the object line:

```
void IGame::Draw()
  {
    //For safety
    glViewport(0, 0, m_window.GetScreenWidth(),
m_window.GetScreenHeight());
    //Check if we have a screen and that the screen is running
    if (m_currentScreen &&
      m_currentScreen->GetScreenState() == ScreenState::RUNNING)
    {
      m_currentScreen->Draw();
    }
  }
```

The last function we need to implement is the `OnSDLEvent` function. Like I mention in the definition section of this class, we will use this function to connect our `InputManager` system to the SDL built in event system.

Every key press or mouse movement is handled as an event. Based on the type of event that has occurred, we again use a switch case statement to create a simple finite state machine. Refer to the manager pattern discussion section preceding for how each function was implemented.

```
void IGame::OnSDLEvent(SDL_Event & event)
  {
    switch (event.type) {
    case SDL_QUIT:
      m_isRunning = false;
      break;
    case SDL_MOUSEMOTION:
      m_inputManager.SetMouseCoords((float)event.motion.x,
(float)event.motion.y);
      break;
    case SDL_KEYDOWN:
      m_inputManager.KeyPress(event.key.keysym.sym);
      break;
    case SDL_KEYUP:
      m_inputManager.KeyRelease(event.key.keysym.sym);
      break;
    case SDL_MOUSEBUTTONDOWN:
      m_inputManager.KeyPress(event.button.button);
      break;
```

```
    case SDL_MOUSEBUTTONUP:
      m_inputManager.KeyRelease(event.button.button);
      break;
    }
  }
}
```

Well, that takes care of the IGame interface. With this created, we can now create a new project that can utilize this and other interfaces in the example engine to create a game and initialize it all with just a few lines of code. Here is the App class of the example project located in the Chapter03 folder of the code repository:

```
#pragma once
#include <BookEngine/IGame.h>
#include ""GamePlayScreen.h""
class App : public BookEngine::IGame
{
public:
  App();
  ~App();
  virtual void OnInit() override;
  virtual void OnExit() override;
  virtual void AddScreens() override;
private:
  std::unique_ptr<GameplayScreen> m_gameplayScreen = nullptr;
};
```

The highlights to note here are that, one, the App class inherits from the BookEngine::IGame interface and two, we have all the necessary overrides that the inherited class requires. Next, if we take a look at the main.cpp file, the entry point for our application, you will see the simple commands to set up and kick off all the amazing things our interfaces, managers, and helpers abstract for us:

```
#include <BookEngine/IGame.h>
#include ""App.h""
int main(int argc, char** argv)
{
  App app;
  app.Run();
  return 0;
}
```

As you can see, this is far simpler to type out every time we want to create a new project than having to recreate the framework constantly from scratch.

To see the output of the framework described throughout this chapter, build the `BookEngine` project, then build and run the example project. The XCode and Visual Studio projects can be found in the `Chapter03` folder of the GitHub code repository.

On Windows, the example project when run will look like the following:

On macOS, the example project when run will look like the following:

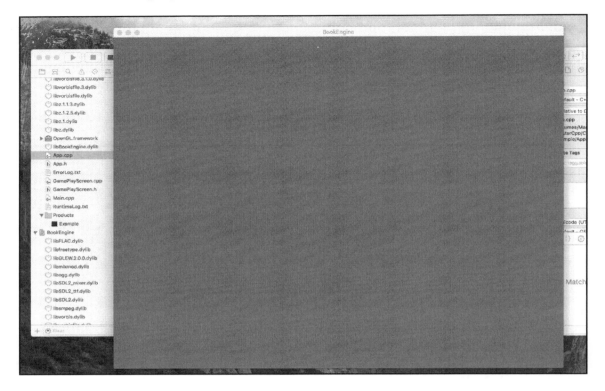

Summary

In this chapter, we covered quite a bit. We took a look at the different methods of using object-oriented programming and polymorphism to create a reusable structure for all your game projects. We walked through the differences in helper, managers, and interfaces classes with examples from real code.

In the rest of chapters, we will see this structure reused and built upon to create the demos. In fact, in the next chapter, we will build even more managers and helper classes to create an asset management pipeline.

4
Building the Asset Pipeline

Games are essentially a collection of assets or content packaged in a fun and engaging way. Handling all the needed content for a video game can be a large challenge in itself. Having a structure in place to import, convert, and consume these assets is a necessity in any real project. In this chapter, we are going to explore the topic of developing and implementing an asset pipeline. The following are the topics we will cover:

- Handling audio
- Working with images
- Importing model meshes

What is an asset pipeline?

In `Chapter 3`, *Building a Strong Foundation*, we took a look at how we can use the structure of helper and manager classes to wrap multiple methods into an easy to consume interface to work with various pieces of the project. We are going to use these techniques throughout the next few sections to build our own custom framework/content pipeline.

Handling audio

To get started, we are going to ease ourselves into the process, by looking at how to handle audio assets in our game projects. To help us with the process we are going to again use a helper library. There are literally hundreds of different libraries to help with the use of audio. Some of the more popular choices are listed here:

- FMOD (`http://www.fmod.org`)
- Wwise (`https://www.audiokinetic.com/products/wwise/`)

- XAudio2 (https://msdn.microsoft.com/en-us/library/windows/desktop/ee415813(v=vs.85).aspx)
- OpenAL (https://www.openal.org/)
- SDL_mixer (https://www.libsdl.org/projects/SDL_mixer/)

Each library has its own strengths and weaknesses. Choosing the right one for your project boils down to a few different questions you should ask yourself.

Does this library meet your technical needs? Does it have all the features you want?

Does it meet the project's budget constraints? A lot of the more robust libraries have a large price tag.

Is this library's learning curve within your own, or team's, skill range? Picking an advanced API with a bunch of cool features might seem like a good idea, but if you spend more time trying to understand the API than implementing it, that could be detrimental.

For the examples in this book, I chose to use SDL_mixer API for a few reasons. First, it is fairly easy to get started with, compared to some of the others. Second, it matches my project's needs very well. It has support for FLAC, MP3, and even Ogg Vorbis files. Third, it connects well with the rest of the project's framework since it is an extension to the SDL library we are already using. Lastly, I chose this API because it is open source and has a simple license that does not require me to pay the creator a share of my game's proceeds in return for using the library.

Let's start by taking a look at the declaration and implementation of a few different classes we will need. The file we are looking at is the AudioManager.h file that can be found in the Chapter04 folder of the code repository.

We begin with the necessary includes, the SDL/SDL_mixer.h, string, and map implementations. Like all other engine components, we have been building, we wrap these declarations in the BookEngine namespace:

```
#pragma once
#include <SDL/SDL_mixer.h>
#include <string>
#include <map>

namespace BookEngine
{
```

Within the "AudioManager.h" file, we have the declaration of a few helper classes. The first one is the SoundEffect class. This class defines the structure of the sound effect object to be used in our game:

```
class SoundEffect
{
  public:
    friend class AudioManager;
    ///Plays the sound file
    ///@param numOfLoops: If == -1, loop forever,
    ///otherwise loop of number times provided + 1
    void Play(int numOfLoops = 0);

  private:
    Mix_Chunk* m_chunk = nullptr;
};
```

These can include sounds like the player jumping, weapon fire, and really anything we will play in a short burst.

Inside the class definition, we need a friend class statement that will allow this class access to the AudioManager class methods and variables, including private ones. Next we have the definition of the Play function. This function will simply play the sound effect and take just one argument, the number of times to loop through the sound. By default, we set this to 0, if you pass -1 as the number of loops it will set the sound effect to loop indefinitely. The last definition is for a private variable of type Mix_Chunk. Mix_Chunk is a SDL_mixer object type that stores the audio data in memory.

The Mix_Chunk object structure is as follows:

```
typedef struct {
        int allocated;
        Uint8 *abuf;
        Uint32 alen;
        Uint8 volume;
} Mix_Chunk;
```

Here are the internals of the object:

- allocated: If this is set to 1, struct has its own allocated buffer
- abuf: This is a pointer to the audio data
- alen: This is the length of the audio data, in bytes
- volume: This is a per sample volume value between 0 and 128

The next helper class we have in the `AudioManager.h` file is the `Music` class. Like the sound effect, the `Music` class defines the structure of a `Music` object. This can be used for sounds like the loading screen music, background music, and really any sound we wish to play for an extended time or will need to stop, start, and pause:

```
class Music
  {
  public:
    friend class AudioManager;
    ///Plays the music file
    ///@param numOfLoops: If == -1, loop forever,
    ///otherwise loop of number times provided
    void Play(int numOfLoops = -1);

    static void Pause() { Mix_PauseMusic(); };
    static void Stop() { Mix_HaltMusic(); };
    static void Resume() { Mix_ResumeMusic(); };

  private:
    Mix_Music* m_music = nullptr;
  };
```

For the class definition, we again start with a `friend` class statement so that the `Music` class will have access to the needed parts of the `AudioManager` class. Next we have a `Play` function, and just like the `SoundEffect` class, it takes a single argument to set the amount of loops the sound will go through. After the `Play` function, we have three more functions, `Pause()`, `Stop()`, and `Resume()` function. These three functions are just wrappers to the underlining SDL_mixer API calls, for pausing, stopping, and resuming the music, respectively.

Finally, we have a private declaration for the `Mix_Music` object. `Mix_Music` is the SDL_mixer datatypes used for music data. It supports the loading of WAV, MOD, MID, OGG, and MP3 sound files. We will see more about this in the implementation section next:

```
class AudioManager
  {
  public:
    AudioManager();
    ~AudioManager();

    void Init();
    void Destroy();

    SoundEffect LoadSoundEffect(const std::string& filePath);
    Music LoadMusicEffect(const std::string& filePath);
```

```
    private:
      std::map<std::string, Mix_Chunk*> m_effectList;
      std::map<std::string, Mix_Music*> m_musicList;
      bool m_isInitialized = false;
    };
}
```

After the two `Music` and `SoundEffect` helper classes, we now come to the `AudioManager` class definition. The `AudioManager` class will do most of the heavy lifting on our side, it will load, hold, and manage creation and deletion of all music and sound effects.

Our declaration of the class starts like most others with a default constructor and destructor. Next we have an `Init()` function. This function will handle the setup or initialization of our audio system. We then have a `Destroy()` function that will handle the deletion and cleanup of our audio system. After the `Init` and `Destroy` functions, we have two loader functions, `LoadSoundEffect()` and `LoadMusicEffent()` function. Both of these functions take a single argument, a standard string that holds the path to the audio file. These functions will load the audio files and return a `SoundEffect` or `Music` object depending on the function.

The private section of our class has three objects. The first two private objects are maps of either type `Mix_Chunk` or `Mix_Music`. This is where we will store all the effects and music we will need. By storing a list of sound effects and music files we load, we are creating a cache. If we need the file at a later time in the project, we can then check these lists and save some valuable loading time. The last variable, `m_isInitialized`, holds a Boolean value to specify whether the `AudioManager` class has been initialized or not.

That completes the declaration of the `AudioManager` and helper classes, let's move on to the implementation where we can take a closer look at some of the functions. You can find the `AudioManager.cpp` file in the `Chapter04` folder of the code repository:

```
#include "AudioManager.h"
#include "Exception.h"
#include "Logger.h"

namespace BookEngine
{

  AudioManager::AudioManager()
  {
  }


  AudioManager::~AudioManager()
```

```
{
  Destroy();
}
```

Our implementation starts out with the includes, default constructor, and destructor. Nothing new here, only thing of note is that we call Destroy() function from the destructor. This allows us two methods of cleaning up the class, through the destructor or by explicitly calling the Destroy() function on the object itself:

```
void BookEngine::AudioManager::Init()
{
  //Check if we have already been initialized
  if (m_isInitialized)
    throw Exception("Audio manager is already initialized");
```

The next function in the AudioManager class implementation is the Init() function. This is the function that will setup all the needed components for our manager. The function starts out with a simple check to see if we have already initialized the class; if we have, we throw an exception with a debug message:

```
//Can be Bitwise combination of
//MIX_INIT_FAC, MIX_INIT_MOD, MIX_INIT_MP3, MIX_INIT_OGG
if(Mix_Init(MIX_INIT_OGG || MIX_INIT_MP3) == -1)
  throw Exception("SDL_Mixer could not initialize! Error: " +
  std::string(Mix_GetError()));
```

After we check that we haven't already, we move on to initializing the SDL_mixer objects. We do this by calling the Mix_Init() function and passing in a bitwise combination of flags to set the supported file types. This can be a combination of FLAC, MOD, MP3, and OGG. In this example, we are passing the flags for OGG and MP3 support. We wrap this call in an if statement to check if the Mix_Init() function call had any issues. If it does run into an error, we throw another exception with a debug message containing the error information returned from the Mix_Init() function:

```
if(Mix_OpenAudio(MIX_DEFAULT_FREQUENCY, MIX_DEFAULT_FORMAT, 2,
  1024) == -1)       throw Exception("Mix_OpenAudio Error: " +
  std::string(Mix_GetError()));
```

Once the SDL_mixer function has been initialized, we can call Mix_OpenAudio to configure the frequency, format, channels, and chunksize to use. It is important to note that this function must be called before any other SDL_mixer functions. The function definition looks like the following:

```
int Mix_OpenAudio(int frequency, Uint16 format, int channels, int
chunksize)
```

Here is what the arguments mean:

- `frequency`: This is the output sampling frequency in samples per second, Hz. In the example, we use `MIX_DEFAULT_FREQUENCY` define, which is 22050, a good value for most cases.
- `format`: This is the output sample format; again, in the example, we set this to the default value by using `MIX_DEFAULT_FORMAT` define, which is the same as using `AUDIO_S16SYS` or Signed 16-bit samples, in system byte order. To see the full format, define list, see the `SDL_audio.h` file.
- `channels`: This is the number of sound channels in the output. 2 channels for stereo, 1 for mono. The value 2 is used for our example.
- `chunksize`: This is the bytes used per output sample. We use `1024` bytes or 1 **megabyte (mb)** for our chunksize.

Finally, the last thing we do in this function is to set the `m_isInitalized` Boolean value to true. This will stop us from accidentally trying to initialize the class again:

```
m_isInitialized = true;
    }
```

The next function in the `AudioManager` class is the `Destroy()` method:

```
void BookEngine::AudioManager::Destroy()
{
  if (m_isInitialized)
  {
    m_isInitialized = false;

    //Release the audio resources
    for(auto& iter : m_effectList)
      Mix_FreeChunk(iter.second);
    for(auto& iter : m_musicList)
      Mix_FreeMusic(iter.second);
    Mix_CloseAudio();
    Mix_Quit();
  }
}
```

I will not go through this function line by line as it is self-explanatory. The basic overview is; check if `AudioManager` has been initialized, if it has then we use the `Mix_FreeChunk()` function to free each of the sound and music resources we have created. Finally we use `Mix_CloseAudio()` and `Mix_Quit()` to shutdown, clean up, and close the SDL_mixer API.

The `LoadSoundEffect` is the next function we have to look at. This function much like its name suggests is the function that loads sound effects:

```
SoundEffect BookEngine::AudioManager::LoadSoundEffect(const std::string &
filePath)
  {
    SoundEffect effect;
```

The first step in this function is to create a `SoundEffect` object to temporarily hold the data until we return the effect to the calling method. We simply call this variable, effect.

After we have created our holding variable, we do a quick check to see if this effect we need has already been created and stored in our cache, the map object, `m_effectList`:

```
//Lookup audio file in the cached list
auto iter = m_effectList.find(filePath);
```

The interesting way we do it here is by creating an iterator variable and assigning it the result of `Map.find()`, where the argument passed is the location of the sound file we want to load. The cool thing about this method is that if the sound effect is not found in the cache, the iterator value will be set to the index of the end object of the map, allowing us to do a simple check that you shall see as follows:

```
//Failed to find in cache, load
    if (iter == m_effectList.end())
    {
      Mix_Chunk* chunk = Mix_LoadWAV(filePath.c_str());
      //Error Loading file
      if(chunk == nullptr)
        throw Exception("Mix_LoadWAV Error: " +
              std::string(Mix_GetError()));

      effect.m_chunk = chunk;
      m_effectList[filePath] = chunk;
    }
```

Using the iterator value trick, we simply do a check to see if the value of `iter` variable matches the return value of the `Map.end()` function; if it does, this means that the sound effect is not in the cache list and should be created.

To load the sound effect, we call the `Mix_LoadWAV()` function with the argument of the files path location as a `c` string. We assign the returning object to a `Mix_Chunk` pointer called chunk.

We then check to see if the value of the chunk is a `nullptr` pointer, indicating that the loading function has hit an error. If it is a `nullptr` pointer, we throw an exception with some debug information provided by the handy `Mix_GetError()` function. If successful, we assign our temporary holder, the effect's member `m_chunk`, the value of chunk, which is our loaded sound effects data.

Next we add this newly loaded effect into our cache so that we can save some effort in the future.

Alternatively, if our check on the `iter` value returns false, that means the sound effect we are trying to load is in the cache:

```
else //Found in cache
    {
       effect.m_chunk = iter->second;
    }

    return effect;
  }
```

The true beauty of the iterator tick is now revealed. The lookup result, that is the result of the line `auto iter = m_effectList.find(filePath);`, when it finds the sound effect will then point to that effect in the list. So all we have to do is assign the holder variable effects member value `m_chunk` to the `iter` second value, which is the data value for the effect. The last thing we do in the `LoadSoundEffect()` function is return the effect variable to the calling method. This completes the process and our sound effect is now ready to be used.

After the `LoadSoundEffect()` function, comes the `LoadMusic()` function:

```
Music BookEngine::AudioManager::LoadMusic(const std::string & filePath)
  {
    Music music;

    //Lookup audio file in the cached list
    auto iter = m_musicList.find(filePath);

    //Failed to find in cache, load
    if (iter == m_musicList.end())
    {
      Mix_Music* chunk = Mix_LoadMUS(filePath.c_str());
      //Error Loading file
      if (chunk == nullptr)
          throw Exception("Mix_LoadMUS Error: " +
            std::string(Mix_GetError()));
```

```
        music.m_music = chunk;
        m_musicList[filePath] = chunk;
    }
    else //Found in cache
    {
        music.m_music = iter->second;
    }

    return music;
}
```

I am not going to go over this function in detail, because as you can see it is very much like the `LoadSoundEffect()` function, but instead of wrapping the `Mix_LoadWAV()` function, it instead wraps the `Mix_LoadMUS()` of the `SDL_mixer` library.

The last two function implementations in the `AudioManager.cpp` file do not belong to the `AudioManager` class itself, but instead are implementations of the `Play` functions for both the `SoundEffect` and `Music` helper classes:

```
    void SoundEffect::Play(int numOfLoops)
    {
        if(Mix_PlayChannel(-1, m_chunk, numOfLoops) == -1)
            if (Mix_PlayChannel(0, m_chunk, numOfLoops) == -1)
                throw Exception("Mix_PlayChannel Error: " +
                        std::string(Mix_GetError()));
    }
    void Music::Play(int numOfLoops)
    {
        if (Mix_PlayMusic(m_music, numOfLoops) == -1)
            throw Exception("Mix_PlayMusic Error: " +
                    std::string(Mix_GetError()));
    }
}
```

I won't step through each function line by line, instead I would like to simply point out how these functions create wrappers around the SDL_mixer, `Mix_PlayChannel`, and `Mix_PlayMusic` functions. This is in essentially the point of the `AudioManager` class, it is simply a wrapper that abstracts the process of loading the files and creating the objects directly. This helps us to create an expandable framework, the pipeline, without the worry of the underlying mechanisms. This means that at any time we could, in theory, replace the underlying library with another or even multiple libraries, without disturbing the code that calls the manager class functions.

To round out this example, let's take a look at how we would use this AudioManager in a demo project. You can find this demo in the Chapter04 folder of the code repository, labeled SoundExample. Credit for the music goes to Bensound (http://www.bensound.com).

Starting with the GameplayScreen.h file:

```
private:
    void CheckInput();
    BookEngine::AudioManager m_AudioManager;
    BookEngine::Music m_bgMusic;
};
```

We add two new objects to the private declarations, one for the AudioManager named m_AudioManager and one for the Music object, named m_bgMusic.

In the GameplayScreen.cpp file:

```
void GameplayScreen::OnEntry()
{
    m_AudioManager.Init();
    m_bgMusic = m_audioManager.LoadMusic("Audio/bensound-epic.mp3");
    m_bgMusic.Play();
}
```

To initialize, load, and play our music file, we need to add three lines to the GameplayScreen classes OnEntry().

- The first line m_AudioManager.Init() sets up the AudioManager and initializes all the components as we saw earlier.

- Next we load the music file, in this case the bensound-epic.mp3 file, and assign it to the m_bgMusic variable.

- The last line, m_bgMusic.Play(), starts the music track playing. By not passing in the amount of times to loop the music track, it defaults to −1, which means it will continue to loop until the program stops.

That handles the playing of the music track, but we need to add a couple of more function calls to clean up the AudioManager when the game is ended and to stop the music if we switch screens.

To stop the music from playing when we leave this screen, we add the following to the GameplayScreen class OnExit function:

```
m_bgMusic.Stop();
```

To clean up the AudioManager and stop any potential memory leaks, we call the following in the GameplayScreen class Destroy function:

```
m_AudioManager.Destroy();
```

This will in turn handle the destruction and clean-up of any audio assets we have loaded as we covered in the previous section.

With all this in place now, if you run the SoundExample demo, you will hear some epic adventure music start to play, and continuously loop if you are patient enough. Now that we have some sound in the game, let's step it up a bit and look at how we can get some visual assets into our project.

Working with textures

A texture, if you are unfamiliar with the term, can basically be thought of as an image. These textures can be applied to a simple geometric square, two triangles, to make an image. This type of image is commonly referred to as a Sprite. We use a Sprite class in the demo at the end of this section. It is also important to note that textures can be applied to more complex geometry and are used in 3D modeling to skin objects. Textures will play a larger part as we continue with the demos later on in the book.

Resource manager

Let's start at the high level class, the ResourceManager. This manager class will be responsible for maintaining resource objects in a cache as well as providing a simple, abstracted interface to acquiring the resource:

```
#pragma once
#include "TextureCache.h"
#include <string>
namespace BookEngine
{
class ResourceManager
  {
  public:
```

```
    static GLTexture GetTexture(std::string pathToTextureFile);
  private:
    static TextureCache m_textureCache;
  };
}
```

The declaration file, `ResourceManager.h`, is a simple class consisting of one public function `GetTexture`, and one private member of type `TextureCache`. The `GetTexure` will be the function we expose to other classes. It will be responsible for returning the texture object. The `TextureCache` is like the cache we used in `AudioManager`, it will hold loaded textures for later use. Let's move on to the implementation so we can see how this is setup:

```
#include "ResourceManager.h"
namespace BookEngine
{

  TextureCache ResourceManager::m_textureCache;

  GLTexture ResourceManager::GetTexture(std::string texturePath)
  {
    return m_textureCache.GetTexture(texturePath);
  }
}
```

The `ResourceManager` implementation is really just an abstracted call to the underlying structure. When we call the `GetTexture` function of the `ResourceManager` class we are expecting to get a `GLTexture` type back. As the caller of this function, I don't need to worry about the internal workings of `TextureCache` or how the object is parsed. All I have to do is specify the path of the texture I wish to load and the asset pipeline does the rest. This should be the ultimate goal of the asset pipeline system regardless of the methods, the interfaces should be sufficiently abstract to allow developers and designers to import and consume assets in the project without the implementation of the underlying systems becoming a blocker.

Next we will look at this example texture system that is the core underneath the simplicity of the `ResourceManager` class interface.

Texture and TextureCache

Earlier we saw two new objects introduced that comprise the structure of the `ResourceManager` class, the `GLTexture` and `TextureCache`. In the coming sections, we will take a look at these two classes in more detail so we can see how these classes connect to other systems to build a robust asset management system, all leading back to the simple interface of `ResourceManager`.

To start with we will take a look at the class, `GLTexture`. This class is comprised solely of a `struct` that describes the attributes of our texture. Here is the code for the `GLTexture` class in its entirety:

```
#pragma once
#include <GL/glew.h>
namespace BookEngine
{
  struct GLTexture
  {
    GLuint id;
    int width;
    int height;
  };
}
```

As mentioned earlier, the `GLTexture` class is really just a wrapper for a `struct`, also called `GLTexture`. This `struct` holds some simple values. A `GLuint id`, used to identify the texture and two integer values, `width` and `height`, which of course hold the textures/images height and width. This `struct` could easily be included in the `TextureClass`, I chose to implement it this way to, one, make it a little easier to read, and two, to allow some flexibility for future development. Again we want to make sure that our asset pipeline allows for the adaption of different needs and the inclusion of new asset types.

Next we have the `TextureCache` class, as we did with our audio assets, it is a good idea to create a cache for our image files. This again will provide us quicker access to the needed image files by saving them in a map and returning them as needed. We only have to create a new texture if it does not already exist in the cache. I tend to favor this type of implementation with a cache mechanism when building any system that works with assets.

While these examples provide a basic implementation, they are a great starting points for creating more robust systems, with memory management and other components integrated. The following is the declaration of the `TextureCache` class, it should look very familiar from the preceding audio example:

```
#pragma once
#include <map>
#include "GLTexture.h"

namespace BookEngine
{
  class TextureCache
  {
  public:
    TextureCache();
    ~TextureCache();

    GLTexture GetTexture(std::string texturePath);
  private:
    std::map<std::string, GLTexture> m_textureMap;

  };
}
```

Moving on to the implementation of the `TextureCache` class, in the `TextureCache.cpp` file, let's take a look at the `GetTexture()`:

```
GLTexture TextureCache::GetTexture(std::string texturePath) {

    //lookup the texture and see if it''''s in the map
    auto mit = m_textureMap.find(texturePath);

    //check if its not in the map
    if (mit == m_textureMap.end())
    {
      //Load the texture
      GLTexture newTexture = ImageLoader::LoadPNG(texturePath);

      //Insert it into the map
      m_textureMap.insert(std::make_pair(texturePath, newTexture));

      //std::cout << "Loaded Texture!\n";
      return newTexture;
    }
    //std::cout << "Used Cached Texture!\n";
    return mit->second;
}
```

This implementation again will look very similar to the `AudioManager` example we saw earlier. The main line to pay attention to here is the line that calls the `ImageLoader` class to load the image file, `GLTexture newTexture = ImageLoader::LoadPNG(texturePath);`. This call is the heavy lifting aspect of the class, and as you can see we again are abstracting the underlying system and simply providing a `GLTexture` as the return type from our `GetTexture` class. Let's jump ahead and look at the implementation of the `ImageLoader` class in the next section.

The ImageLoader class

Now that we have the structure in place to pass our texture object back up to our calling resource manager, we need to implement to class that actually loads the image file. The `ImageLoader` is that class. It will handle the loading, processing, and creating of the texture. This simple example will load a **Portable Network Graphics (PNG)** format image.

Since we are focusing on the structure of the asset pipe here, I am going to stick to the core sections of the class. I will assume some knowledge of OpenGL's buffer and texture creation. If you are not familiar with OpenGL, I highly recommend the OpenGL bible series as a great reference. We will be looking at some of these features later on when we look at some of the advanced rendering and animation techniques in the future chapters.

For this example, the `ImageLoader.h` file has only a single declaration for a `LoadPNG` function. This function takes one parameter, which is the path to the image file and it will return a `GLTexture`. Here is the `ImageLoader` in its entirety:

```
#pragma once
#include "GLTexture.h"
#include <string>
namespace BookEngine
{
  class ImageLoader
  {
  public:
    static GLTexture LoadPNG(std::string filePath);
    static GLTexture LoadDDS(const char * imagepath);
  };
}
```

Moving on to the implementation, inside of the `ImageLoader.cpp` file, let's go through the `LoadPNG` function:

```
   ...
   GLTexture ImageLoader::LoadPNG(std::string filePath) {
unsigned long width, height;
GLTexture texture = {};
std::vector<unsigned char> in;
   std::vector<unsigned char> out;
```

The first thing we do is create a few temporary variables to hold our working data. An unsigned `long` for `height` and `width`, a `GLTexture` object, which we then initialize all its fields to `0`. Then we have two vector containers of unsigned char's. The `in` vector will be the container that will house the raw encoded data to be read in from the PNG. The `out` vector will hold the decoded data that has been converted.

```
   ...
   //Read in the image file contents into a buffer
      if (IOManager::ReadFileToBuffer(filePath, in) == false) {
        throw Exception("Failed to load PNG file to buffer!");
      }

      //Decode the .png format into an array of pixels
      int errorCode = DecodePNG(out, width, height, &(in[0]), in.size());
      if (errorCode != 0) {
        throw Exception("decodePNG failed with error: " +
std::to_string(errorCode));
      }
   ...
```

Next we have two function calls. The first we call a function that uses the `IOManager` class `ReadFileToBuffer` function to read in the image files raw data. We pass in the `pathToFile`, and the vector in; the function will then fill the vector with the raw encoded data. The second call is to the `DecodePNG` function; this is the call to the single function library I mentioned before. This library will handle the reading of the raw data, decoding, and filling of the out vector container with the decoded data. The function takes four parameters:

- The first is the vector to hold the decoded data, in our case the `out` vector
- The second is the `width` and the `height` variables, which the `DecodePNG` function will fill in with the images values
- The third is a reference to a container that holds the encoded data, in our case, the `in` vector
- The last parameter is the size of the buffer, the size of the vector `in`

These two calls are the major part of this class, they complete the system that comprise the image loading component of our asset pipeline. We won't dive into the reading of the raw data and decoding right now. In the next section, we will see a similar technique to load 3D models, where we will see how to read and decode data in detail.

The rest of the function will handle the uploading and processing of the image in OpenGL, again I am not going to spend time on this section of the function. We will see more of the OpenGL framework's calls as we move forward and I will go into more depth at that time. This example is built specifically for OpenGL, it however could easily be replaced with more generic code, or code specific to another graphics library.

Minus the `IOManger` and `DecodePNG` classes, this rounds out the image handling of the asset pipeline. As hopefully you can see, having a structure in place, such as we have seen, allows a lot of flexibility under the hood while providing a simple interface that requires little knowledge of the underlying system.

Now that we have a texture returned with a simple one line call, `ResourceManger::GetTexture(std::string pathToTextureFile)`, let's bring this example full circle and see how we plug into this system to create a `Sprite` (2D image) from the loaded texture:

```
void Sprite::Init(float x, float y, float width, float height, std::string
texturePath) {
        //Set up our private vars
        m_x = x;
        m_y = y;
        m_width = width;
        m_height = height;

        m_texture = ResourceManager::GetTexture(texturePath);
```

In the texture example project, jumping into the `Sprite` class, if we focus on the `Init()`, we see where our simple interface allows us to call the `ResourceManager` classes `GetTexture` to return the handled image. That's it, very simple! Of course this is not limited to just sprites we can use this function to load textures for other uses, such as modeling and GUI uses. We can also expand this system to load more than just PNG's, in fact I would challenge you to spend some time building this out for more file formats, DDS, BMP, JPG, and others. The `ResourceManager` itself has a lot of room for improvement and growth. This basic structure is easily repeatable for other assets, such as sound, 3D models, fonts, and everything else. In the next section, we dive a little deeper and will look at the loading of 3D models or meshes as they are commonly referred to.

To see the whole system at work, run the texture example project, you will be presented with a very nice image of the sun, provided by the kind folks at NASA.

The following is the output on Windows:

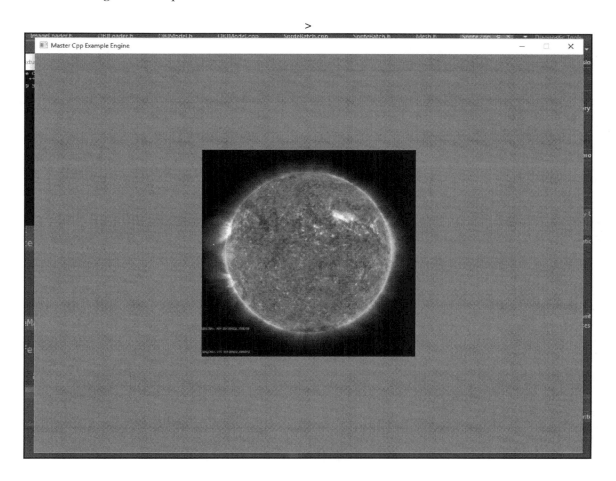

The following is the output on macOS:

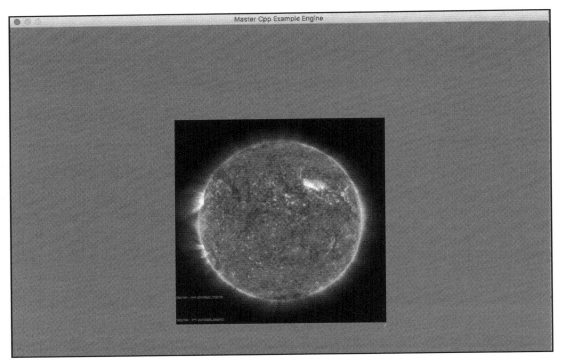

Importing models – meshes

Models or meshes are representations of objects in a three-dimensional space. These models could be anything from the player's character to a small scenery object, such as a table or chair. Loading and manipulating these object is a huge part of the game engine and the underlying systems. In this section, we will look at the process of loading in a 3D mesh. We will walk through a simple file format that describes the object in three-dimensional terms. We will look at how to load this file format and parse it into a readable format to share with the graphics processor. Finally, we will touch on the steps used by OpenGL to render the object. Let's dive right in and begin with the Mesh class:

```
namespace BookEngine
{
  class Mesh
  {
  public:
```

```
      Mesh();
      ~Mesh();
      void Init();
      void Draw();
    private:
      GLuint m_vao;
      GLuint m_vertexbuffer;
      GLuint m_uvbuffer;
      GLTexture m_texture;
      std::vector<glm::vec3> m_vertices;
      std::vector<glm::vec2> m_uvs;
      std::vector<glm::vec3> m_normals;
      // Won''''t be used at the moment.
    };
}
```

Our `Mesh` class declaration file, `Mesh.h`, is pretty simple. We have the `normal` constructor and destructors. Then we have two more functions exposed as `public`. The `Init()` function, which will initialize all of the `Mesh` components, and the `Draw` function, which will do the actual processing to pass the information to the renderer. In the `private` declarations, we have a bunch of variables to hold the mesh's data. The first is the `GLuint` `m_vao` variable. This variable will hold a handle to the OpenGL vertex array object, I won't go into this in detail right now, refer to the OpenGL documentation for a quick break down.

The next two `GLuint` variables, `m_vertexbuffer` and `m_uvbuffer` are holders for, like their names suggest, buffers of data for the `vertex` and `uv` information. More on this in the implementation that follows. After the buffers, we have a `GLTexture` variable `m_texture`. You will remember this object type from earlier; this will house the mesh's texture. The last three variables are vectors of `glm vec3`. These hold the Cartesian coordinates for the `vertices`, texture `uvs`, and `normal` of the `Mesh`. In this current example, we will not be using the normal values.

That gives us a good understanding of what our `Mesh` class will need; now we can move on to the implementation. We will walk through the class, diverting to other classes as they arise. Let's begin in the `Mesh.cpp` file:

```
namespace BookEngine
{
  Mesh::Mesh()
  {
    m_vertexbuffer = 0;
    m_uvbuffer = 0;
    m_vao == 0;
  }
```

The `Mesh.cpp` file starts out with the constructor implementation. The `Mesh` constructor sets the values of the two buffers and the vertex array object to zero. We do this so we can do a simple check later on to see if they have been initialized or for deletion, which we will see next:

```
OBJModel::~OBJModel()
  {
    if (m_vertexbuffer != 0)
      glDeleteBuffers(1, &m_vertexbuffer);
    if (m_uvbuffer != 0)
      glDeleteBuffers(1, &m_uvbuffer);
if (m_vao != 0)
      glDeleteVertexArrays(1, &m_vao);
  }
```

The destructor for the `Mesh` class handles the deletion of the `Buffer` and `Vertex` arrays. We do a simple check to see if they are not set to zero, meaning they have been created, and then delete them if they are not:

```
void OBJModel::Init()
  {
    bool res = LoadOBJ("Meshes/Dwarf_2_Low.obj", m_vertices, m_uvs,
m_normals);
    m_texture =
ResourceManager::GetTexture("Textures/dwarf_2_1K_color.png");
```

Moving on to the `Init()` function, we start off with the loading of our assets. Here we the texture that our model will need using a familiar helper function the `ResourceManager` class `GetTexture` function. We also load `Mesh`, in this case an OBJ format model called `Dwarf_2_Low.obj`, provided by andromeda vfx on TurboSquid.com. This happens through the use of the `LoadOBJ` function. Let's jump out of our `Mesh` class for a minute and look at how this function is implemented.

In the `MeshLoader.h` file, we see the declaration of the `LoadOBJ` function:

```
bool LoadOBJ(
    const char * path,
    std::vector<glm::vec3> & out_vertices,
    std::vector<glm::vec2> & out_uvs,
    std::vector<glm::vec3> & out_normals
  );
```

The `LoadOBJ` function takes four parameters, the file path to the OBJ file to load, and three vectors that will be filled with the data found in the OBJ file. The function also has a return type of a Boolean, this is for a simple error checking ability.

Before we move on and see how this function is put together and how it will parse the data to fill the vectors we created, it is important to understand the structure of the file we are using. Luckily for us the OBJ file is an open file format and can actually be read in plain text in any text editor. It is also possible for you to create very simple models by hand with the OBJ format. To give you an example let's look at the cube.obj file as viewed in a text editor. Side note, you can view an OBJ formatted model 3D rendering in Visual Studio; it even has basic editing tools:

```
# Simple 3D Cube Model
mtllib cube.mtl
v 1.000000 -1.000000 -1.000000
v 1.000000 -1.000000 1.000000
v -1.000000 -1.000000 1.000000
v -1.000000 -1.000000 -1.000000
v 1.000000 1.000000 -1.000000
v 0.999999 1.000000 1.000001
v -1.000000 1.000000 1.000000
v -1.000000 1.000000 -1.000000
vt 0.748573 0.750412
vt 0.749279 0.501284
vt 0.999110 0.501077
vt 0.999455 0.750380
vt 0.250471 0.500702
vt 0.249682 0.749677
vt 0.001085 0.750380
vt 0.001517 0.499994
vt 0.499422 0.500239
vt 0.500149 0.750166
vt 0.748355 0.998230
vt 0.500193 0.998728
vt 0.498993 0.250415
vt 0.748953 0.250920
vn 0.000000 0.000000 -1.000000
vn -1.000000 -0.000000 -0.000000
vn -0.000000 -0.000000 1.000000
vn -0.000001 0.000000 1.000000
vn 1.000000 -0.000000 0.000000
vn 1.000000 0.000000 0.000001
vn 0.000000 1.000000 -0.000000
vn -0.000000 -1.000000 0.000000
usemtl Material_ray.png
s off
f 5/1/1 1/2/1 4/3/1
f 5/1/1 4/3/1 8/4/1
f 3/5/2 7/6/2 8/7/2
f 3/5/2 8/7/2 4/8/2
```

```
f  2/9/3  6/10/3  3/5/3
f  6/10/4  7/6/4  3/5/4
f  1/2/5  5/1/5  2/9/5
f  5/1/6  6/10/6  2/9/6
f  5/1/7  8/11/7  6/10/7
f  8/11/7  7/12/7  6/10/7
f  1/2/8  2/9/8  3/13/8
f  1/2/8  3/13/8  4/14/8
```

As you can see, there is a lot of data packed into these files. Remember this is just a simple cube model being described. Take a look at the dwarf OBJ file to get an even deeper sense of the data contained. The important parts to us are the v, vt, vn, and f lines. The v lines describe the geometric vertices of the Mesh, that is the x, y, z values of the model in local space (coordinates with a origin that is relative to the model itself). The vt lines describe the texture vertices for the model, this time the values are normalized x and y coordinates, normalized meaning they are a value between 0 and 1. The vn lines are the descriptions of the vertex normals, we won't use these in our current example, but these values give normalized vector units that are perpendicular to the vertex. These are very useful values to know when computing things like lighting and shading. The following figure depicts the vertex normals of a dodecahedral shaped mesh:

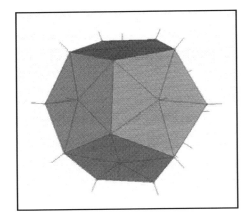

The last set of lines, the f lines, describe the faces of the mesh. These are groups of three vector values that make a single face, a triangle, of the mesh. These are again local space x, y, and z coordinates.

This file once rendered in our example engine will look like the following:

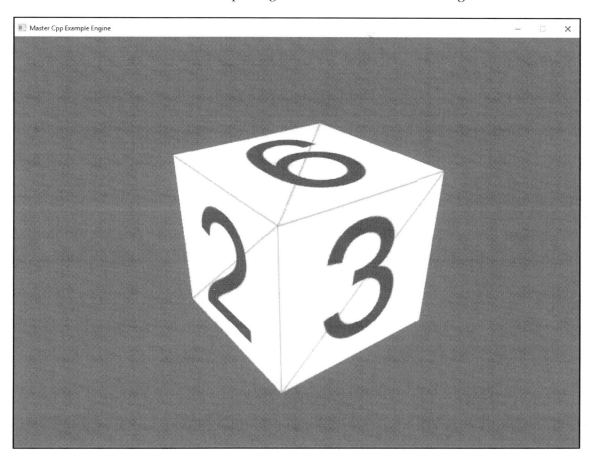

Okay that is the OBJ file format in a nutshell, now let's move ahead and take a look at how we will parse this data and store it in buffers for our renderer to use. Inside the MeshLoader.cpp file, we find the implementation of the LoadOBJ() function:

```cpp
...
bool LoadOBJ(
    std::string path,
    std::vector<glm::vec3> & out_vertices,
    std::vector<glm::vec2> & out_uvs,
    std::vector<glm::vec3> & out_normals
    )
{
    WriteLog(LogType::RUN, "Loading OBJ file " + path + " ...");
```

```
std::vector<unsigned int> vertexIndices, uvIndices, normalIndices;
std::vector<glm::vec3> temp_vertices;
std::vector<glm::vec2> temp_uvs;
std::vector<glm::vec3> temp_normals;
```

To start the LoadOBJ function, a few holder variables are created. The first line of variable declarations is a set of three vectors of integers. These will hold the indices of the vertices, uvs, and normals. After the indices, we have three more vectors. Two vec3 vectors for the vertices and normal, and one vec2 vector for the uvs. These vectors will hold the temporary values for each, allowing us to perform some calculations:

```
try
{
std::ifstream in(path, std::ios::in);
```

Next we start a try block that will house the core logic for the function. We do this so we can throw some exception if any issues arise and catch them internally at the end of this function. The first line in the try block, std::ifstream in(path, std::ios::in); attempts to load the file at the location we passed in. The ifstream, which, as you might have noticed, is part of the standard library, is used to define a stream object that can be used to read in character data from a file. It is very common to see ifstream used in modern I/O systems, it is the C++ replacement for the commonly seen fopen, which is actually C:

```
if (!in) {
throw Exception("Error opening OBJ file: " + path); }
```

We can then test to see if there were any errors loading the file with the simple if statement if(!in), which is the same as checking the state flags directly such as in.bad() == true; or in.fail() == true. If we do encounter an error, we throw an exception with a debug message. We handle this exception later in the function:

```
std::string line;
while (std::getline(in, line))
  {
```

Next we need to create a loop so we can traverse the file and parse the data as needed. We do this using a `while()` loop using the `std::getline(in, line)` function as the parameter. The `std::getline` returns a single line of characters until it reaches an end of line character. The `parameters std::getline()` takes are the stream containing the characters, in our case `in` and a `std::string` object that will hold the function's output.

By using this as the `while` loop's condition parameter, we will continue to step through the input file, line by line, until we reach the end of the file. The time during which the condition will become false, we will stop the loop. This is a very handy method of stepping through files to parse:

```
if (line.substr(0, 2) == "v ") {
  std::istringstream v(line.substr(2));
  glm::vec3 vert;
  double x, y, z;
  v >> x; v >> y; v >> z;
  vert = glm::vec3(x, y, z);
  temp_vertices.push_back(vert);
}
```

Inside of our `while` loop, the first thing we want to try and parse is the vertex data in the OBJ file. If you remember from our earlier explanation, the vertex data is contained in a single line, denoted by a v. Then to parse our vertex data, we should first test to see if the line is a vertex (v) line. The `std::string()` object has a handy method that allows you to select a defined amount of characters from the string. This method is the `substr()`, the `substr()` method can take two arguments, the starting position and the ending position of the characters in the string. This creates a substring object that we can then test against.

In this example, we use the `substr()` method to take the first two characters of the string, line, and then test to see if they match the string `"v "` (notice the space). If this condition is `true`, that means we have a vertex line and can then move on to parsing it into a useful form for our system.

The code is pretty self-explanatory, but let's highlight some important parts. The first is the `std::istringstream` object v. A `stringstream` is a special object that provides a string buffer with a convenient way to manipulate strings much like it was an I/O object (`std::cout`). This means you can treat it like a stream using the `>>` and `<<` operators, but also use it like a `std::string` using the `str()` method. We use our string stream object to house a new collection of characters. These new characters are provided by the method call to `line.substr(2)`. This time by only passing one argument, `2`, to the `substr` method, we are telling it to return the rest of the line starting at the second character. What this does is return the values x, y, and z of the vertex line without the v denotation. Once we have this new collection of characters, we can step through each one and assign it to the double variable it matches. As you can see, this is where we use the unique nature of the string stream object to stream out the character to its variable, the `v >> x;v >> y;  v >> x;` line. At the end of the `if` statement we then turn these x,y,z doubles into a `vec3` and finally push the newly created `vec3` to the back of the temp `vertices` vector:

```
else if (line.substr(0, 2) == "vt")
{
std::istringstream v(line.substr(3));
        glm::vec2 uv;
        double U, V;
        v >> U;v >> V;
        uv = glm::vec2(U, V);
        uv.y = -uv.y;
        temp_uvs.push_back(uv);
    }
```

For the textures we do much of the same thing. The major difference, besides checking for `"vt"`, is that we are only looking for two values, or `vec2` vector's. The other note here is that we invert the v coordinate since we are using texture formats, which are inverted. Remove if you want to use TGA or BMP format loaders:

```
else if (line.substr(0, 2) == "vn")
{

        std::istringstream v(line.substr(3));
        glm::vec3 normal;
        double x, y, z;
        v >> x;v >> y;v >> z;
        normal = glm::vec3(x, y, z);
        temp_normals.push_back(normal);
    }
```

For the normals, we do the exact same as we did for the vertices, but look for vn lines:

```
else if (line.substr(0, 2) == "f ")
```

```
{
    unsigned int vertexIndex[3], uvIndex[3], normalIndex[3];
    const char* cstring = line.c_str();
    int matches = sscanf_s(cstring, "f %d/%d/%d %d/%d/%d %d/%d/%d\n",
&vertexIndex[0], &uvIndex[0], &normalIndex[0], &vertexIndex[1],
&uvIndex[1], &normalIndex[1], &vertexIndex[2], &uvIndex[2],
&normalIndex[2]);
```

For the faces, a collection of triangles, we do something a little differently. First we check to see if we have a "f " line. If we do, we setup a few arrays to hold the indexes of the vertex, uv, and normal. We then convert our std::string, line, to a character array, which is referred to as C string, with the line const char* cstring = line.c_str();. We then use another C function, sscanf_s to parse the actual string and separate out each character into the specific index array element. Once this statement finishes, the sscanf_s() function will return an integer value of the element's set, which we give to the variable matches:

```
if (matches != 9)
    throw Exception("Unable to parse format");
```

We then use the matches variable to check and see if it is equal to 9, which means we have nine elements and it is a format we can work with. If the value of matches is not 9, that means we have a format that we are not setup to handle, so we throw an exception with a simple debug message:

```
        vertexIndices.push_back(vertexIndex[0]);
        vertexIndices.push_back(vertexIndex[1]);
        vertexIndices.push_back(vertexIndex[2]);
        uvIndices.push_back(uvIndex[0]);
        uvIndices.push_back(uvIndex[1]);
        uvIndices.push_back(uvIndex[2]);
        normalIndices.push_back(normalIndex[0]);
        normalIndices.push_back(normalIndex[1]);
        normalIndices.push_back(normalIndex[2]);
    }
}
```

The last thing we do in the "f " or face line if statement, is to take all the separated elements and push them into the corresponding indices vector. We use these values to build the actual mesh data next:

```
for (unsigned int i = 0; i < vertexIndices.size(); i++)
{
    // Get the indices of its attributes
    unsigned int vertexIndex = vertexIndices[i];
    unsigned int uvIndex = uvIndices[i];
    unsigned int normalIndex = normalIndices[i];
```

To create our final mesh data to give the output vectors, we create another loop to step through the model data, this time using a for loop and the amount of vertices as the condition. We then create three variables to hold the current index to each `vertex`, `uv`, and `normal`. Each time we go through this loop, we set this index to the value of `i`, which increments each step through:

```
glm::vec3 vertex = temp_vertices[vertexIndex - 1];
glm::vec2 uv = temp_uvs[uvIndex - 1];
glm::vec3 normal = temp_normals[normalIndex - 1];
```

Then thanks to these index values, we can get the attributes for each `vertex`, `uv`, and `normal`. We set these in either a `vec2` or `vec3`, which is what we will need for the output vectors:

```
out_vertices.push_back(vertex);
out_uvs.push_back(uv);
out_normals.push_back(normal);
    }
}
```

Finally, the last step is to push these new values into their specific output vectors:

```
catch (Exception e)
{
    WriteLog(LogType::ERROR, e.reason);
    return false;
}
return true;
}
...
```

Lastly, we have the `catch` block to match the `try` block from the top. This catch is very simple, we take the reason member object from the incoming `Exception` object and use it to print the debug message to the error log file. We also return false from the `LoadOBJ()` function to let the calling object know that there was an error. If there is nothing to catch, we simply return true, to let the calling object know everything worked as expected. We are now ready to use this function to load our OBJ files and produce useful data for the rendering system.

Now, moving back to the `Mesh.cpp` file, we will continue on and use this loaded data to draw the model with the example engine. I won't spend too much time on each function, again this is specific to the OpenGL API, but could be written in a more generic way or to use another graphics library such as DirectX:

```
if (m_vao == 0)
  glGenVertexArrays(1, &m_vao);
glBindVertexArray(m_vao);
```

Here we check to see if the vertex array object has already been generated; if it has not, we go ahead a make one using our `m_vao` as the referenced object. Next we bind the VAO, this will allow us to use it for all subsequent OpenGL calls in this class:

```
    if (m_vertexbuffer == 0)
  glGenBuffers(1, &m_vertexbuffer);
    if (m_uvbuffer == 0)
      glGenBuffers(1, &m_uvbuffer);
```

Next we check if our vertex buffer has been created; if not we create one using the `m_vertexbuffer` variable as the referenced object. We do the same for the `uvbuffer`:

```
    glBindBuffer(GL_ARRAY_BUFFER, m_vertexbuffer);
    glBufferData(GL_ARRAY_BUFFER, m_vertices.size() * sizeof(glm::vec3),
&m_vertices[0], GL_STATIC_DRAW);
    glBindBuffer(GL_ARRAY_BUFFER, m_uvbuffer);
    glBufferData(GL_ARRAY_BUFFER, m_uvs.size() * sizeof(glm::vec2),
&m_uvs[0], GL_STATIC_DRAW);
    }
```

The last things we do in our `Meshes Init()` function, is to bind the `vertex` and `uv` buffers and then upload the data to those buffers on the graphics card with the use of the OpenGL, `glBindBuffer()` and `glBufferData()` functions. Check out the OpenGL documentation for more detailed information on these functions:

```
void Mesh::Draw()
{
  glActiveTexture(GL_TEXTURE0);
  glBindTexture(GL_TEXTURE_2D, m_texture.id);
```

For the `Mesh` class `Draw()` function, we start out setting up the texture in the OpenGL API framework. We do this with the function calls `glActiveTexture()`, which activates the texture, and `glBindTexture()`, which does the actual binding of the texture data in memory:

```
  glBindBuffer(GL_ARRAY_BUFFER, m_vertexbuffer);
  glVertexAttribPointer( 0,  3,  GL_FLOAT,  GL_FALSE,  0,  (void*)0);
  glBindBuffer(GL_ARRAY_BUFFER, m_uvbuffer);
  glVertexAttribPointer(1, 2, GL_FLOAT, GL_FALSE, 0, (void*)0);
```

Next we bind the buffers and set the attributes for both the vertex data and texture coordinate data. Again, I won't focus on the details here, the code has comments to explain the parameters of each. For more information on the functions, I recommend viewing the OpenGL documentation online.

```
  glDrawArrays(GL_TRIANGLES, 0, m_vertices.size());
```

After all the data is bound, and all the attributes are set, we can call the function to actually draw the `Mesh` object. In this case, we use the `glDrawArrays()` function, passing in `GL_TRIANGLES` as the method of drawing. This means we want to render the vertex data using triangles. For fun try changing this value to `GL_POINTS`.

```
  glDisableVertexAttribArray(0);
  glDisableVertexAttribArray(1);
  glBindBuffer(GL_ARRAY_BUFFER, 0);
  }
}
```

At the end of our draw call, we have one last step to complete, the clean up. After every OpenGL draw call, it is required to disable the used attributes that have been set, and to unbind the used buffers. The `glDisableVertexAttribArray()` and `glBindBuffer()` functions are used for these tasks.

In the `GameplayScreen.cpp` file, we add our call to initialize the model:

```
    . . .
  //Init Model
    m_model.Init("Meshes/Dwarf_2_Low.obj", "Textures/dwarf_2_1K_color.png");
    . . .
```

We can then start to draw it by simply adding a call to the model's `Draw()` function in the `Draw()` function of `GameplayScreen`:

```
    . . .
  //Draw Model
    m_model.Draw();
  . . .
```

And that's it! If you run the `ModelExample`, you will see the output of the dwarf model on screen. I have also added a simple 3D camera to the game so you can move around the model. `W`, `A`, `S`, and `D` for moving the camera up, left, right, and down in game space. Use the mouse to look around.

The following is the output on Windows:

The following is the output on macOS:

Summary

In this chapter, we covered a very important part of development, the handling of assets. We took a look at the process of importing, processing, and managing content, such as sound, images, and 3D objects. With this groundwork system in place, we can move on to rounding out the rest of the systems needed for game development.

In the next chapter, we will look at developing the core gameplay systems needed, including state systems, physics, cameras, and GUI/HUD systems.

5
Building Gameplay Systems

We have come to the point on our journey where we are able to start piecing together the various systems that we will be using to drive our games and tools. These systems are the parts of the engine that power the interactions with all the amazing assets we are now able to import into our game:

- Understanding states
- Designing camera systems
- Working with physics

Understanding states

We use states in many different ways. They can be used for controlling the game flow, handling the different ways characters can act and react, even for simple menu navigation. Needless to say, states are an important requirement for a strong and manageable code base.

There are many different types of states machines; the one we will focus on in this section is the **Finite State Machine (FSM)** pattern. Observant readers among you will have noticed that we have already seen an FSM pattern in the function of the screen system that has been implemented. In fact, what we will be creating here is very similar to what was created for that system with some key differences that will make this a more generic and flexible state machine.

There are a few ways we can implement a simple state machine in our game. One way would be to simply use a switch case set up to control the states and an enum structure for the state types. An example of this would be as follows:

```
enum PlayerState
{
    Idle,
      Walking
}
...
PlayerState currentState = PlayerState::Idle; //A holder variable for the
state currently in
...
// A simple function to change states
void ChangeState(PlayState nextState)
{
    currentState = nextState;
}
void Update(float deltaTime)
{
    ...
    switch(currentState)
{
    case PlayerState::Idle:
        ... //Do idle stuff
        //Change to next state
ChangeState(PlayerState::Walking);
break;
        case PlayerState::Walking:
            ... //Do walking stuff
            //Change to next state
            ChangeState(PlayerState::Idle);
break;
    }
    ...
}
```

Using a switch/case like this can be effective for a lot of situations, but it does have some strong drawbacks. What if we decide to add a few more states? What if we decide to add branching and more if conditionals?

The simple switch/case we started out with has suddenly become very large and undoubtedly unwieldy. Every time we want to make a change or add some functionality, we multiply the complexity and introduce more chances for bugs to creep in. We can help mitigate some of these issues and provide more flexibility by taking a slightly different approach and using classes to represent our states. Through the use of inheritance and polymorphism, we can build a structure that will allow us to chain together states and provide the flexibility to reuse them in many situations.

Let's walk through how we can implement this in our demo examples, starting with the base class we will inherit from in the future, `IState`:

```
...
namespace BookEngine
{
    class IState {
    public:
        IState() {}
        virtual ~IState(){}
        // Called when a state enters and exits
        virtual void OnEntry() = 0;
        virtual void OnExit() = 0;

        // Called in the main game loop
        virtual void Update(float deltaTime) = 0;
    };
}
```

As you can see, this is just a very simple class that has a constructor, a virtual destructor, and three completely virtual functions that each inherited state must override. `OnEntry`, which will be called as the state is first entered, will only execute once per state change. `OnExit`, like `OnEntry`, will only be executed once per state change and is called when the state is about to be exited. The last function is the `Update` function; this will be called once per game loop and will contain much of the state's logic. Although this seems very simple, it gives us a great starting point to build more complex states. Now let's implement this basic `IState` class in our examples and see how we can use it for one of the common needs of a state machine: creating game states.

First, we will create a new class called `GameState` that will inherit from `IState`. This will be the new base class for all the states our game will need. The `GameState.h` file consists of the following:

```
#pragma once
#include <BookEngine\IState.h>
class GameState : BookEngine::IState
```

```
{
public:
    GameState();
    ~GameState();
    //Our overrides
    virtual void OnEntry() = 0;
    virtual void OnExit() = 0;
    virtual void Update(float deltaTime) = 0;
    //Added specialty function
    virtual void Draw() = 0;
};
```

The GameState class is very much like the IState class it inherits from, except for one key difference. In this class, we add a new virtual method Draw() that all classes will now inherit from GameState will be implemented. Each time we use IState and create a new specialized base class, player state, menu state, and so on, we can add these new functions to customize it to the requirements of the state machine. This is how we use inheritance and polymorphism to create more complex states and state machines.

Continuing with our example, let's now create a new GameState. We start by creating a new class called GameWaiting that inherits from GameState. To make it a little easier to follow, I have grouped all of the new GameState inherited classes into one set of files GameStates.h and GameStates.cpp. The GamStates.h file will look like the following:

```
#pragma once
#include "GameState.h"

class GameWaiting: GameState
{
    virtual void OnEntry() override;
    virtual void OnExit() override;
    virtual void Update(float deltaTime) override;
    virtual void Draw() override;
};

class GameRunning: GameState
{
    virtual void OnEntry() override;
    virtual void OnExit() override;
    virtual void Update(float deltaTime) override;
    virtual void Draw() override;
};

class GameOver : GameState
{
    virtual void OnEntry() override;
```

```
        virtual void OnExit() override;
        virtual void Update(float deltaTime) override;
        virtual void Draw() override;
};
```

Nothing new here; we are just declaring the functions for each of our GameState classes.
Now, in our GameStates.cpp file, we can implement each individual state's functions as
described in the preceding code:

```
#include "GameStates.h"
    void GameWaiting::OnEntry()
{
...
//Called when entering the GameWaiting state's OnEntry function
...
}

void GameWaiting::OnExit()
{
...
//Called when entering the GameWaiting state's OnEntry function
...
}

void GameWaiting::Update(float deltaTime)
{
...
//Called when entering the GameWaiting state's OnEntry function
...

}

void GameWaiting::Draw()
{
...
//Called when entering the GameWaiting state's OnEntry function
...

}
...
//Other GameState implementations
...
```

For the sake of page space, I am only showing the GameWaiting implementation, but the same goes for the other states. Each one will have its own unique implementation of these functions, which allows you to control the code flow and implement more states as necessary without creating a hard-to-follow maze of code paths.

Now that we have our states defined, we can implement them in our game. Of course, we could go about this in many different ways. We could follow the same pattern that we did with our screen system and implement a GameState list class, a definition of which could look like the following:

```cpp
class GameState;

class GameStateList {
public:
    GameStateList (IGame* game);
    ~ GameStateList ();

    GameState* GoToNext ();
    GameState * GoToPrevious ();

    void SetCurrentState (int nextState);
    void AddState (GameState * newState);

    void Destroy ();

    GameState* GetCurrent ();

protected:
    IGame* m_game = nullptr;
    std::vector< GameState*> m_states;
    int m_currentStateIndex = -1;
};
}
```

Or we could simply use the GameState classes we created with a simple enum and a switch case. The use of the state pattern allows for this flexibility. In the examples case, I chose to follow the same design as the screen system; you can see the full implementation of the GameStateExample project in the source code repository. It's worth going through the source code, as we will continue to use these state designs throughout the book. Try to modify the example; add a new state that creates a different print out on the screen than the others. You could even try nesting states within states to create even more powerful code branching abilities.

Working with cameras

At this point, we have discussed a good amount about the structure of systems and have now been able to move on to designing ways of interacting with our game and 3D environment. This brings us to an important topic: the design of virtual camera systems. A camera is what provides us with a visual representation of our 3D world. It is how we immerse ourselves and it provides us with feedback on our chosen interactions. In this section, we are going to go over the concept of a virtual camera in computer graphics.

Before we dive into writing the code for our camera, it is important to have a strong understanding of how, exactly, it all works. Let's start with the idea of being able to navigate around the 3D world. In order to do this, we need to use what is referred to as a transformation pipeline. A transformation pipeline can be thought of as the steps that are taken to transform all objects and points relative to the position and orientation of a camera viewpoint. The following is a simple diagram that details the flow of a transformation pipeline:

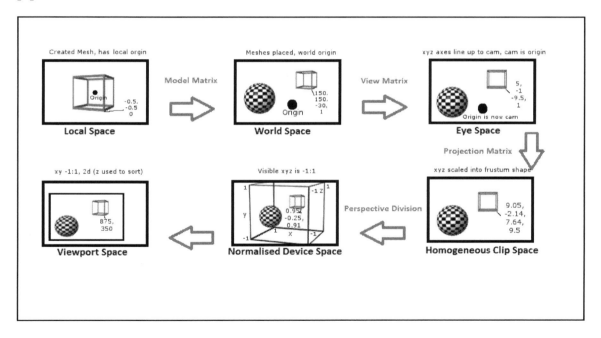

Beginning with the first step in the pipeline, local space, when a mesh is created it has a local origin 0 x, 0 y, 0 z. This local origin is typically located in either the center of the object or in the case of some player characters, the center of the feet. All points that make up that mesh are then based on that local origin. When talking about a mesh that has not been transformed, we refer to it as being in local space:

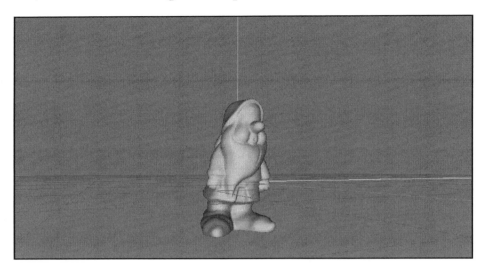

The preceding image pictures the gnome mesh in a model editor. This is what we would consider local space.

In the next step, we want to bring a mesh into our environment, the world space. In order to do this, we have to multiply our mesh points by what is referred to as a model matrix. This will then place the mesh in world space, which sets all the mesh points to be relative to a single world origin. It's easiest to think of world space as being the description of the layout of all the objects that make up your game's environment. Once meshes have been placed in world space, we can start to do things such as compare distances and angles. A great example of this step is when placing game objects in a world/level editor; this is creating a description of the model's mesh in relation to other objects and a single world origin (0,0,0). We will discuss editors in more detail in the next chapter.

Next, in order to navigate this world space, we have to rearrange the points so that they are relative to the camera's position and orientations. To accomplish this, we perform a few simple operations. The first is to translate the objects to the origin. First, we would move the camera from its current world coordinates.

In the following example figure, there is **20** on the *x* axis, **2** on the *y* axis, and **-15** on the *z* axis, to the world origin or **0,0,0**. We can then map the objects by subtracting the camera's position, the values used to translate the camera object, which in this case would be **-20, -2, 15**. So if our game object started out at **10.5** on the *x̂* axis, **1** on the *y* axis, and **-20** on the *z* axis, the newly translated coordinates would be **-9.5, -1, -5**. The last operation is to rotate the camera to face the desired direction; in our current case, that would be pointing down the -*z* axis. For the following example, that would mean rotating the object points by **-90** degrees, making the example game object's new position **5, -1, -9.5**. These operations combine into what is referred to as the view matrix:

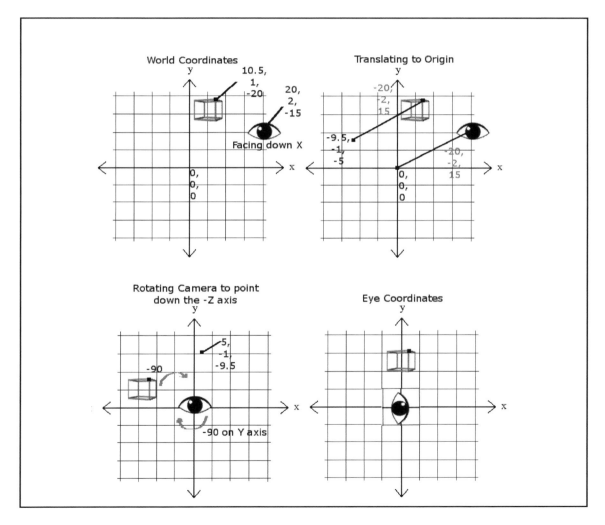

Before we go any further, I want to briefly cover some important details when it comes to working with matrices, in particular, handling matrix multiplication and the order of operations. When working with OpenGL, all matrices are defined in a column-major layout. The opposite being row-major layout, found in other graphics libraries such as Microsoft's DirectX. The following is the layout for column-major view matrices, where U is the unit vector pointing up, F is our vector pointing forward, R is the right vector, and P is the position of the camera:

$$
V = \begin{bmatrix}
Rx, & Ry, & Rz, & -Px \\
Ux, & Uy, & Uz, & -Py \\
-Fx & -Fy, & -Fz, & -Pz \\
0, & 0, & 0, & 1
\end{bmatrix}
$$

When constructing a matrix with a combination of translations and rotations, such as the preceding view matrix, you cannot, generally, just stick the rotation and translation values into a single matrix. In order to create a proper view matrix, we need to use matrix multiplication to combine two or more matrices into a single final matrix. Remembering that we are working with column-major notations, the order of the operations is therefore right to left. This is important since, using the orientation (R) and translation (T) matrices, if we say V = T x R, this would produce an undesired effect because this would first rotate the points around the world origin and then move them to align to the camera position as the origin. What we want is V = R x T, where the points would first align to the camera as the origin and then apply the rotation. In a row-major layout, this is the other way around of course:

A bird's eye view matrix

$$
R = \begin{bmatrix}
1, & 0, & 0, & 0 \\
0, & 0, & -1, & 0 \\
0, & 1, & 0, & 0 \\
0, & 0, & 0, & 1
\end{bmatrix}
\quad
T = \begin{bmatrix}
1, & 0, & 0, & -Px \\
0, & 1, & 0, & -Py \\
0, & 0, & 1, & -Pz \\
0, & 0, & 0, & 1
\end{bmatrix}
$$

Orientation   Translation

The good news is that we do not necessarily need to handle the creation of the view matrix manually. Older versions of OpenGL and most modern math libraries, including GLM, have an implementation of a `lookAt()` function. Most take a version of camera position, target or look position, and the up direction as parameters, and return a fully created view matrix. We will be looking at how to use the GLM implementation of the `lookAt()` function shortly, but if you want to see the full code implementation of the ideas described just now, check out the source code of GLM which is included in the project source repository.

Continuing through the transformation pipeline, the next step is to convert from eye space to homogeneous clip space. This stage will construct a projection matrix. The projection matrix is responsible for a few things.

First is to define the near and far clipping planes. This is the visible range along the defined forward axis (usually *z*). Anything that falls in front of the near distance and anything that falls past the far distance is considered out of range. Any geometrical objects that are on the outside of this range will be *clipped* (removed) from the pipeline in a later step.

Second is to define the **Field of View (FOV)**. Despite the name, the field of view is not a field but an angle. For the FOV, we actually only specify the vertical range; most modern games use 66 or 67 degrees for this. The horizontal range will be calculated for us by the matrix once we provide the aspect ratio (how wide compared to how high). To demonstrate, a 67 degree vertical angle on a display with a 4:3 aspect ratio would have a FOV of 89.33 degrees (*67 * 4/3 = 89.33*).

These two steps combine to create a volume that takes the shape of a pyramid with the top chopped off. This created volume is referred to as the view frustum. Any of the geometry that falls outside of this frustum is considered to be out of view.

The following diagram illustrates what the view frustum looks like:

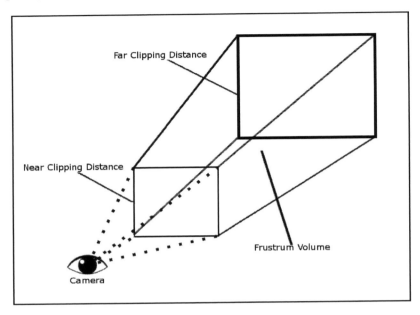

You might note that there is more visible space available at the end of the frustum than in the front. In order to properly display this on a 2D screen, we need to tell the hardware how to calculate the perspective. This is the next step in the pipeline. The larger, far end of the frustum will be pushed together creating a box shape. The collection of objects visible at this wide end will also be squeezed together; this will provide us with a perspective view. To understand this, imagine the phenomenon of looking along a straight stretch of railway tracks. As the tracks continue into the distance, they appear to get smaller and closer together.

The next step in the pipeline, after defining the clipping space, is to use what is called the perspective division to normalize the points into a box shape with the dimensions of (-1 to 1, -1 to 1, -1 to 1). This is referred to as the **normalized device space**. By *normalizing* the dimensions into unit size, we allow the points to be multiplied to scale up or down to any viewport dimensions.

The last major step in the transformation pipeline is to create the 2D representation of the 3D that will be displayed. To do this, we flatten the normalized device space with the objects further away being drawn behind the objects that are closer to the camera (draw depth). The dimensions are scaled from the *X* and *Y* normalized values into actual pixel values of the viewport. After this step, we have a 2D space referred to as the **Viewport space**.

That completes the transformation pipeline stages. With that theory covered, we can now shift to implementation and write some code. We are going to start by looking at the creation of a basic, first person 3D camera, which means we are looking through the eyes of the player's character. Let's start with the camera's header file, Camera3D.h, which can be found in the Chapter05 project folder in the source code repository:

```
. . .
#include <glm/glm.hpp>
#include <glm/gtc/matrix_transform.hpp>
. . .,
```

We start with the necessary includes. As I just mentioned, GLM includes support for working with matrices, so we include both glm.hpp and the matrix_transform.hpp to gain access to GLM's lookAt() function:

```
. . .
    public:
        Camera3D();
        ~Camera3D();
        void Init(glm::vec3 cameraPosition = glm::vec3(4,10,10),
                float horizontalAngle = -2.0f,
                float verticalAngle = 0.0f,
                float initialFoV = 45.0f);
        void Update();
```

Next, we have the public accessible functions for our Camera3D class. The first two are just the standard constructor and destructor. We then have the Init() function. We declare this function with a few defaults provided for the parameters; this way if no values are passed in, we will still have values to calculate our matrices in the first update call. That brings us to the next function declared, the Update() function. This is the function that the game engine will call each loop to keep the camera updated:

```
glm::mat4 GetView() { return m_view; };
glm::mat4 GetProjection() { return m_projection; };
glm::vec3 GetForward() { return m_forward; };
glm::vec3 GetRight() { return m_right; };
glm::vec3 GetUp() { return m_up; };
```

After the `Update()` function, there is a set of five getter functions to return both the View and Projection matrices, as well as the camera's forward, up, and right vectors. To keep the implementation clean and tidy, we can simply declare and implement these *getter* functions right in the header file:

```
void SetHorizontalAngle(float angle) { m_horizontalAngle = angle; };
void SetVerticalAngle(float angle) { m_verticalAngle = angle; };
```

Directly after the set of getter functions, we have two setter functions. The first will set the horizontal angle, the second will set the vertical angle. This is useful for when the screen size or aspect ratio changes:

```
void MoveCamera(glm::vec3 movementVector) { m_position +=   movementVector;
};
```

The last public function in the Camera3D class is the `MoveCamera()` function. This simple function takes in a vector 3, then cumulatively adds that vector to the `m_position` variable, which is the current camera position:

```
...
   private:
     glm::mat4 m_projection;
     glm::mat4 m_view; // Camera matrix
```

For the private declarations of the class, we start with two `glm::mat4` variables. A `glm::mat4` is the datatype for a 4x4 matrix. We create one for the view or camera matrix and one for the projection matrix:

```
glm::vec3 m_position;
float m_horizontalAngle;
float m_verticalAngle;
float m_initialFoV;
```

Next, we have a single vector 3 variable to hold the position of the camera, followed by three float values—one for the horizontal and one for the vertical angles, as well as a variable to hold the field of view:

```
glm::vec3 m_right;
glm::vec3 m_up;
glm::vec3 m_forward;
```

We then have three more vector 3 variable types that will hold the right, up, and forward values for the camera object.

Now that we have the declarations for our 3D camera class, the next step is to implement any of the functions that have not already been implemented in the header file. There are only two functions that we need to provide, the `Init()` and the `Update()` functions. Let's begin with the `Init()` function, found in the `Camera3D.cpp` file:

```cpp
void Camera3D::Init(glm::vec3 cameraPosition,
    float horizontalAngle,
    float verticalAngle,
    float initialFoV)
{
    m_position = cameraPosition;
    m_horizontalAngle = horizontalAngle;
    m_verticalAngle = verticalAngle;
    m_initialFoV = initialFoV;
    Update();
}
...
```

Our `Init()` function is straightforward; all we are doing in the function is taking in the provided values and setting them to the corresponding variable we declared. Once we have set these values, we simply call the `Update()` function to handle the calculations for the newly created camera object:

```cpp
...
void Camera3D::Update()
{
    m_forward = glm::vec3(
        glm::cos(m_verticalAngle) * glm::sin(m_horizontalAngle),
        glm::sin(m_verticalAngle),
        glm::cos(m_verticalAngle) * glm::cos(m_horizontalAngle)
    );
```

The `Update()` function is where all of the heavy lifting of the classes is done. It starts out by calculating the new forward for our camera. This is done with a simple formula leveraging GLM's cosine and sine functions. What is occurring is that we are converting from spherical coordinates to cartesian coordinates so that we can use the value in the creation of our view matrix.

```cpp
m_right = glm::vec3(
    glm::sin(m_horizontalAngle - 3.14f / 2.0f),
    0,
    glm::cos(m_horizontalAngle - 3.14f / 2.0f)
);
```

After we calculate the new forward, we then calculate the new right vector for our camera, again using a simple formula that leverages GLM's sine and cosine functions:

```
m_up = glm::cross(m_right, m_forward);
```

Now that we have the forward and up vectors calculated, we can use GLM's cross-product function to calculate the new up vector for our camera. It is important that these three steps happen every time the camera changes position or rotation, and before the creation of the camera's view matrix:

```
float FoV = m_initialFoV;
```

Next, we specify the FOV. Currently, I am just setting it back to the initial FOV specified when initializing the camera object. This would be the place to recalculate the FOV if the camera was, say, zoomed in or out (hint: mouse scroll could be useful here):

```
m_projection = glm::perspective(glm::radians(FoV), 4.0f / 3.0f, 0.1f,
100.0f);
```

Once we have the field of view specified, we can then calculate the projection matrix for our camera. Luckily for us, GLM has a very handy function called `glm::perspective()`, which takes in a field of view in radians, an aspect ratio, the near clipping distance, and a far clipping distance, which will then return a created projection matrix for us. Since this is an example, I have specified a 4:3 aspect ratio (4.0f/3.0f) and a clipping space of 0.1 units to 100 units directly. In production, you would ideally move these values to variables that could be changed during runtime:

```
m_view = glm::lookAt(
        m_position,
        m_position + m_forward,
        m_up
    );
}
```

Finally, the last thing we do in the `Update()` function is to create the view matrix. As I mentioned before, we are fortunate that the GLM library supplies a `lookAt()` function to abstract all the steps we discussed earlier in the section. This `lookAt()` function takes three parameters. The first is the position of the camera. The second is a vector value of where the camera is pointed, or *looking at*, which we provide by doing a simple addition of the camera's current position and it's calculated forward. The last parameter is the camera's current up vector which, again, we calculated previously. Once finished, this function will return the newly updated view matrix to use in our graphics pipeline.

That is a simple 3D camera class in a nutshell. Go ahead and run the CameraDemo project to see the system in action. You can move the camera around with the WASD keys and change the viewing angle with the mouse. Next, we will move onto another important game engine system, physics!

Working with physics

Nowadays, it tends to be very rare that a game does not implement at least some basic form of physics. The topic of game physics is rather large and complex and could easily fill a few volumes before you could consider it well covered. It's because of this that entire teams are dedicated to the creation of the *physics engines* and it can take years of development to build production-level systems. Since this is the case, we won't attempt to cover all aspects here, but instead take a higher-level approach. We will cover some of the more commonly needed aspects of physics systems, specifically basic collision detection. For more advanced needs, such as the support for gravity, friction, and advanced collision detection, we will cover the implementation of a third-party physics library. At the end of this section, our demo engine will have advanced physics support.

Point in AABB

To start, let's take a look at one of the easier collision checks you can perform in 3D, finding out whether a point is inside or outside an **Axis Aligned Bounding Box (AABB)**. AABBs are very easy to create. You can basically think of these as non-rotatable cubes or boxes. The following image depicts an AABB and point—collision:

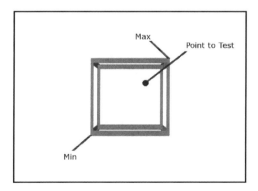

To create a bounding box, you can specify a max point and a min point in vector format or by having a center point and then specifying a height, width, and depth. For this example, we will create our AABB's with the min and max points approach:

```
struct BoundingBox
{
 glm::vec3 m_vecMax;
 glm::vec3 m_vecMin;
};
```

The preceding code is a simple example struct for an AABB.

Now that we have an AABB, we can develop a way to check if a single point falls inside of the AABB. This check is very simple; all we need to do is check if all its values, x, y, and z, are greater than the AABB's min values and less than the AABB's max values. This check in the code would look something like the following, in its simplest form:

```
bool PointInAABB(const BoundingBox& box, const glm::vec3 & vecPoint)
  {
    if(vecPoint.x > tBox.m_vecMin.x && vecPoint.x < tBox.m_vecMax.x &&
       vecPoint.y > tBox.m_vecMin.y && vecPoint.y < tBox.m_vecMax.y &&
       vecPoint.z > tBox.m_vecMin.z && vecPoint.z < tBox.m_vecMax.z)
    {
        return true;
    }
    return false;
  }
```

AABB to AABB

Now that we have seen how to test if a point is within a certain AABB, the next very useful collision check we will look at is the AABB to AABB check—a quick test to find out if two AABBs are colliding. The following image depicts this collision check:

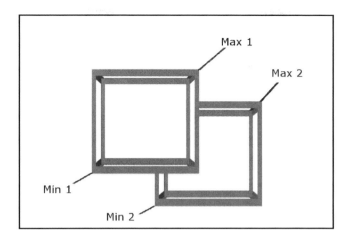

The collision check between two AABBs is very simple and fast. It is a very common choice for most objects that need a form of collision detection.

The bad thing about AABBs is that they can't be rotated. Once they are rotated, they stop being AABBs since they are not aligned to the *x*, *y*, and *z* axes anymore. For objects that rotate, a better option would be to use spheres, capsules, or even **oriented bounding boxes (OBBs)**.

To check if two AABBs are colliding, we just need to check that the first AABB's max point is greater than the second one's min point and that the first one's min point is less than the second one's max point. The following is what this check would look like in code, in its simplest form:

```
bool AABBtoAABB(const BoundingBox& box1, const BoundingBox& box2)
{
  if (box1.m_vecMax.x > tBox2.m_vecMin.x &&
      box1.m_vecMin.x < tBox2.m_vecMax.x &&
      box1.m_vecMax.y > tBox2.m_vecMin.y &&
      box1.m_vecMin.y < tBox2.m_vecMax.y &&
      box1.m_vecMax.z > tBox2.m_vecMin.z &&
      box1.m_vecMin.z < tBox2.m_vecMax.z)
  {
    return true;
  }
  return false;
}
```

Of course, the order of the boxes, which one is first and which one is the second, doesn't matter.

Since this check contains a lot of `&&` comparisons, if the first check is false, it will not continue to check the rest; this is what allows for a very fast test.

Sphere to sphere

The last simple collision check I want to touch on here is the test to find out if two spheres are colliding with each other. Testing collisions between spheres is very simple and easy to perform. An advantage that spheres have over things such as AABBs is that it doesn't matter if the object rotates, the sphere will remain the same. The following is an image that depicts the collision check between two spheres:

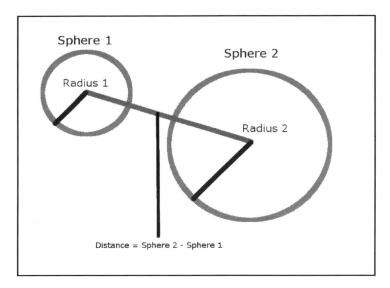

To perform the check, we simply need to calculate the distance between the centers of the spheres and compare it to the sum of their radii. If this distance is less than the sum of their radii, then the spheres are overlapping. If it's the same, then the spheres are just touching. The following is how this collision test would look like in code, in its simplest form:

```
...
struct BoundingSphere
{
glm::vec3    m_vecCenter;
float        m_radius;
```

```
};
...
bool SphereToSphere(const BoundingSphere & Sphere1, const BoundingSphere &
Sphere2)
{

glm::vec3 distance(Sphere2.m_vecCenter - Sphere1.m_vecCenter);
float distanceSqaured(glm::dot( & distance, & distance) );
```

To get the distance between the centers of the spheres, we need to create a vector between their center points:

```
float radiiSumSquared( Sphere1.m_radius + Sphere2.m_radius );
radiiSumSquared *= radiiSumSquared;
```

We can then calculate the length of that vector with the sum of the radii:

 There is a more efficient way to do this. Since the dot product of a vector with itself equals the squared length of that vector, we could just calculate the squared length of the vector against the square of the sum of the radii. If we do it this way, we don't need to calculate the length of the vector, which is an expensive operation in itself.

```
if( distanceSqaured <= radiiSumSquared )
{
    return true;
}
return false;
}
...
```

Finally, we can perform the collision check. If the distance squared is less than or equal to the square sum, then the spheres have collided, otherwise, the object has not collided and we return false.

Armed with these simple checks, most basic collision detection can be handled. In fact, as we will see in the next section, most advanced checks are comprised of many smaller checks. However, there will come a point when you will find yourself needing more advanced or optimized ways of handling physics; this is when you can turn to a third-party library to provide this support. In the next section, we will look at the implementation of one of these third-party libraries.

Implementing the Bullet physics library.

Bullet is a physics engine that simulates collision detection and soft and rigid body dynamics. It has been used in many released video games as well as for visual effects in movies. The Bullet physics library is free and open-source software subject to the terms of the zlib License.

Some of the features Bullet has to offer include:

- Rigid body and soft body simulation with discrete and continuous collision detection
- Collision shapes: sphere, box, cylinder, cone, convex hull using GJK, non-convex, and triangle mesh
- Soft body support: cloth, rope, and deformable objects

A rich set of rigid body and soft body constraints with constraint limits and motors

You can find the source code link and more information at: http://bulletphysics.org.

Let's take a look at how you can incorporate Bullet into your own game project. I am not going to spend the time going over how to link the libraries to our demo project since we have covered this a few times now. If you do need a refresher, flip back a few chapters to see how. What we are going to do is incorporate the Bullet engine into our demo engine and then use the Bullet engine's calculations to position our game objects in real time. In this example, we are going to create a simple ground plane and then a ball (sphere) to fall and collide with the ground. We will be using Bullet's built-in types to support this, including gravity to give it a realistic effect.

Beginning with the Ground GameObject, we set up variables to hold some of our needed physics values. The first is of type btCollisionShape. This is a Bullet type that allows the definition of simple shapes to use when creating bounding objects for the physics tests. The next is of type btDefaultMotionState, which again is a Bullet datatype that describes the way the object should behave when in motion. The last variable we need is of type btRigidBody, which is a Bullet datatype that will hold all the physical properties of the object that our physics engine would be concerned with:

```
class GroundObject : BookEngine::GameObject
{
    ...

    btCollisionShape* groundShape = nullptr;
    btDefaultMotionState* groundMotionState = nullptr;
    btRigidBody* groundRigidBody = nullptr;
```

Once we have these variables defined, we can then construct the physics representation of the ground object in its `Init()` function:

```
void GroundObject::Init(const glm::vec3& pos, const glm::vec3& scale)
{
    ...
    groundShape = new btStaticPlaneShape(btVector3(0, 1, 0), 1);
    groundMotionState =
        new btDefaultMotionState(btTransform(btQuaternion(0, 0, 0, 1),
    btVector3(m_position.x, m_position.y, m_position.z)));
```

We start by setting our `groundShape` variable to be a `btStaticPlanShape`. This is a Bullet object that specifies a simple plane object, which is perfect for our needs and a simple ground object. Next, we set the `groundMotionState`. We do this by using the `btDefaultMotionState` Bullet object. The `btDefaultMotionState` is the type used for specifying the way an object will behave in motion. When creating a new `btDefaultMotionState`, we need to pass in some information about the object's transform, that is the rotation and position of the object. To do this we pass a `btTransform` object with its own parameters of a rotation in quaternion format (`btQuaternion(0, 0, 0, 1)`) and a position in vector 3 format (`btVector3(m_position.x, m_position.y, m_position.z)`):

```
btRigidBody::btRigidBodyConstructionInfo
  groundRigidBodyCI(0, groundMotionState, groundShape, btVector3(0, 0, 0));
  groundRigidBody = new btRigidBody(groundRigidBodyCI);
```

Now, with the `groundShape` and `groundMotionState` set, we can move on to creating and setting the rigid body info. First we define a holder `btRigidBodyConstuctionInfo` variable for the construction information called `groundRigidBodyCI`. This object takes in a few parameter values, a scaler value to specify mass, the motion state of the object, the collision shape, and a vector 3 to specify the local Inertia value. Inertia is the resistance of any physical object to any change in its state of motion. It is basically the tendency of objects to keep moving in a straight line at constant velocity.

Since our ground object is static and does not require any changes based on the physics input, we can forego an `Update()` function and move on to the Ball object that we will be using to test out the system.

Moving into the `BallObject.h` file, we define some variables that we need, much like we did for our ground object. We create a motion state, a scalar (an integer) value for mass, collision shape, and, finally, a rigid body:

```
btDefaultMotionState* fallMotionState;
btScalar mass = 1;
btCollisionShape* fallShape;
btRigidBody* fallRigidBody;
...
```

Now, moving into the `BallObject.cpp` file, we assign some values to the variables we have just defined:

```
void BallObject::Init(const glm::vec3& pos, const glm::vec3& scale)
  {
    ...
    fallShape = new btSphereShape(10);
    btVector3 fallInertia(0.0f, 0.0f, 0.0f);
```

First, we set our collision shape. In this case, we are going to use the type `btSphereShape`. This is the default shape for spheres and takes in a parameter to set the radius for the sphere. Next, we create a vector 3 holder for the sphere's inertia. We are setting this to be all zeros since we want this ball to fall freely with no resistance based on the mass of the object and a gravity value we will set shortly:

```
fallMotionState =
        new btDefaultMotionState(btTransform(btQuaternion(0, 0, 0, 1),
        btVector3(m_position.x, m_position.y, m_position.z)));
```

Next, we set the ball's motion state, just like we did for the ground object. We set the rotation to be 0 and the position to the current position of the ball object:

```
fallShape->calculateLocalInertia(mass, fallInertia);
    btRigidBody::btRigidBodyConstructionInfo fallRigidBodyCI(mass,
fallMotionState, fallShape, fallInertia);
    fallRigidBody = new btRigidBody(fallRigidBodyCI);
    }
```

We then calculate the local inertia value using the handy `calculateLocalInertia()` function, passing in the mass and `fallInertia` values. This will set the falling vector for our ball object to be used in the first tick of the physics engine. Finally, we end with setting up the rigid body object, exactly like we did previously with the ground object.

With the ball object, we do expect the physics engine output to affect the ball object. It's because of this that we need to make some adjustments in the Update() function of the ball object:

```
void BallObject::Update(float deltaTime)
{
    btTransform trans;
    fallRigidBody->getMotionState()->getWorldTransform(trans);
    m_position.x = trans.getOrigin().getX();
    m_position.y = trans.getOrigin().getY();
    m_position.z = trans.getOrigin().getZ();
}
```

The first step in the update loop for the ball object is to get the physics object's transform from the rigid body. Once we have this transform object, we can then set the ball object's mesh (the visible object) to make the position of the physics transform object. That's it for the object itself. The ball and ground objects now house all the needed physics information. We can now implement the physics engine loop into our game loop and get the ball rolling, no pun intended!

For the implementation of the physics engine into our existing game engine's loop, we need to set up a few values first. Jumping into our Gameplayscreen.h, we define the variables to hold these values:

```
btBroadphaseInterface* broadphase = new btDbvtBroadphase();
```

First is a definition of a btBroadphaseInterface class object, which provides a Bullet interface to detect AABB-overlapping object pairs. In this case, we are setting it to a btDbvtBroadphase, which implements a btBroadphase using two dynamic AABB bounding volume hierarchies/trees. This tends to be the best broadphase when working with many moving objects; its insertion/addition and removal of objects is generally faster than the sweep and prune broad phases found in the btAxisSweep3 and bt32BitAxisSweep3:

```
btDefaultCollisionConfiguration* collisionConfiguration = new
        btDefaultCollisionConfiguration();
btCollisionDispatcher* dispatcher = new
        btCollisionDispatcher(collisionConfiguration);
btSequentialImpulseConstraintSolver* solver = new
        btSequentialImpulseConstraintSolver;
```

Next, we have defined for the collision configuration, collision dispatcher, and sequential impulse constraint solver. We won't go too deep on each of these, but the main points are that the collision configuration sets up some Bullet internal values, such as collision detection stack allocators and pool memory allocators. The collision dispatcher is the definition of how the collisions will be handled. It supports algorithms that handle *ConvexConvex* and *ConvexConcave* collision pairs, time of impact, closest points, and penetration depth. Finally, the sequential impulse constraint solver, which defines what can be thought of as the algorithm, will determine how to solve the collisions between objects. For those wishing to know, it is a **Single Instruction, Multiple Data (SIMD)** implementation of the Projected Gauss-Seidel (iterative LCP) method:

```
btDiscreteDynamicsWorld* dynamicsWorld = new
    btDiscreteDynamicsWorld(dispatcher, broadphase, solver,
    collisionConfiguration);
```

The last variable we need to define is for our dynamics world object. A `btDiscreteDynamicsWorld` provides a discrete rigid body simulation. This can be thought of as the environment or *world* in which the physics simulation occurs. Once we have this defined, we have all the pieces in place to start our physics simulation.

Let's jump into the `GameplayScreen.cpp` file and look at the `OnEntry()` function that we will use to initialize the physics simulation:

```
void GameplayScreen::OnEntry()
{
    ...

    dynamicsWorld->setGravity(btVector3(0, -1, 0));
    dynamicsWorld->addRigidBody(m_ground.groundRigidBody);
    dynamicsWorld->addRigidBody(m_ball.fallRigidBody);
    ...
}
```

The first thing we set is our gravity vector. In our simple example, we are setting this to be -1 on the *y* axis. Next, we add the two created rigid bodies to the simulation environment, one for the ground and one for the ball. That handles the initialization of our physics engine; now we need to handle updating it on each engine tick:

```
void GameplayScreen::Update(float deltaTime)
{
    CheckInput(deltaTime);
    dynamicsWorld->stepSimulation(1 / 60.f, 10);
    m_ball.Update(deltaTime);
```

Inside of the `GameplayScreen::Update()` function, we first check the input, then call the update on the physics engine, before finally calling the update on the game objects themselves. It is important to note this order. We want to accept the user's input first, but we want to make sure we have updated the physics engine before the objects. The reason is that the physics calculations should have some effect on the objects and we don't want to cause a case where our drawing loop is ahead of the physics loop, as this would definitely cause some unwanted effects. You will also notice the physics update function, `stepSimulation`, takes in two parameters. The first is the amount of time to step the simulation by. This is typically the time since you last called it. In this case, we are setting this to 1/60 of a second, or 60 FPS. The second parameter is the maximum number of steps that Bullet is allowed to take each time you call it. If you pass a very large value as the first parameter, say, something like five times the size of the fixed internal time step or game clock, then you must increase the number of `maxSubSteps` to compensate for this; otherwise, your simulation is *losing* time, which will again result in some unwanted physics calculation output.

That's it! We now have a physics engine running its simulation and effecting the objects in our world that we are drawing on the screen. You can see this in action by running the `PhysicsDemo` example project in the `Chapter05` GitHub repository. The output will look something like the following:

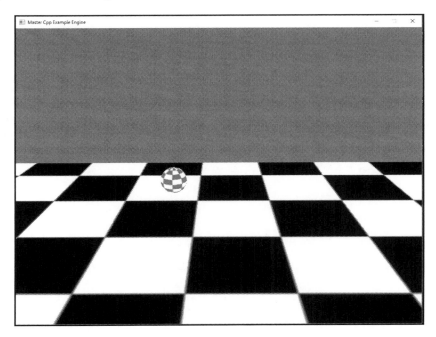

Summary

In this chapter, we covered a lot of ground and made strong progress in developing the core game systems needed for developing professional-grade projects. We now have our own custom game state system that can be adopted by many of the other components in the game engine itself. We developed our own custom camera system while building an understanding of how cameras work at a lower level. Finally, we looked at how we can add complete third-party game systems to our projects by adding the Bullet physics engine to our example engine.

6
Creating a Graphical User Interface

In games, user interaction is an extremely important part of the design. Being able to provide the user with visual information and a visual selection of choices is where the **Graphical User Interface (GUI)** comes in. Like many other systems discussed in this book, there are existing libraries available for use. One of the most commonly known in the open source game development world is **Crazy Eddies GUI (CEGUI)**. While CEGUI is a very robust GUI system implementation, with that robustness comes complexity, and to be honest, most of the time you will really just need a text label, a simple button, and maybe a checkbox and icon support. With these simple building blocks, you can create a lot.

In this chapter, we will construct the building blocks and create a simple GUI system. It should be noted that creating a complete, production-ready GUI system from scratch is an enormous task, not one for a single chapter. So, we will focus on the core concepts and build a system that can be extended and scaled later on. Our GUI will not use any API specifics and will continue to build off of the created structure from previous chapters. The topics covered in this chapter are the following:

- Coordinate systems and positioning
- Adding control logic
- Rendering the GUI

The complete code example for this chapter can be found in the Chapter06 folder in the code repository. For brevity's sake, I will be omitting some of the non-essential lines of code from the sections and may jump around files and classes more frequently.

Coordinate systems and positioning

One of the most important parts of every GUI system is how objects/elements are positioned on the screen. For the most part, graphics APIs use coordinates known as screen space, usually expressed in an absolute range [-1, 1]. While this is good for rendering, this can cause some issues when trying to develop our GUI system. Let's take, for example, the idea of using an absolute system. In this system, we would explicitly set each element in the GUI to a real pixel coordinate. This could be very simple to implement, but would only work if the game's resolution stayed the same. If at any time we changed the resolution, the elements would stay locked to their pixel coordinates and would not scale to match the new resolution.

Another option would be to create a relative system, where each GUI element's position would be described in relation to other elements or screen locations. This approach is much better than an absolute system but still poses some scaling issues. For example, if we had an element that we placed at the top left of the screen, with a small offset, if at any time the game's resolution changed, the spacing that we used would change as well.

What we are going to build is a somewhat similar approach employed by CEGUI, which is a combination of the two solutions mentioned previously. While we are at it, we are also going to add another common convention used in modern GUIs: containing grouped elements in *panels*. There are a couple of good reasons why we want to group our GUI elements in panels. The first is that if we wanted to move a bunch of elements, say a status bar with health, ammo, and items indicators, if we group them in a panel, we only have to move the panel and all the elements will follow, correctly positioned. Which brings us to reason two: by grouping elements together in panels, we can define the position of the elements relative to the panel's position, as opposed to setting the elements positions as pixel coordinates or even relative to a screen location.

The following is a diagram depicting this design layout:

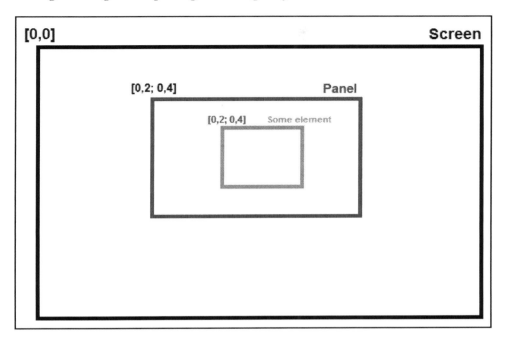

As you can see, a combination of relative and absolute positioning is used, but this time the relative starting point is not the origin **[0,0]** of the entire screen, but the origin **[0,0]** of our panel. While the panel's origin point already has some coordinates on the screen, we don't use those for setting the position of the element.

In theory, we now have scalable elements inside the panel(s), but we still need a way to *lock* or *stickie* panels in place, regardless of the screen resolution. This is where the concept of GUI anchor systems comes in. Chances are, if you have ever worked with a GUI before, you have seen anchors in action. In our example, we are going to slightly simplify the concept for the sake of time. In our system, every panel will have the ability to set its origin relative to one of five anchor points: top left, top right, bottom left, bottom right, and center.

The following diagram demonstrates this concept:

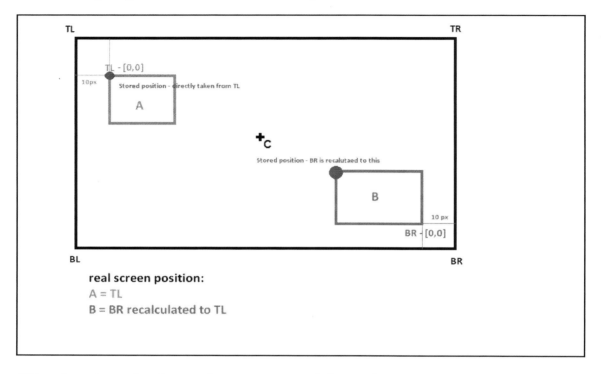

OK, so how do we implement these concepts and design them in code? Let start with a IGUIElement class that all other elements will inherit from. Take a look at the IGUIElement class:

```
class IGUIElement
{
public:
virtual void Update() = 0;
glm::vec2 GetPosition() { return m_position; };
protected:
glm::vec2 m_position;
};
}
```

To start with, our elements are not that complicated. Each element will have an Update() function, as well as a getter function to return the position of the element. We will be expanding on this class later on in this chapter.

The next part of the system we can implement is the concept of panels. Let's start by taking a look at the header file of `IGUIPanel.h`:

```
...
static enum class GUIAnchorPos {
TopRight,
TopLeft,
BottomRight,
BottomLeft,
Center
};
...
```

The file starts off with the declaration of an `enum class` called `GUIAnchorPos`; this `enum` will give the elements access to the calculated anchor points. We are making this an enum class instead of just an `enum` inside of the `IGUIPanel` class, as this will allow elements to access the anchor points without the need for an `IGUIPanel` instance. Later on, we will see a function that connects these enumerated values to the screen positions that have been calculated:

```
...
IGUIPanel(glm::vec4 panelBounds = glm::vec4(0,0,200,480),
glm::vec2 panelAnchor = glm::vec2(0,0),
glm::vec2 offset = glm::vec2(0,0));
...
```

The next part of the file that is of interest is the constructor. Here, we are requesting a vector 4 to be passed in to define the bounds of the panel to be created. Next, we are requesting a vector two for the panel anchor's origin location, as well as a vector two to provide the offset or *padding* for the panel's position. You will also notice that we are also providing some defaults for each parameter. We are doing this for a couple of reasons, but the biggest one is that we want to be able to create GUI elements and attach them to a panel by default. By providing defaults, if we do create a GUI element and there is no existing panel to attach it to, we can create one without the need to pass in values when it's created. We will revisit this later on in the chapter. Let's move on to the implementation:

```
IGUIPanel::IGUIPanel(glm::vec4 panelBounds, glm::vec2 panelAnchor,
glm::vec2 offset)  : m_bounds(panelBounds), m_offset(offset)
{
  m_Pos = panelAnchor + m_offset;
  m_panelWidth = m_bounds.z;
  m_panelHeight = m_bounds.w;
}
```

For the implementation of the `IGUIPanel` constructor, the first thing we will calculate is the panel's position on the screen. We do this by adding the panel's anchor point with the offset that has been passed in and storing it in the protected member variable `m_Pos`. Next, we calculate the panel's width and height; we do this using the bounds values being passed in. We store them in protected member variables named `m_panelWidth` and `m_panelHeight` respectively.

Now that we have the panel constructor in place, we can move on to setting up how the panels will hold their elements. To accomplish this, we simply create a vector of `IGUIElements` pointers called `m_GUIElementList`. We can then start to create some public methods to access and manipulate the panel's element list:

```
. . .
  void IGUIPanel::AddGUIElement(IGUIElement & GUIElement)
  {
      m_GUIElement.List.push_back(&GUIElement);
  }
. . .
```

First, in the `IGUIPanel.cpp` file, we create an `AddGUIElement()` function to add new elements to the panel. This function implements a call to the `push_back()` method of the panel's element list, pushing in the giving `GUIElement` reference:

```
virtual std::vector<IGUIElements*>& GetGUIElementList()
{
    return m_ GetGUIElementList;
};
```

Jumping to the `IGUIPanel.h` file, we implement a getter function, `GetGUIElementList()`, to provide public access to the private element list:

```
void IGUIPanel::Update()
{
  for (auto const& element : m_ m_GUIElement.List)
  {
      element ->Update();
  }
}
```

Switching back to the `IGUIPanel.cpp` file, we can look at the implementation of the `Update()` function for the panel class. This update will step through the panel's element list and then call the `Update()` function for each of the elements in the list. This will allow the panel to control the updates of its elements, and provides the structure for implementing concepts such as pausing element updates on the panel being hidden:

```
IGUIPanel::~IGUIPanel()
{
  std::for_each(m_GUIElementList.begin(),
  m_ GUIElementList.end(),
  std::default_delete<IGUIElement>());
}
```

Finally, we need to remember to clean up all the elements belonging to the panel when the destructor is called. To do this, we are going to use the `for_each()` method of the `standard` library. We are using this method mostly because this is an example and due to the sheer fact that I want to introduce you to it. The `for_each()` method takes three parameters. The first two are applied to the range, and the third is the function to execute. In our example, we are going to call `default_delete()` on each element we step through, and again we are using this method as a means to introduce you to the function. The `default_delete()` function is actually a function object class, whose function-like invocation takes a templated object type and deletes it. This can be compared the non-specialized version that simply uses delete for the delete operation or the specialization for arrays, `delete[]`. This class is specifically designed to be used with `unique_ptr` and provides a way to delete `unique_ptr` objects with no overhead.

OK, now that we have the `IGUIPanel` class in place, we can move on to constructing some more complex elements needed for our GUI system. For this example, we will add a basic button with label support:

```
...
class IGUIButton : public IGUIElement
{
 public:
 IGUIButton(glm::vec4& bounds,
 glm::vec2& position,
 GLTexture* texture,
 std::string label,
 SpriteFont* font,
 glm::vec2& fontScale = glm::vec2(1.0f),
 IGUIPanel* panel = NULL);
 ~IGUIButton();
 virtual void Update() override;
...
```

In the `IGUIButton.h` file, we can see that the button inherits from our basic `IGUIElement`. This of course means we have access to all the functions and protected members of the parent class, including the `m_position` and `GetPosition()` functions, so we do not redefine them here. While we are looking at the `IGUIButton.h`, we can also peek at the constructor, where we are defining what the button will require to be passed in when creating. In our example button, we are looking for the bounds (size) of the button, the position, a texture to use when drawing the button, a label for the button (text to be displayed), the font to use for the label, the scale of the font (which we give as a default of `1.0f`), and finally a panel to add the button to which we default to `NULL` unless otherwise specified. We will take a deeper look at these parameters as we continue on with the chapter.

Shifting to the implementation of the constructor, in the `IGUIButton.cpp` before `IGUIButton::IGUIButton(glm::vec4 & bounds, glm::vec2 & position, std::string label, GLTexture * texture, SpriteFont* font, glm::vec2& fontScale, IGUIPanel* panel):`

```
    m_texture(*texture),
    m_buttonLabel(label),
    m_spriteFont(font),
    m_fontScale(fontScale),
    m_panel(panel)
    {
        m_bounds = bounds;
        if (m_panel != NULL)
        {
        m_position = *m_panel->GetPosition() + position;
```

For the most part, we are just setting the internal member variables to the passed in values, but the one thing of note is how we handle the panel value. In the constructor body, we perform a check to see if the value stored in `m_panel` is not null. If this check is true, we can move on to setting the position of the button element relative to the panel's position. We do this by first calling the panel's `GetPosition()` function, adding the returned value to our passed in position value, and saving that calculation in the `m_position` member variable. This will give us, partially, what we want by setting the position of our button to the relation origin of the panel, but since the origin of our default panel elements is the lower left corner, the outcome would be the button being placed at the bottom of the panel. This is not necessarily the desired behavior. To correct this, we need to calculate our button's new *y* axis value based on the top of the panel, and of course any already existing elements in the panel:

```
    //Move to just below the last element in the list
    if (!m_panel->GetGUIElementList().empty())
```

```
  {
    IGUIElement* lastElement = m_panel-> GetGUIElementList().back();
    m_position.y = lastElement ->GetPosition().y -
    lastElement ->GetBounds().w -
    10.0f; // Used as default padding (should be dynamic)
  }
  else
  {
    //Move to top of panel
    m_position.y += m_panel->GetBounds()->w - m_bounds.w;
    }
  }
}
```

First, we want to check if the panel we are adding the button to has any existing elements in it already. We do this by checking the panel's vector with the GetGUIElementList().empty() function. If the panel's element list is not empty, we then need the position the of the last element in the panel's list. We do this by creating a temporary element called lastElement and assigning it to the last element in the panel's list using GetGUIElementList().back(). With the element stored, we can then use it to calculate the button's *y* axis value. We do this by subtracting the stored element's *y* axis value from the stored element's height (GetBounds().w) and a default padding value, which we are setting at 10.0f in this example. In a full GUI implementation, you would want to make this padding value dynamic. Finally, if the panel is empty, and this is the first element, we set the button's *y* axis by calculating the panel's height (GetBounds()->w) minus the new button's height. This will place the button element at the very top of the panel.

We now have a panel system with an element class and an implemented button element created. The last thing we need to do is build a high-level class to glue the system together. We are going to create an IGUI class that will house panels, provide access to the GUI methods to other game systems, and, as we will see in the next sections, provide input, update, and draw mechanisms. Let's jump into the constructor implementation in the IGUI.cpp file:

```
IGUI::IGUI(Window& window) : m_window(window)
{
...
m_BL = new glm::vec2(
                      0,
                      0
                     );
m_BR = new glm::vec2(
                      m_window.GetScreenWidth(),
```

```
                              0
                              );
    m_TL = new glm::vec2(
                              0,
                              m_window.GetScreenHeight()
                              );
    m_TR = new glm::vec2(
                              m_window.GetScreenWidth(),
                              m_window.GetScreenHeight()
                              );
    m_C = new glm::vec2(
                              m_window.GetScreenWidth() * 0.5f,
                              m_window.GetScreenHeight() * 0.5f
                              );
    ...
```

In the constructor for the IGUI class, we are going to define the anchor points that we will use for all the panels held by the IGUI instance. We are going to store these values in private member variables: m_BL for the bottom left of the screen, m_BR for the bottom right of the screen, m_TL for the top left, m_TR for the top right, and m_C for the center of the screen. We use the set m_window Window object to return the width and height of the screen used to calculate the anchor points. We will see how these points are used to provide anchors to the panels later in the class.

Next, let's look at the functions we will use to add the elements and panels to the IGUI instances:

```
void IGUI::AddGUIElement(IGUIElement& GUIElement)
{
    if (!m_GUIPanelsList.empty())
    {
    m_GUIPanelsList[0]->AddGUIObject(GUIElement);
    }
    else
    {
    IGUIPanel* panel = new IGUIPanel();
    m_GUIPanelsList.push_back(panel);
    m_GUIPanelsList[0]->AddGUIObject(GUIElement);
    }
}
```

Starting with the `AddGUIElement` function, this function, as its name implies, adds a GUI element to the GUI. By default, the element will be added to the first panel found in the GUI's panel list, which is stored in the `m_GUIPanelsList` vector. If the panel list is empty we then create a new panel, add it to the list, and then finally add the element to that panel:

```
void IGUI::AddGUIPanel(IGUIPanel& GUIPanel)
{
  m_GUIPanelsList.push_back(&GUIPanel);
}
```

The `AddGUIPanel()` function is very simple. We take the passed in `IGUIPanel` object and add it to the GUI's panel list using the `push_back()` vector method.

The last part of the positioning system that we need to look at is the `GetAnchorPos()` function. This function will return the panel's anchor position based on the calculated screen values, which we saw previously in the `IGUI` constructor and the size of the panel itself:

```
...
glm::vec2* IGUI::GetAnchorPos(GUIAnchorPos anchorPos, glm::vec4 bounds)
{
  switch (anchorPos)
  {
    case(GUIAnchorPos::TopRight):
    m_TR->y -= bounds.w;
    m_TR->x -= bounds.z;
    return m_TR;
    break;
    case(GUIAnchorPos::TopLeft):
    m_TL->y -= bounds.w;
    return m_TL;
    break;
    case(GUIAnchorPos::BottomRight):
    m_BR->x -= bounds.z;
    return m_BR;
    break;
    case(GUIAnchorPos::BottomLeft):
    return m_BL;
    break;
    case(GUIAnchorPos::Center):
    m_C->y -= bounds.w;
    return m_C;
    break;
  }
}
...
```

We start off by passing in two values. The first is GUIAnchorPos, which you might remember from earlier on in the chapter when we defined an enum class in the IGUIPanel.h file. The second is the bounds of the panel, described with a vector four object. Inside the function, we have a switch case statement which we are using to determine what anchor point to calculate.

If the case matches the TopRight enum value, first we modify the *y* axis value of the anchor point. We do this because we use the bottom left corner as the default origin, so we need to modify this so the top left corner is the new origin for the anchor point. Next, we modify the *x* axis value of the anchor point. We do this because we need to move the anchor point in from the top right corner of the screen by the width of the panel object. If we don't modify the *x* axis value, the panel will draw off screen to the right.

Next, if the case matches the TopLeft enum value, we modify the *y* axis value of the anchor point. As stated previously, we do this to account for the origin of our coordinate system being the lower left-hand corner. We do not have to modify the *x* axis value this time, since when we draw left to right, our panel will appear on screen.

If the case matches the BottomRight enum value, we need to modify the *x* axis value. As mentioned before, we need to move the anchor point to the left by the width of the panel, to make sure the panel will draw on the screen. We do not need to modify the *y* axis this time, since the anchor will match the default coordinate system's *y* origin of the bottom of the screen.

If the case matches the BottomLeft enum value, we simply return the anchor point unmodified since it matches the default origin of the coordinate system.

Finally, if the case matches the Center enum value, we will only modify the *y* axis value since we only have to account for the default origin being in the lower left corner. The *x* axis value calculated in the constructor will move the panel to the right to position it properly in the center of the screen.

That takes care of the positioning and anchor system for our GUI system. We now have a solid framework to continue building on throughout the rest of the chapter. Next, we will look at how we can add input control to our GUI system.

Adding control logic

A GUI is much more than just what you can see on screen. There is also logic running behind the scenes, so to speak, that provides the functionality needed to interact with objects. Handling what happens if a mouse is moved over an element, if a checkbox is selected, or if a button is clicked is all part of the GUI input system. In this section, we are going to construct the necessary architecture to handle mouse input for our GUI.

While there are a few different ways we could implement the system to handle input for our GUI, I think this is a perfect opportunity to introduce you to one of my favorite programming patterns, the Observer. The `Observer` is one of the most widely known patterns from the **Gang of Four**. The `Observer` is so commonly used that Java has a core library dedicated to it, `java.util.Observer` and C# has it incorporated into the language itself in the form of the event keyword.

I think the easiest way to explain the `Observer` pattern is that when you have objects doing various things that are of interest to another class or object, you can *subscribe* to *events* and get notified when these objects perform their interesting functions. It's very likely you have seen and/or used the `Observer` pattern before in your development adventures. In fact, we have seen it already in this book. The SDL library uses its own `Observer` pattern for handling input. We tap into it to perform tasks based on the user's input. The following is the SDL event implementation we use to handle our game input:

```
SDL_Event event;
while (SDL_PollEvent(&event))
{
  m_game->OnSDLEvent(event);
}
```

What we are going to build is something a little more basic, but it will provide you with a good understanding of how you can implement an input system for a GUI, and you can hopefully familiarize yourself with a flexible pattern for future development.

To start with, inside the `IGUIElement` header file, we create a new `enum` class called `GUIEvent`:

```
enum class GUIEvent
{
 HoverOver,
 Released,
 Clicked,
};
```

This enum class defines the different types of events that our GUI elements can listen for. Next, still in our IGUIElement class header file, we need to add a completely virtual function, OnNotify():

```
virtual void OnNotify(IGUIElement& element, GUIEvent event) = 0;
```

This function will be overridden by each of the element types and will be called when events occur. The elements that have this function implemented can *listen* to the events that matter to them and perform actions as necessary. OnNotify() takes two parameters: an IGUIElement() which defines which element is affected, and the event type. These two parameters will give us all the information we need to determine what to do with each event sent.

Let's take a look at the OnNotify() implementation in our IGUIButton() object class:

```
void IGUIButton::OnNotify(IGUIElement & button, GUIEvent event)
{
   If(event == GUIEvent::HoverOver)
  {
  //Handle Hover
  }
}
```

In the IGUIButton::OnNotify implementation, we can listen to different types of events being passed in. In this example case, we are checking if the event passed in is a HoverOver event. If it is, we add a comment for where we will perform any actions we need to when the button is hovered over. That's really it when it comes to setting up the *listener*. Next, we need to connect our GUI input system to the current input system and start sending out the event notifications. Let's move on and look at the CheckInput() function implementation in the IGUI object class:

```
void IGUI::CheckInput(InputManager inputManager)
{
   float pointX = inputManager.GetMouseCoords().x;
   float pointY = inputManager.GetMouseCoords().y;
   for (auto &panel : m_GUIPanelsList) // access by reference to avoid
                                       copying
  {
  for (auto& object : panel->GetGUIElementList())
  {
  //Convert Y coordinate position to top upper left origin, y-down
   float convertedY =
   m_window.GetScreenHeight() -
   (object->GetPosition().y + object->GetBounds().w);
   if (pointX < object->GetPosition().x + (object->GetBounds().z) &&
```

```
      pointX >(object->GetPosition().x - (object->GetBounds().z)) &&
      pointY < convertedY + object->GetBounds().w &&
      pointY > convertedY - object->GetBounds().w)
    {
      object->OnNotify(*object, GUIEvent::HoverOver);
      }
    }
  }
}
```

We will take a look at it piece by piece. To start with, we get the current mouse coordinates from the passed in `InputManager` object and save them to temporary variables:

```
void IGUI::CheckInput(InputManager inputManager)
{
float pointX = inputManager.GetMouseCoords().x;
float pointY = inputManager.GetMouseCoords().y;
```

Next, we need to use a nested `for` loop to step through all the panels in the GUI and, in turn, all the elements attached to each one of those panels:

```
for (auto &panel : m_GUIPanelsList) // access by reference to avoid copying
{
for (auto& object : panel->GetGUIElementList())
{
```

Inside of the nested loop, we are going to do a simple *hit* test to see if we are in the button's bound. However, first, we need to do a quick calculation. In the coordinate and position section earlier in this chapter, you might remember we made a conversion to have the anchor point's *y* axis moved to the top left corner. Now we need to do the opposite and convert the *y* axis of the element's position back to the lower left corner. The reason we need to do this is so the mouse cursor's screen coordinate system is in the same as the buttons position:

```
float convertedY = m_window.GetScreenHeight() -
                    (object->GetPosition().y + object->GetBounds().w);
```

The last thing we need to do in the loop is to perform the actual *hit* or bounds check. To do this, we check and see if the mouse cursor's, *x* axis value is within the button's screen area. We also check the same thing on the *y* axis using the converted *y* values from earlier. If all these conditions are met, then we can send a `HoverOver` event notification to the element:

```
if (pointX <element->GetPosition().x + (element->GetBounds().z) &&
pointX >(element->GetPosition().x - (element->GetBounds().z)) &&
pointY < convertedY + element->GetBounds().w &&
pointY > convertedY - element->GetBounds().w)
```

```
{
    object->OnNotify(*object, GUIEvent::HoverOver);
}
...
```

With that, we have, while crude, a working event system. The last piece of the puzzle we need to put in place is connecting it to the current input handling system of the game engine. To do that, we add one simple line to the `CheckInput()` function of the `ExampleScreen` class, `m_gui->CheckInput(m_game->GetInputManager());`:

```
void ExampleScreen::CheckInput(float deltaTime)
{
    SDL_Event event;
    while (SDL_PollEvent(&event))
    {
    m_game->OnSDLEvent(event);
    }
    ...
    m_gui->CheckInput(m_game->GetInputManager());
    ...
}
```

That takes care of the logic implementation for this chapter's example. There is definitely room for refactoring and tuning, but this should provide you with a good starting point to expand upon. I would recommend going through the next steps and adding more functionality, maybe even new elements to work with. In the next section, we are going to close out the chapter by adding rendering to our GUI system and finally drawing our example on the screen.

Rendering the GUI

With all the positioning and input logic in place, we can now finish up our GUI system by implementing some basic rendering. The good news is we already have a strong infrastructure for our main rendering that we built earlier on in the book. We are going to tap into this infrastructure to render our GUI on the screen. Basically, you have two real choices when it comes to rendering the GUI. You could render the GUI to a texture and then blend the created texture into your final drawn scene. The other option is to render everything as geometry in each frame on top of your scene. Both have their issues, but I would argue that in most cases creating a texture and blending that texture will be slower than rendering the GUI elements as geometry.

To keep things slightly simple and to focus more on the implementation, we start with an easier approach and render each of the elements separately. This, of course, is not the most performance-friendly way of rendering if we have lots of elements in the GUI. In our example, we will not have a large number of elements, and if you are building something such as a start game/menu GUI, this solution in its current form will be more than sufficient. Keep an eye on your framerate, as if you notice a drop then chances are you have too many draw calls.

The best way we can approach our solution is to use the same approach we took when rendering our models, with some slight differences. We will use shaders again to draw the geometry, as this will provide us with lots of control and the ability to perform any blend, masks, patterns, and effects we might want to add. For our GUI example, we are going to reuse our texture vertex and fragment shaders from the previous chapters. In the next chapter, we are going to dive deeper into advanced shaders and drawing techniques.

So, let's dive into the implementation. Add this to the `IGUI.h` file:

```
std::unique_ptr<Camera2D> m_camera = nullptr;

    std::unique_ptr<ShaderManager> m_textureProgram = nullptr;
    std::unique_ptr<SpriteBatch> m_spriteBatch = nullptr;
```

And then add this in the constructor for the `IGUI` object:

```
IGUI::IGUI(Window& window) : m_window(window)
{
   m_camera = std::make_unique<Camera2D>();
   ...
   m_textureProgram = std::make_unique<BookEngine::ShaderManager>();
   m_spriteBatch = std::make_unique<BookEngine::SpriteBatch>();
}
```

Here, we are specifying a shader texture program, a sprite batch, and a 2D camera. This camera is slightly different to the 3D version we created earlier in the book. I won't go too deep into the 2D camera since its slightly out of the scope of this chapter, but I will mention that the major change is that we are constructing an orthographic matrix for 2D drawing. We are giving each GUI instance its own shader, camera, and sprite batch. It will be up to the instance to handle the final setup.

The `ExampleGUI` is the implementation of the `IGUI` class for our example. Taking a look at the `OnInit()` function, we can see the setup of these resources:

```
void ExampleGUI::OnInit()
{
m_textureProgram->CompileShaders(
```

```
                        "Shaders/textureShading.vert",
                        "Shaders/textureShading.frag");
   m_textureProgram->AddAttribute("vertexPosition");
   m_textureProgram->AddAttribute("vertexColor");
   m_textureProgram->AddAttribute("vertexUV");
   m_textureProgram->LinkShaders();
   m_spriteBatch->Init();
   m_camera->Init(m_window.GetScreenWidth(),
                m_window.GetScreenHeight());
   m_camera->SetPosition(glm::vec2(
                        m_window.GetScreenWidth() * 0.5f,
                        m_window.GetScreenHeight()* 0.5f));
   panel = new BookEngine::IGUIPanel(
                        glm::vec4(0, 0, 150, 500),
                        *GetAnchorPos(
                            BookEngine::GUIAnchorPos:BottomLeft,
                            glm::vec4(0, 0, 150, 500)
                        ),
                        glm::vec2(0,0));
   AddGUIPanel(*panel);
        BookEngine::GLTexture texture
        =BookEngine::ResourceManager::GetTexture("Textures/button.png");

   button = new BookEngine::IGUIButton(
        glm::vec4(0, 0, 100, 50),
        glm::vec2(10, -10),"My Button", &texture,
        new BookEngine::SpriteFont("Fonts/Impact_Regular.ttf", 72),
            glm::vec2(0.2f), panel);

        AddGUIElement (*button);
   }
```

We will break it down piece by piece. To start with, we need to compile the Shaders we need for our GUI, so we add the attributes we need for the shaders, and finally link them for use. This should be familiar:

```
   m_textureProgram->CompileShaders(
   "Shaders/textureShading.vert",
   "Shaders/textureShading.frag");
   m_textureProgram->AddAttribute("vertexPosition");
   m_textureProgram->AddAttribute("vertexColor");
   m_textureProgram->AddAttribute("vertexUV");
   m_textureProgram->LinkShaders();
   Next, we call Init on the sprite batch for the GUI instance:
   m_spriteBatch->Init();
```

We then call `Init` on our 2D camera instance, passing the screen width and height. After the `Init`, we then set the position of the camera to the middle of the screen by dividing the screen's height and width values in half:

```
m_camera->Init(m_window.GetScreenWidth(),
                m_window.GetScreenHeight());
m_camera->SetPosition(glm::vec2(
                m_window.GetScreenWidth() * 0.5f,
                m_window.GetScreenHeight()* 0.5f));
```

Now that we have the shader program, the sprite batch, and camera setup, we move on to the creation of the GUI elements. First up is the panel element, which we create using the architecture we created earlier in the chapter. We set its anchor point as the bottom left of the screen. Once the panel is created, we add it to the GUI instance by calling the `AddGUIPanel` function that the class has inherited:

```
panel = new BookEngine::IGUIPanel(glm::vec4(0, 0, 150, 500),
                            *GetAnchorPos(
                            BookEngine::GUIAnchorPos:BottomLeft,
                            glm::vec4(0, 0, 150, 500)
                            ),
    glm::vec2(0,0));
AddGUIPanel(*panel);
```

With the panel created and added to the GUI instance's panel list, we then add a button to that panel. To do that, we first create a temporary variable to hold the texture we want to load for this button. Then we create the button itself. We again use the structure we built earlier on in the chapter. We pass in the label of `My Button` and the texture we just loaded. Once complete, we call the `AddGUIElement()` function and add the button to the panel:

```
BookEngine::GLTexture texture =
BookEngine::ResourceManager::GetTexture("Textures/button.png");
button = new BookEngine::IGUIButton(
        glm::vec4(0, 0, 100, 50),
        glm::vec2(10, -10),
        "My Button",
        &texture,
        new BookEngine::SpriteFont("Fonts/Impact_Regular.ttf", 72),
glm::vec2(0.2f), panel);
AddGUIElement (*button);
```

Now our elements are in place, and the rendering components have been created and set up, we can finalize the rendering pipeline for the GUI system. To do this, we are going to fall back on the inheritance structure we have created in our objects. To start the draw call chain, we begin with the `ExampleGUI` class and its `Draw()` function implementation:

```
void ExampleGUI::Draw()
{
    ...

    m_textureProgram->Use();

    ...

    m_spriteBatch->Begin();

    //Draw all of the panels
    for (auto const&panel : m_GUIPanelsList)
    {
        panel->Draw(*m_spriteBatch);
    }
    m_spriteBatch->End();
    m_spriteBatch->BatchRender();
    m_textureProgram->UnUse();
}
```

Focusing on an important aspect of our GUI implementation, we begin the `Draw()` function by specifying the shader program we want to use when rendering the GUI elements. Next, we start the sprite batch that will be used for the GUI elements. Then, between the start of the sprite batch and the end of the sprite batch, we use a `for` loop to step through all the panels in the GUI's panel list and call its `Draw()` function implementation. Once the `for` loop has completed, we then end the sprite batch, call the `BatchRender()` method to render all the objects in the batch, and finally close out the function by calling the `UnUse()` method on our shader program.

Let's go down one level in the draw chain and look at the IGUIPanel's Draw function implementations:

```
void IGUIPanel::Draw(SpriteBatch& spriteBatch)
    {
spriteBatch.Draw(glm::vec4(m_Pos.x,
m_Pos.y,
m_panelWidth,
m_panelHeight),
  glm::vec4(0,0,1,1),
BookEngine::ResourceManager::GetTexture(
```

```
"Textures/background.png").id,
-0.1f,
ColorRGBA8(0,0,0,75)
);

        for (auto const&element : m_GUIElementList)
        {
            element->Draw(spriteBatch);
        }
    }
```

In the `IGUIPanel::Draw()` function, we start by adding the panel itself to the sprite batch that we passed in from the calling object. This will draw a slightly opaque black background. Ideally, you want to make the texture used for the background a non-hardcoded value and allow it to be set for each instance. After we have added the panel to the sprite batch for drawing, we again use a `for` loop to step through each element in the panel's element list and call its `Draw()` function implementation. This effectively pushes its use to the next layer down in the draw chain.

For the `IGUIElement` class, we simply create a pure virtual function that the elements inheriting will have to implement:

```
virtual void Draw(SpriteBatch& spriteBatch) = 0;
```

So this means we can now step down to the last link in our draw chain example and look at the `IGUIButton::Draw()` function implementation:

```
void IGUIButton::Draw(SpriteBatch& spriteBatch)    {
        ...

        spriteBatch.Draw(glm::vec4(m_position.x,
  m_position.y,
m_bounds.z,
m_bounds.w),
uvRect,
m_texture.id,
0.0f,
ColorRGBA8(255, 255, 255, 255));

        char buffer[256];
        m_spriteFont->Draw(spriteBatch,
buffer,
glm::vec2(
m_position.x + (m_bounds.z * 0.5f),
(m_position.y + (m_bounds.w * 0.5f)) - ((m_spriteFont->GetFontHeight() *
m_fontScale.y) * 0.5f)
```

```
        ),
                                 m_fontScale,
        0.2f,
        BookEngine::ColorRGBA8(255, 255, 255, 255),
        Justification::MIDDLE);
            }
```

Again, this implementation of the functions is not too complicated. We are adding the element to the sprite batch passed in by the calling object to be drawn. The effect of this is that all panels and their elements will be added to a single GUI instance's sprite batch, which will be far more performant than each panel and object drawing itself in sequence. The last code block in the Draw() function is a call to a Sprite Font instance's Draw() method. I won't go into detail about how the Sprite Font class works since it is out of the scope of this chapter, but have a look at the code files to understand how things are working under its hood. The role of the SpriteFont class is much like the Sprite class, except it provides a means to draw fonts/text on screen. Here in this example, we are using it to draw the label for the button.

That wraps up the draw chain. All we need to do now is connect the GUI's head Draw() call to the main game's Draw() call. To do this, we add one line to call the Draw() method of the GUI's instance in the ExampleScreen class's Draw() function:

```
void EditorScreen::Draw()
{
...
    m_gui->Draw();
}
```

Now, I am happy to say, we have a simple but complete, working GUI system in place. You can run the example demo to see the completed GUI running. If you want to see how the panel is effected by each of the defined anchor points, you just need to change the BookEngine::GUIAnchorPos value when setting the panel in the ExampleGUI class:

```
panel = new BookEngine::IGUIPanel(glm::vec4(0, 0, 150, 500),
*GetAnchorPos(
BookEngine::GUIAnchorPos::BottomRight,
glm::vec4(0, 0, 150, 500)
),
 glm::vec2(0,0));
```

The following are screenshots of the GUI in action, with its anchor points changed to BottomLeft, BottomRight, TopLeft, TopRight, and Center:

The screenshot for BottomRight is as shown in the following figure:

The screenshot for `BottomLeft` is as shown in the following figure:

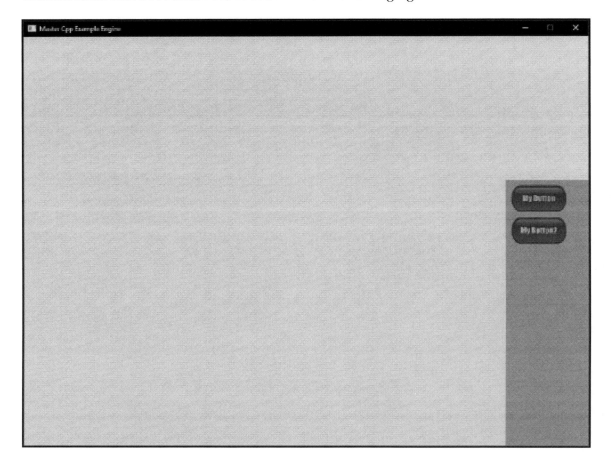

The screenshot for `TopLeft` is as shown in the following figure:

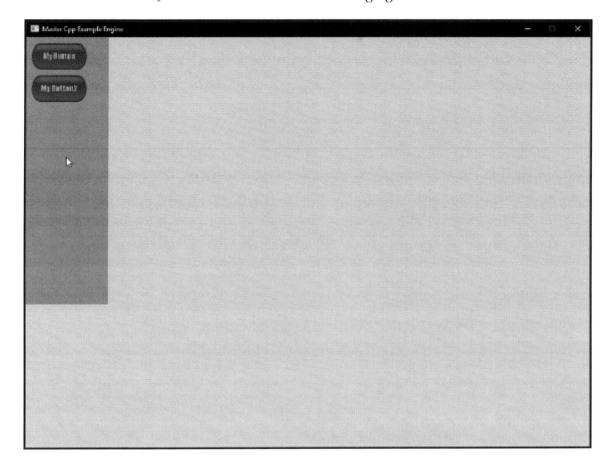

The screenshot for `TopRight` is as shown in the following figure:

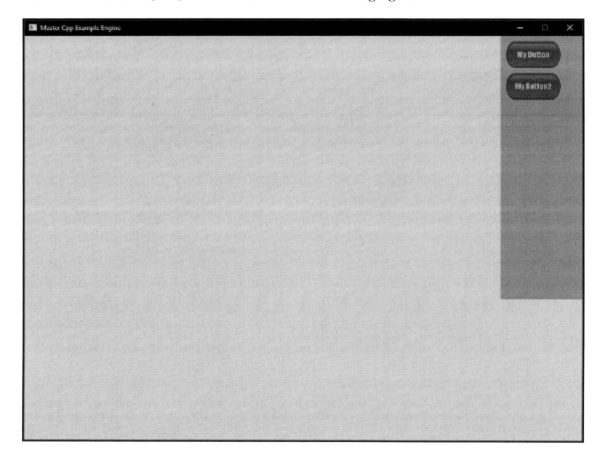

The screenshot for Center is as shown in the following figure:

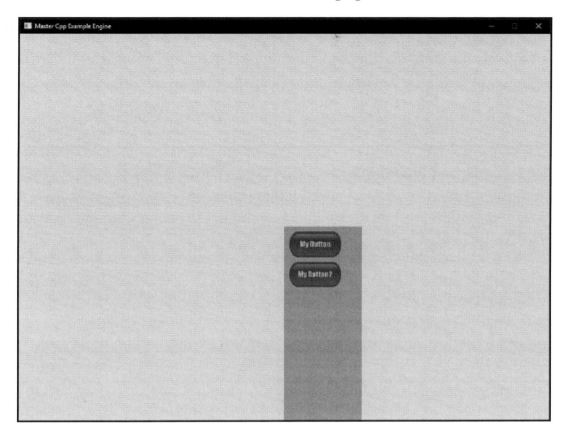

Summary

In this chapter, we covered a large amount of information. We discussed the different aspects needed to create a GUI. We walked through its implementation, diving deep into the core architecture behind a working GUI. We developed a panel and element architecture complete with anchor points for controlling positioning. We implemented a user input structure using the Observer design pattern and rounded it out by coding up the rendering pipe needed to display the GUI elements on the screen. In the next chapter, we will dive deep into some of the advanced rendering techniques used in game development.

7
Advanced Rendering

Often, the first impression that a player will get off your game is from the visuals on the screen. Having a strong understanding of creating advanced rendering techniques is crucial in building a compelling and immersive experience. In this chapter, we look at how we can create some advanced rendering effects by implementing shader techniques.

- Introduction to shaders
- Lighting techniques
- Using shaders to create effects

Introduction to shaders

Simply put, a shader is a computer program that is used to do image processing such as special effects, color effects, lighting, and, well, shading. The position, brightness, contrast, hue, and other effects on all pixels, vertices, or textures used to produce the final image on the screen can be altered during runtime, using algorithms constructed in the shader program(s). These days, most shader programs are built to run directly on the **Graphical Processing Unit** (**GPU**). Shader programs are executed in parallel. This means, for example, that a shader might be executed once per pixel, with each of the executions running simultaneously on different threads on the GPU. The amount of simultaneous threads depends on the graphics card specific GPU, with modern cards sporting processors in the thousands. This all means that shader programs can be very performant and provide developers with lots of creative flexibility. In this section, we are going to get acquainted with shaders and implement our own shader infrastructure for the example engine.

Shader languages

With advances in graphics card technology, more flexibility has been added to the rendering pipeline. Where at one time developers had little control over concepts such as fixed-function pipeline rendering, new advancements have allowed programmers to take deeper control of graphics hardware for rendering their creations. Originally, this deeper control was achieved by writing shaders in assembly language, which was a complex and cumbersome task. It wasn't long before developers yearned for a better solution. Enter the shader programming languages. Let's take a brief look at a few of the more common languages in use.

C for graphics (Cg) is a shading language originally developed by the Nvidia graphics company. Cg is based on the C programming language and, although they share the same syntax, some features of C were modified and new data types were added to make Cg more suitable for programming GPUs. Cg compilers can output shader programs supported by both DirectX and OpenGL. While Cg was mostly deprecated, it has seen a resurgence in a new form with its use in the Unity game engine.

High-Level Shading Language (HLSL) is a shading language developed by the Microsoft Corporation for use with the DirectX graphics API. HLSL is again modeled after the C programming language and shares many similarities to the Cg shading language. HLSL is still in development and continues to be the shading language of choice for DirectX. Since the release, DirectX 12 the HLSL language supports even lower level hardware control and has seen dramatic performance improvements.

OpenGL Shading Language (GLSL) is a shading language that is also based on the C programming language. It was created by the **OpenGL Architecture Review Board (OpenGL ARB)** to give developers more direct control of the graphics pipeline without having to use ARB assembly language or other hardware-specific languages. The language is still in open development and will be the language we will focus on in our examples.

Building a shader program infrastructure

Most modern shader programs are composed of up to five different types of shader files: fragment or pixel shaders, vertex shaders, geometry shaders, compute shaders, and tessellation shaders. When building a shader program, each of these shader files must be compiled and linked together for use, much like how a C++ program is compiled and linked. Next, we are going to walk you through how this process works and see how we can build an infrastructure to allow for easier interaction with our shader programs.

To get started, let's look at how we compile a GLSL shader. The GLSL compiler is part of the OpenGL library itself, and our shaders can be compiled within an OpenGL program. We are going to build an architecture to support this internal compilation. The whole process of compiling a shader can be broken down into some simple steps. First, we have to create a shader object, then provide the source code to the shader object. We can then ask the shader object to be compiled. These steps can be represented in the following three basic calls to the OpenGL API.

First, we create the shader object:

```
GLuint vertexShader = glCreateShader(GL_VERTEX_SHADER);
```

We create the shader object using the `glCreateShader()` function. The argument we pass in is the type of shader we are trying to create. The types of shaders can be `GL_VERTEX_SHADER`, `GL_FRAGMENT_SHADER`, `GL_GEOMETRY_SHADER`, `GL_TESS_EVALUATION_SHADER`, `GL_TESS_CONTROL_SHADER`, or `GL_COMPUTE_SHADER`. In our example case, we are trying to compile a vertex shader, so we use the `GL_VERTEX_SHADER` type.

Next, we copy the shader source code into the shader object:

```
GLchar* shaderCode = LoadShader("shaders/simple.vert");
glShaderSource(vertexShader, 1, shaderCode, NULL);
```

Here we are using the `glShaderSource()` function to load our shader source to memory. This function accepts an array of strings, so before we call `glShaderSource()`, we create a pointer to the start of the `shaderCode` array object using a still-to-be-created method. The first argument to `glShaderSource()` is the handle to the shader object. The second is the number of source code strings that are contained in the array. The third argument is a pointer to an array of source code strings. The final argument is an array of `GLint` values that contains the length of each source code string in the previous argument.

Finally, we compile the shader:

```
glCompileShader(vertexShader);
```

The last step is to compile the shader. We do this by calling the OpenGL API method, `glCompileShader()`, and passing the handle to the shader that we want compiled.

Of course, because we are using memory to store the shaders, we should know how to clean up when we are done. To delete a shader object, we can call the `glDeleteShader()` function.

Deleting a Shader `ObjectShader` objects can be deleted when no longer needed by calling `glDeleteShader()`. This frees the memory used by the shader object. It should be noted that if a shader object is already attached to a program object, as in linked to a shader program, it will not be immediately deleted, but rather flagged for deletion. If the object is flagged for deletion, it will be deleted when it is detached from the linked shader program object.

Once we have compiled our shaders, the next step we need to take before we can use them in our program is to link them together into a complete shader program. One of the core aspects of the linking step involves making the connections between input variables from one shader to the output variables of another and making the connections between the input/output variables of a shader to appropriate locations in the OpenGL program itself.

Linking is much like compiling the shader. We create a new shader program and attach each shader object to it. We then tell the shader program object to link everything together. The steps to accomplish this in the OpenGL environment can be broken down into a few calls to the API, as follows:

First, we create the shader program object:

```
GLuint shaderProgram = glCreateProgram();
```

To start, we call the `glCreateProgram()` method to create an empty program object. This function returns a handle to the shader program object which, in this example, we are storing in a variable named `shaderProgram`.

Next, we attach the shaders to the program object:

```
glAttachShader(shaderProgram, vertexShader);
glAttachShader(shaderProgram, fragmentShader);
```

To load each of the shaders into the shader program, we use the `glAttachShader()` method. This method takes two arguments. The first argument is the handle to the shader program object, and the second is the handle to the shader object to be attached to the shader program.

Finally, we link the program:

```
glLinkProgram(programHandle);
```

When we are ready to link the shaders together we call the `glLinkProgram()` method. This method has only one argument: the handle to the shader program we want to link.

It's important that we remember to clean up any shader programs that we are not using anymore. To remove a shader program from the OpenGL memory, we call `glDeleteProgram()` method. The `glDeleteProgram()` method takes one argument: the handle to the shader program that is to be deleted. This method call invalidates the handle and frees the memory used by the shader program. It is important to note that if the shader program object is currently in use, it will not be immediately deleted, but rather flagged for deletion. This is similar to the deletion of shader objects. It is also important to note that the deletion of a shader program will detach any shader objects that were attached to the shader program at linking time. This, however, does mean the shader object will be deleted immediately unless those shader objects have already been flagged for deletion by a previous call to the `glDeleteShader()` method.

So those are the simplified OpenGL API calls required to create, compile, and link shader programs. Now we are going to move onto implementing some structure to make the whole process much easier to work with. To do this, we are going to create a new class called `ShaderManager`. This class will act as the interface for compiling, linking, and managing the cleanup of shader programs. To start with, let's look at the implementation of the `CompileShaders()` method in the `ShaderManager.cpp` file. I should note that I will be focusing on the important aspects of the code that pertain to the implementation of the architecture. The full source code for this chapter can be found in the `Chapter07` folder in the GitHub repository.

```
void ShaderManager::CompileShaders(const std::string&
                    vertexShaderFilePath, const std::string&
                    fragmentShaderFilepath)
{
    m_programID = glCreateProgram();
    m_vertexShaderID = glCreateShader(GL_VERTEX_SHADER);
    if (m_vertexShaderID == 0){
        Exception("Vertex shader failed to be created!");
    }
    m_fragmentShaderID = glCreateShader(GL_FRAGMENT_SHADER);
    if (m_fragmentShaderID == 0){
        Exception("Fragment shader failed to be created!");
    }
    CompileShader(vertexShaderFilePath, m_vertexShaderID);
    CompileShader(fragmentShaderFilepath, m_fragmentShaderID);
}
```

To begin, for this example we are focusing on two of the shader types, so our `ShaderManager::CompileShaders()` method accepts two arguments. The first argument is the file path location of the vertex shader file, and the second is the file path location to the fragment shader file. Both are strings. Inside the method body, we first create the shader program handle using the `glCreateProgram()` method and store it in the `m_programID` variable. Next, we create the handles for the vertex and fragment shaders using the `glCreateShader()` command. We check for any errors when creating the shader handles, and if we find any we throw an exception with the shader name that failed. Once the handles have been created, we then call the `CompileShader()` method, which we will look at next. The `CompileShader()` function takes two arguments: the first is the path to the shader file, and the second is the handle in which the compiled shader will be stored.

The following is the full `CompileShader()` function. It handles the look and loading of the shader file from storage, as well as calling the OpenGL compile command on the shader file. We will break it down chunk by chunk:

```
void ShaderManager::CompileShader(const std::string& filePath, GLuint id)
{
  std::ifstream shaderFile(filePath);
  if (shaderFile.fail()){
    perror(filePath.c_str());
    Exception("Failed to open " + filePath);
  }
    //File contents stores all the text in the file
    std::string fileContents = "";
    //line is used to grab each line of the file
    std::string line;
   //Get all the lines in the file and add it to the contents
    while (std::getline(shaderFile, line)){
    fileContents += line + "n";
  }
  shaderFile.close();
  //get a pointer to our file contents c string
  const char* contentsPtr = fileContents.c_str();   //tell opengl that
  we want to use fileContents as the contents of the shader file
  glShaderSource(id, 1, &contentsPtr, nullptr);
  //compile the shader
  glCompileShader(id);
  //check for errors
  GLint success = 0;
  glGetShaderiv(id, GL_COMPILE_STATUS, &success);
  if (success == GL_FALSE){
    GLint maxLength = 0;
    glGetShaderiv(id, GL_INFO_LOG_LENGTH, &maxLength);
    //The maxLength includes the NULL character
```

```
        std::vector<char> errorLog(maxLength);
        glGetShaderInfoLog(id, maxLength, &maxLength, &errorLog[0]);
        //Provide the infolog in whatever manor you deem best.
        //Exit with failure.
        glDeleteShader(id); //Don't leak the shader.
        //Print error log and quit
        std::printf("%sn", &(errorLog[0]));
            Exception("Shader " + filePath + " failed to compile");
    }
}
```

To start the function, we first use an `ifstream` object to open the file with the shader code in it. We also check to see if there were any issues loading the file and if, there were, we throw an exception notifying us that the file failed to open:

```
std::ifstream shaderFile(filePath);
if (shaderFile.fail()) {
  perror(filePath.c_str());
  Exception("Failed to open " + filePath);
}
```

Next, we need to parse the shader. To do this, we create a string variable called `fileContents` that will hold the text in the shader file. We then create another string variable named line; this will be a temporary holder for each line of the shader file we are trying to parse. Next, we use a `while` loop to step through the shader file, parsing the contents line by line and saving each loop into the `fileContents` string. Once all the lines have been read into the holder variable, we call the close method on the `shaderFile` `ifstream` object to free up the memory used to read the file:

```
std::string fileContents = "";
std::string line;
while (std::getline(shaderFile, line)) {
   fileContents += line + "n";
}
shaderFile.close();
```

You might remember from earlier in the chapter that I mentioned that when we are using the `glShaderSource()` function, we have to pass the shader file text as a pointer to the start of a character array. In order to meet this requirement, we are going to use a neat trick where we use the C string conversation method built into the string class to allow us to pass back a pointer to the start of our shader character array. This, in case you are unfamiliar, is essentially what a string is:

```
const char* contentsPtr = fileContents.c_str();
```

Now that we have a pointer to the shader text, we can call the `glShaderSource()` method to tell OpenGL that we want to use the contents of the file to compile our shader. Then, finally, we call the `glCompileShader()` method with the handle to the shader as the argument:

```
glShaderSource(id, 1, &contentsPtr, nullptr);
glCompileShader(id);
```

That handles the compilation, but it is a good idea to provide ourselves with some debug support. We implement this compilation debug support by closing out the `CompileShader()` function by first checking to see if there were any errors during the compilation process. We do this by requesting information from the shader compiler through `glGetShaderiv()` function, which, among its arguments, takes an enumerated value that specifies what information we would like returned. In this call, we are requesting the compile status:

```
GLint success = 0;
glGetShaderiv(id, GL_COMPILE_STATUS, &success);
```

Next, we check to see if the returned value is `GL_FALSE`, and if it is, that means we have had an error and should ask the compiler for more information about the compile issues. We do this by first asking the compiler what the max length of the error log is. We use this max length value to then create a vector of character values called errorLog. Then we can request the shader compile log by using the `glGetShaderInfoLog()` method, passing in the handle to the shader file the number of characters we are pulling, and where we want to save the log:

```
if (success == GL_FALSE){
  GLint maxLength = 0;
  glGetShaderiv(id, GL_INFO_LOG_LENGTH, &maxLength);
  std::vector<char> errorLog(maxLength);
  glGetShaderInfoLog(id, maxLength, &maxLength, &errorLog[0]);
```

Once we have the log file saved, we go ahead and delete the shader using the `glDeleteShader()` method. This ensures we don't have any memory leaks from our shader:

```
glDeleteShader(id);
```

Finally, we first print the error log to the console window. This is great for runtime debugging. We also throw an exception with the shader name/file path, and the message that it failed to compile:

```
std::printf("%sn", &(errorLog[0]));
Exception("Shader " + filePath + " failed to compile");
}
...
```

That really simplifies the process of compiling our shaders by providing a simple interface to the underlying API calls. Now, in our example program, to load and compile our shaders we use a simple line of code similar to the following:

```
shaderManager.CompileShaders("Shaders/SimpleShader.vert",
"Shaders/SimpleShader.frag");
```

Having now compiled the shaders, we are halfway to a useable shader program. We still need to add one more piece, linking. To abstract away some of the processes of linking the shaders and to provide us with some debugging capabilities, we are going to create the `LinkShaders()` method for our `ShaderManager` class. Let's take a look and then break it down:

```
void ShaderManager::LinkShaders() {
//Attach our shaders to our program
glAttachShader(m_programID, m_vertexShaderID);
glAttachShader(m_programID, m_fragmentShaderID);
//Link our program
glLinkProgram(m_programID);
//Note the different functions here: glGetProgram* instead of glGetShader*.
GLint isLinked = 0;
glGetProgramiv(m_programID, GL_LINK_STATUS, (int *)&isLinked);
if (isLinked == GL_FALSE){
  GLint maxLength = 0;
  glGetProgramiv(m_programID, GL_INFO_LOG_LENGTH, &maxLength);
  //The maxLength includes the NULL character
  std::vector<char> errorLog(maxLength);
  glGetProgramInfoLog(m_programID, maxLength, &maxLength,
  &errorLog[0]);
  //We don't need the program anymore.
  glDeleteProgram(m_programID);
  //Don't leak shaders either.
  glDeleteShader(m_vertexShaderID);
  glDeleteShader(m_fragmentShaderID);
  //print the error log and quit
  std::printf("%sn", &(errorLog[0]));
  Exception("Shaders failed to link!");
```

```
}
  //Always detach shaders after a successful link.
  glDetachShader(m_programID, m_vertexShaderID);
  glDetachShader(m_programID, m_fragmentShaderID);
  glDeleteShader(m_vertexShaderID);
  glDeleteShader(m_fragmentShaderID);
}
```

To start our `LinkShaders()` function, we call the `glAttachShader()` method twice, using the handle to the previously created shader program object, and the handle to each shader we wish to link, respectively:

```
glAttachShader(m_programID, m_vertexShaderID);
glAttachShader(m_programID, m_fragmentShaderID);
```

Next, we perform the actual linking of the shaders into a usable shader program by calling the `glLinkProgram()` method, using the handle to the program object as its argument:

```
glLinkProgram(m_programID);
```

We can then check to see if the linking process has completed without any errors and provide ourselves with any debug information that we might need if there were any errors. I am not going to go through this code chunk line by line since it is nearly identical to what we did with the `CompileShader()` function. Do note, however, that the function to return the information from the linker is slightly different and uses `glGetProgram*` instead of the `glGetShader*` functions from before:

```
GLint isLinked = 0;
glGetProgramiv(m_programID, GL_LINK_STATUS, (int *)&isLinked);
if (isLinked == GL_FALSE){
  GLint maxLength = 0;
  glGetProgramiv(m_programID, GL_INFO_LOG_LENGTH, &maxLength);
  //The maxLength includes the NULL character
  std::vector<char> errorLog(maxLength);
  glGetProgramInfoLog(m_programID, maxLength, &maxLength,
  &errorLog[0]);
  //We don't need the program anymore.
  glDeleteProgram(m_programID);
  //Don't leak shaders either.
  glDeleteShader(m_vertexShaderID);
  glDeleteShader(m_fragmentShaderID);
  //print the error log and quit
  std::printf("%sn", &(errorLog[0]));
  Exception("Shaders failed to link!");
}
```

Lastly, if we are successful in the linking process, we need to clean it up a bit. First, we detach the shaders from the linker using the `glDetachShader()` method. Next, since we have a completed shader program, we no longer need to keep the shaders in memory, so we delete each shader with a call to the `glDeleteShader()` method. Again, this will ensure we do not leak any memory in our shader program creation process:

```
    glDetachShader(m_programID, m_vertexShaderID);
    glDetachShader(m_programID, m_fragmentShaderID);
    glDeleteShader(m_vertexShaderID);
    glDeleteShader(m_fragmentShaderID);
}
```

We now have a simplified way of linking our shaders into a working shader program. We can call this interface to the underlying API calls by simply using one line of code, similar to the following one:

```
    shaderManager.LinkShaders();
```

So that handles the process of compiling and linking our shaders, but there is another key aspect to working with shaders, which is the passing of data to and from the running program/the game and the shader programs running on the GPU. We will look at this process and how we can abstract it into an easy-to-use interface for our engine next.

Working with shader data

One of the most important aspects of working with shaders is the ability to pass data to and from the shader programs running on the GPU. This can be a deep topic, and much like other topics in this book has had its own dedicated books. We are going to stay at a higher level when discussing this topic and again will focus on the two needed shader types for basic rendering: the vertex and fragment shaders.

To begin with, let's take a look at how we send data to a shader using the vertex attributes and **Vertex Buffer Objects** (**VBO**). A vertex shader has the job of processing the data that is connected to the vertex, doing any modifications, and then passing it to the next stage of the rendering pipeline. This occurs once per vertex. In order for the shader to do its thing, we need to be able to pass it data. To do this, we use what are called vertex attributes, and they usually work hand in hand with what is referred to as VBO.

For the vertex shader, all per-vertex input attributes are defined using the keyword `in`. So, for example, if we wanted to define a vector 3 input attribute named VertexColour, we could write something like the following:

```
    in vec3 VertexColour;
```

Now, the data for the `VertexColour` attribute has to be supplied by the program/game. This is where VBO come in. In our main game or program, we make the connection between the input attribute and the vertex buffer object, and we also have to define how to parse or step through the data. That way, when we render, the OpenGL can pull data for the attribute from the buffer for each call of the vertex shader.

Let's take a look a very simple vertex shader:

```
#version 410
in vec3 VertexPosition;
in vec3 VertexColour;
out vec3 Colour;
void main(){
  Colour = VertexColour;
  gl_Position = vec4(VertexPosition, 1.0);
}
```

In this example, there are just two input variables for this vertex shader, `VertexPosition` and `VertexColor`. Our main OpenGL program needs to supply the data for these two attributes for each vertex. We will do so by mapping our polygon/mesh data to these variables. We also have one output variable named Colour, which will be sent to the next stage of the rendering pipeline, the fragment shader. In this example, Colour is just an untouched copy of `VertexColour`. The `VertexPosition` attribute is simply expanded and passed along to the OpenGL API output variable `gl_Position` for more processing.

Next, let's take a look at a very simple fragment shader:

```
#version 410
in vec3 Colour;
out vec4 FragColour;
void main(){
  FragColour = vec4(Colour, 1.0);
}
```

In this fragment shader example, there is only one input attribute, `Colour`. This input corresponds to the output of the previous rendering stage, the vertex shader's `Colour` output. For simplicity's sake, we are just expanding the `Colour` and outputting it as the variable `FragColour` for the next rendering stage.

That sums up the shader side of the connection, so how do we compose and send the data from inside our engine? We can accomplish this in basically four steps.

First, we create a **Vertex Array Object (VAO)** instance to hold our data:

```
GLunit vao;
```

Next, we create and populate the VBO for each of the shaders' input attributes. We do this by first creating a VBO variable, then, using the `glGenBuffers()` method, we generate the memory for the buffer objects. We then create handles to the different attributes we need buffers for, assigning them to elements in the VBO array. Finally, we populate the buffers for each attribute by first calling the `glBindBuffer()` method, specifying the type of object being stored. In this case, it is a `GL_ARRAY_BUFFER` for both attributes. Then we call the `glBufferData()` method, passing the type, size, and handle to bind. The last argument for the `glBufferData()` method is one that gives OpenGL a hint about how the data will be used so that it can determine how best to manage the buffer internally. For full details about this argument, take a look at the OpenGL documentation:

```
GLuint vbo[2];
glGenBuffers(2, vbo);
GLuint positionBufferHandle = vbo[0];
GLuint colorBufferHandle = vbo[1];
glBindBuffer(GL_ARRAY_BUFFER,positionBufferHandle);
glBufferData(GL_ARRAY_BUFFER,
             9 * sizeof(float),
             positionData,
             GL_STATIC_DRAW);
glBindBuffer(GL_ARRAY_BUFFER,
             colorBufferHandle);
glBufferData(GL_ARRAY_BUFFER,
             9 * sizeof(float),
             colorData,
             GL_STATIC_DRAW);
```

The third step is to create and define the VAO. This is how we will define the relationship between the input attributes of the shader and the buffers we just created. The VAO contains this information about the connections. To create a VAO, we use the `glGenVertexArrays()` method. This gives us a handle to our new object, which we store in our previously created VAO variable. Then, we enable the generic vertex attribute indexes 0 and 1 by calling the `glEnableVertexAttribArray()` method. By making the call to enable the attributes, we are specifying that they will be accessed and used for rendering. The last step makes the connection between the buffer objects we have created and the generic vertex attribute indexes the match too:

```
glGenVertexArrays( 1, &vao );
glBindVertexArray(vao);
glEnableVertexAttribArray(0);
glEnableVertexAttribArray(1);
```

```
glBindBuffer(GL_ARRAY_BUFFER, positionBufferHandle);
glVertexAttribPointer(0, 3, GL_FLOAT, GL_FALSE, 0, NULL);
glBindBuffer(GL_ARRAY_BUFFER, colorBufferHandle);
glVertexAttribPointer(1, 3, GL_FLOAT, GL_FALSE, 0, NULL);
```

Finally, in our `Draw()` function call, we bind to the VAO and call `glDrawArrays()` to perform the actual render:

```
glBindVertexArray(vaoHandle);glDrawArrays(GL_TRIANGLES, 0, 3 );
```

Before we move on to another way to pass data to the shader, there is one more piece of this attribute connection structure we need to discuss. As mentioned, the input variables in a shader are linked to the generic vertex attribute we just saw, at the time of linking. When we need to specify the relationship structure, we have a few different choices. We can use what are known as layout qualifiers within the shader code itself. The following is an example:

```
layout (location=0) in vec3 VertexPosition;
```

Another choice is to just let the linker create the mapping when linking, and then query for them afterward. The third and the one I personally prefer is to specify the relationship prior to the linking process by making a call to the `glBindAttribLocation()` method. We will see how this is implemented shortly when we discuss how to abstract these processes.

We have described how we can pass data to a shader using attributes, but there is another option: uniform variables. Uniform variables are specifically used for data that changes infrequently. For example, matrices are great candidates for uniform variables. Within a shader, a uniform variable is read-only. That means the value can only be changed from outside the shader. They can also appear in multiple shaders within the same shader program. They can be declared in one or more shaders within a program, but if a variable with a given name is declared in more than one shader, its type must be the same in all shaders. This gives us insight into the fact that the uniform variables are actually held in a shared namespace for the whole of the shader program.

To use a uniform variable in your shader, you first have to declare it in the shader file using the uniform identifier keyword. The following is what this might look like:

```
uniform mat4 ViewMatrix;
```

We then need to provide the data for the uniform variable from inside our game/program. We do this by first finding the location of the variable using the `glGetUniformLocation()` method. Then we assign a value to the found location using one of the `glUniform()` methods. The code for this process could look something like the following:

```
GLuint location = glGetUniformLocation(programHandle," ViewMatrix ");
if( location >= 0 )
{
glUniformMatrix4fv(location, 1, GL_FALSE, &viewMatrix [0][0])
}
```

We then assign a value to the uniform variable's location using the `glUniformMatrix4fv()` method. The first argument is the uniform variable's location. The second argument is the number of matrices that are being assigned. The third is a GL `bool` type specifying whether or not the matrix should be transposed. Since we are using the GLM library for our matrices, a transpose is not required. If you were implementing the matrix using data that was in row-major order, instead of column-major order, you might need to use the `GL_TRUE` type for this argument. The last argument is a pointer to the data for the uniform variable.

Uniform variables can be any GLSL type, and this includes complex types such as structures and arrays. The OpenGL API provides a `glUniform()` function with the different suffixes that match each type. For example, to assign to a variable of type vec3, we would use `glUniform3f()` or `glUniform3fv()` methods. (the *v* denotes multiple values in the array).

So, those are the concepts and techniques for passing data to and from our shader programs. However, as we did for the compiling and linking of our shaders, we can abstract these processes into functions housed in our `ShaderManager` class. We are going to focus on working with attributes and uniform variables. We do have a great class that abstracts the creation of VAO and VBO for models/meshes, that we walked through in great detail back in Chapter 4, *Building Gameplay Systems*, when we discussed building an asset pipeline. To see how that was constructed, either flip back to Chapter 4, *Building Gameplay Systems,* or check out the implementation in the `Mesh.h` and `Mesh.cpp` files of the `BookEngine` solution.

First, we will look at the abstraction of adding attribute bindings using the AddAttribute() function of the ShaderManger class. This function takes one argument, the attribute's name, to be bound as a string. We then call the glBindAttribLocation() function, passing the program's handle and the current index or number of attributes, which we increase on call, and finally the C string conversion of the attributeName string, which provides a pointer to the first character in the string array. This function must be called after compilation, but before the linking of the shader program:

```
void ShaderManager::AddAttribute(const std::string& attributeName)
{
glBindAttribLocation(m_programID,
                     m_numAttributes++,
                     attributeName.c_str());
}
```

For the uniform variables, we create a function that abstracts looking up the location of the uniform in the shader program, the GetUniformLocation() function. This function again takes only one variable which is a uniform name in the form of a string. We then create a temporary holder for the location and assign it the returned value of the glGetUniformLocation() method call. We check to make sure the location is valid, and if not we throw an exception letting us know about the error. Finally, we return the valid location if found:

```
GLint ShaderManager::GetUniformLocation(const std::string& uniformName)
{
    GLint location = glGetUniformLocation(m_programID,
    uniformName.c_str());
    if (location == GL_INVALID_INDEX)
    {
     Exception("Uniform " + uniformName + " not found in shader!");
    }
   return location;
}
```

This gives us the abstraction for binding our data, but we still need to assign which shader should be used for a certain draw call, and to activate any attributes we need. To accomplish this, we create a function in the ShaderManager called Use(). This function will first set the current shader program as the active one using the glUseProgram() API method call. We then use a for loop to step through the list of attributes for the shader program, activating each one:

```
void ShaderManager::Use(){
  glUseProgram(m_programID);
  for (int i = 0; i < m_numAttributes; i++) {
    glEnableVertexAttribArray(i);
```

```
    }
  }
```

Of course, since we have an abstracted way to enable the shader program, it only makes sense that we should have a function to disable the shader program. This function is very similar to the `Use()` function, but in this case, we are setting the program in use to 0, effectively making it `NULL`, and we use the `glDisableVertexAtrribArray()` method to disable the attributes in the for loop:

```
void ShaderManager::UnUse() {
  glUseProgram(0);
  for (int i = 0; i < m_numAttributes; i++) {
    glDisableVertexAttribArray(i);
  }
}
```

The net effect of this abstraction is we can now set up our entire shader program structure with a few simple calls. Code similar to the following would create and compile the shaders, add the necessary attributes, link the shaders into a program, locate a uniform variable, and create the VAO and VBO for a mesh:

```
shaderManager.CompileShaders("Shaders/SimpleShader.vert",
                             "Shaders/SimpleShader.frag");
shaderManager.AddAttribute("vertexPosition_modelspace");
shaderManager.AddAttribute("vertexColor");
shaderManager.LinkShaders();
MatrixID = shaderManager.GetUniformLocation("ModelViewProjection");
m_model.Init("Meshes/Dwarf_2_Low.obj", "Textures/dwarf_2_1K_color.png");
```

Then, in our `Draw` loop, if we want to use this shader program to draw, we can simply use the abstracted functions to activate and deactivate our shader, similar to the following code:

```
shaderManager.Use();
m_model.Draw();
shaderManager.UnUse();
```

This makes it much easier for us to work with and test out advanced rendering techniques using shaders. We will be using this structure to build out the examples in the rest of this chapter and in fact the rest of the book.

Lighting effects

One of the most common uses for shaders is creating lighting and reflection effects. Lighting effects achieved from the use of shaders help provide a level of polish and detail that every modern game strives for. In the next section, we will look at some of the well-known models for creating different surface appearance effects, with examples of shaders you can implement to replicate the discussed lighting effect.

Per-vertex diffuse

To start with, we will look at one of the simpler lighting vertex shaders, the diffuse reflection shader. Diffuse is considered simpler since we assume that the surface we are rendering appears to scatter the light in all directions equally. With this shader, the light makes contact with the surface and slightly penetrates before being cast back out in all directions. This means that some of the light's wavelength will be at least partially absorbed. A good example of what a diffuse shader looks like is to think of matte paint. The surface has a very dull look with no shine.

Let's take a quick look at the mathematical model for a diffuse reflection. This reflection model takes two vectors. One is the direction of the surface contact point to the initial light source, and the second is the normal vector of that same surface contact point. This would look something like the following:

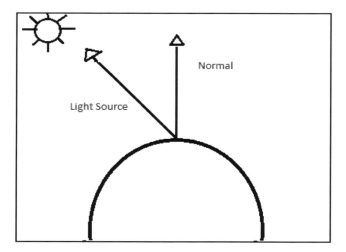

It's worth noting that the amount of light that strikes the surface is partially dependent on the surface in relation to the light source and that the amount of light that reaches a single point will be at its maximum along the normal vector, and its lowest when perpendicular to the normal vector. Dusting off our physics knowledge toolbox, we are able to express this relationship given the amount of light making contact with a point by calculating the dot product of the point normal vector and incoming light vector. This can be expressed by the following formula:

Light Density(Source Vector) Normal Vector

The source and normal vector in this equation are assumed to be normalized.

As mentioned before, some of the light striking the surface will be absorbed before it is re-cast. To add this behavior to our mathematical model, we can add a reflection coefficient, also referred to as the diffuse reflectivity. This coefficient value becomes the scaling factor for the incoming light. Our new formula to specify the outgoing intensity of the light will now look like the following:

Outgoing Light = (Diffuse Coefficient x Light Density x Source Vector) Normal Vector

With this new formula, we now have a lighting model that represents an omnidirectional, uniform scattering.

OK, now that we know the theory, let's take a look at how we can implement this lighting model in a GLSL shader. The full source for this example can be found in the `Chapter07` folder of the GitHub repository, starting with the Vertex Shader shown as follows:

```
#version 410
in vec3 vertexPosition_modelspace;
in vec2 vertexUV;
in vec3 vertexNormal;
out vec2 UV;
out vec3 LightIntensity;
uniform vec4 LightPosition;
uniform vec3 DiffuseCoefficient ;
uniform vec3 LightSourceIntensity;
uniform mat4 ModelViewProjection;
uniform mat3 NormalMatrix;
uniform mat4 ModelViewMatrix;
uniform mat4 ProjectionMatrix;
void main(){
    vec3 tnorm = normalize(NormalMatrix * vertexNormal);
    vec4 CameraCoords = ModelViewMatrix *
    vec4(vertexPosition_modelspace,1.0);
    vec3 IncomingLightDirection = normalize(vec3(LightPosition -
```

```
                 CameraCoords));
        LightIntensity = LightSourceIntensity * DiffuseCoefficient *
                        max( dot( IncomingLightDirection, tnorm ), 0.0 );
        gl_Position = ModelViewProjection *
                        vec4(vertexPosition_modelspace,1);
                        UV = vertexUV;
    }
```

We'll go through this shader block by block. To start out, we have our attributes, `vertexPosition_modelspace`, `vertexUV`, and `vertexNormal`. These will be set by our game application, which we will look at after we go through the shader. Then we have our out variables, UV and `LightIntensity`. These values will be calculated in the shader itself. We then have our uniforms. These include the needed values for our reflection calculation, as we discussed. It also includes all the necessary matrices. Like the attributes, these uniform values will be set via our game.

Inside of the main function of this shader, our diffuse reflection is going to be calculated in the camera relative coordinates. To accomplish this, we first normalize the vertex normal by multiplying it by the normal matrix and storing the results in a vector 3 variable named `tnorm`. Next, we convert the vertex position that is currently in model space to camera coordinates by transforming it with the model view matrix. We then calculate the incoming light direction, normalized, by subtracting the vertex position in the camera coordinates from the light's position. Next, we calculate the outgoing light intensity by using the formula we went through earlier. A point to note here is the use of the max function. This is a situation when the light direction is greater than 90 degrees, as in the light is coming from inside the object. Since in our case we don't need to support this situation, we just use a value of `0.0` when this arises. To close out the shader, we store the model view projection matrix, calculated in clip space, in the built-in outbound variable `gl_position`. We also pass along the UV of the texture, unchanged, which we are not actually using in this example.

Now that we have the shader in place, we need to provide the values needed for the calculations. As we learned in the first section of this chapter, we do this by setting the attributes and uniforms. We built an abstraction layer to help with this process, so let's take a look at how we set these values in our game code. Inside the `GamePlayScreen.cpp` file, we are setting these values in the `Draw()` function. I should point out this is for the example, and in a production environment, you would only want to set the changing values in a loop for performance reasons. Since this is an example, I wanted to make it slightly easier to follow:

```
GLint DiffuseCoefficient =
        shaderManager.GetUniformLocation("DiffuseCoefficient ");
glUniform3f(DiffuseCoefficient, 0.9f, 0.5f, 0.3f);
```

```
GLint LightSourceIntensity =
        shaderManager.GetUniformLocation("LightSourceIntensity ");
glUniform3f(LightSourceIntensity, 1.0f, 1.0f, 1.0f);
glm::vec4 lightPos = m_camera.GetView() * glm::vec4(5.0f, 5.0f, 2.0f,
                    1.0f);
GLint lightPosUniform =
                shaderManager.GetUniformLocation("LightPosition");
glUniform4f(lightPosUniform, lightPos[0], lightPos[1], lightPos[2],
            lightPos[3]);
glm::mat4 modelView = m_camera.GetView() * glm::mat4(1.0f);
GLint modelViewUniform =
                shaderManager.GetUniformLocation("ModelViewMatrix");
glUniformMatrix4fv(modelViewUniform, 1, GL_FALSE, &modelView[0][0]);
glm::mat3 normalMatrix = glm::mat3(glm::vec3(modelView[0]),
                        glm::vec3(modelView[1]),
                        glm::vec3(modelView[2]));
GLint normalMatrixUniform =
                shaderManager.GetUniformLocation("NormalMatrix");
glUniformMatrix3fv(normalMatrixUniform, 1, GL_FALSE, &normalMatrix[0][0]);
glUniformMatrix4fv(MatrixID, 1, GL_FALSE, &m_camera.GetMVPMatrix()[0][0]);
```

I won't go through each line since I am sure you can see the pattern. We first use the shader manager's `GetUniformLocation()` method to return the location for the uniform. Next, we set the value for this uniform using the OpenGL `glUniform*()` method that matches the value type. We do this for all uniform values needed. We also have to set our attributes, and as discussed in the beginning of the chapter, we do this in between the compilation and linking processes. In this example case, we are setting these values in the `OnEntry()` method of the `GamePlayScreen()` class:

```
shaderManager.AddAttribute("vertexPosition_modelspace");
shaderManager.AddAttribute("vertexColor");
shaderManager.AddAttribute("vertexNormal");
```

That takes care of the vertex shader and passed in values needed, so next, let's look at the fragment shader for this example:

```
#version 410
in vec2 UV;
in vec3 LightIntensity;
// Ouput data
out vec3 color;
// Values that stay constant for the whole mesh.
uniform sampler2D TextureSampler;
void main(){
  color = vec3(LightIntensity);
}
```

For this example, our fragment shader is extremely simple. To begin, we have the in values for our UV and `LightIntensity`, and we will only use the `LightIntensity` this time. We then declare our out color value, specified as a vector 3. Next, we have the `sampler2D` uniform that we use for texturing, but again we won't be using this value in the example. Finally, we have the main function. This is where we set the final output color by simply passing the `LightIntensity` through to the next stage in the pipeline.

If you run the example project, you will see the diffuse reflection in action. The output should look like the following screenshot. As you can see, this reflection model works well for surfaces that are very dull but has limited use in a practical environment. Next, we will look at a reflection model that will allow us to depict more surface types:

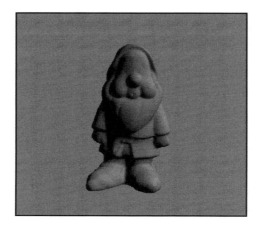

Per-vertex ambient, diffuse, and specular

The **ambient, diffuse, and specular (ADS)** reflection model, also commonly known as the **Phong reflection model**, provides a method of creating a reflective lighting shader. This technique models the interaction of light on a surface using a combination of three different components. The ambient component models the light that comes from the environment; this is intended to model what would happen if the light was reflected many times, where it appears as though it is emanating from everywhere. The diffuse component, which we modeled in our previous example, represents an omnidirectional reflection. The last component, the specular component, is meant to represent the reflection in a preferred direction, providing the appearance of a light *glare* or bright spot.

This combination of components can be visualized using the following diagram:

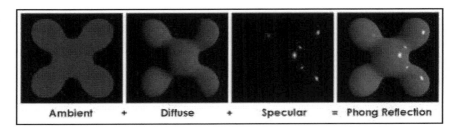

Ambient + Diffuse + Specular = Phong Reflection

Source: Wikipedia

This process can be broken down into separate components for discussion. First, we have the ambient component that represents the light that will illuminate all of the surfaces equally and reflect uniformly in all directions. This lighting effect does not depend on the incoming or the outgoing vectors of the light since it is uniformly distributed and can be expressed by simply multiplying the light source's intensity with the surface reflectivity. This is shown in the mathematical formula $I_a = L_a K_a$.

The next component is the diffuse component we discussed earlier. The diffuse component models a dull or rough surface that scatters light in all directions. Again, this can be expressed with the mathematical formula $I_d = L_d K_d(sn)$.

The final component is the specular component, and it is used to model the *shininess* of the surface. This creates a *glare* or bright spot that is common on surfaces that exhibit glossy properties. We can visualize this reflection effect using the following diagram:

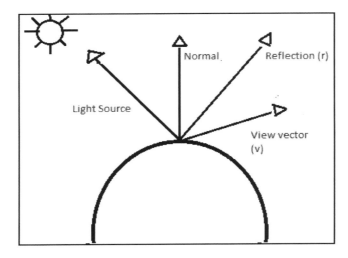

For the specular component, ideally, we would like the reflection to be at is most apparent when viewed aligned with the reflection vector, and then to fade off as the angle is increased or decreased from this alignment. We can model this effect using the cosine of the angle between our viewing vector and the reflection angle, which is then raised by some power, as shown in this equation: $(r\,v)^p$. In this equation, p represents the specular highlight, the *glare* spot. The larger the value input for p, the smaller the spot will appear, and the *shinier* the surface will look. After adding the values to represent the reflectiveness of the surface and the specular light intensity, the formula for calculating the specular effect for the surface looks like so: $I_s = L_s K_s (r\,v)^p$.

So, now, if we take all of our components and put them together in a formula, we come up with $I = I_a + I_d + I_s$ or breaking it down more, $I = L_a K_a + L_d K_d (sn) + L_s K_s (r\,v)^p$.

With our theory in place, let's see how we can implement this in a per-vertex shader, beginning with our vertex shader as follows:

```
#version 410
// Input vertex data, different for all executions of this shader.
in vec3 vertexPosition_modelspace;
in vec2 vertexUV;
in vec3 vertexNormal;
// Output data ; will be interpolated for each fragment.
out vec2 UV;
out vec3 LightIntensity;
struct LightInfo {
  vec4 Position; // Light position in eye coords.
  vec3 La; // Ambient light intensity
  vec3 Ld; // Diffuse light intensity
  vec3 Ls; // Specular light intensity
};
uniform LightInfo Light;
struct MaterialInfo {
  vec3 Ka; // Ambient reflectivity
  vec3 Kd; // Diffuse reflectivity
  vec3 Ks; // Specular reflectivity
  float Shininess; // Specular shininess factor
};
  uniform MaterialInfo Material;
  uniform mat4 ModelViewMatrix;
  uniform mat3 NormalMatrix;
  uniform mat4 ProjectionMatrix;
  uniform mat4 ModelViewProjection;
  void main(){
    vec3 tnorm = normalize( NormalMatrix * vertexNormal);
    vec4 CameraCoords = ModelViewMatrix *
```

```
                    vec4(vertexPosition_modelspace,1.0);
    vec3 s = normalize(vec3(Light.Position - CameraCoords));
    vec3 v = normalize(-CameraCoords.xyz);
    vec3 r = reflect( -s, tnorm );
    float sDotN = max( dot(s,tnorm), 0.0 );
    vec3 ambient = Light.La * Material.Ka;
    vec3 diffuse = Light.Ld * Material.Kd * sDotN;
    vec3 spec = vec3(0.0);
    if( sDotN > 0.0 )
      spec = Light.Ls * Material.Ks *
      pow( max( dot(r,v), 0.0 ), Material.Shininess );
      LightIntensity = ambient + diffuse + spec;
      gl_Position = ModelViewProjection *
              vec4(vertexPosition_modelspace,1.0);
}
```

Let's take a look at the what is different to start with. In this shader, we are introducing a new concept, the uniform struct. We are declaring two struct, one to describe the light, LightInfo, and one to describe the material, MaterialInfo. This is a very useful way of containing values that represent a portion in the formula as a collection. We will see how we can set the values of these struct elements from the game code shortly. Moving on to the main function of the function. First, we start as we did in the previous example. We calculate the tnorm, CameraCoords, and the light source vector(s). Next, we calculate the vector in the direction of the viewer/camera (v), which is the negative of the normalized CameraCoords. We then calculate the direction of the *pure* reflection using the provided GLSL method, reflect. Then we move on to calculating the values of our three components. The ambient is calculated by multiplying the light ambient intensity and the surface's ambient reflective value. The diffuse is calculated using the light intensity, the surface diffuse reflective value of the surface, and the result of the dot product of the light source vector and the tnorm, which we calculated just before the ambient value. Before computing the specular value, we check the value of sDotN. If sDotN is zero, then there is no light reaching the surface, so there is no point in computing the specular component. If sDotN is greater than zero, we compute the specular component. As in the previous example, we use a GLSL method to limit the range of values of the dot product to between 1 and 0. The GLSL function pow raises the dot product to the power of the surface's shininess exponent, which we defined as p in our shader equation previously.

Finally, we add all three of our component values together and pass their sum to the fragment shader in the form of the out variable, LightIntensity. We end by transforming the vertex position to clip space and passing it off to the next stage by assigning it to the gl_Position variable.

For the setting of the attributes and uniforms needed for our shader, we handle the process just as we did in the previous example. The main difference here is that we need to specify the elements of the `struct` we are assigning when getting the uniform location. An example would look similar to the following, and again you can see the full code in the example solution in the `Chapter07` folder of the GitHub repository:

```
GLint Kd = shaderManager.GetUniformLocation("Material.Kd");
glUniform3f(Kd, 0.9f, 0.5f, 0.3f);
```

The fragment shader used for this example is the same as the one we used for the diffuse example, so I won't cover it again here.

When you run the ADS example from the `Chapter07` code solution of the GitHub repository, you will see our newly created shader in effect, with an output looking similar to the following:

In this example, we calculated the shading equation within the vertex shader; this is referred to as a per-vertex shader. One issue that can arise from this approach is that our *glare* spots, the specular highlights, might appear to warp or disappear. This is caused by the shading being interpolated and not calculated for each point across the face. For example, a spot that was set near the middle of the face might not appear due to the fact that the equation was calculated at the vertices where the specular component was near to zero. In the next example, we will look at a technique that can eliminate the issue by calculating the reflection in the fragment shader.

Per-fragment Phong interpolation

In the previous examples, we have been using the vertex shaders to handle the lighting calculations. One issue when using a vertex shader to evaluate the color of each vertex, as mentioned in the last example, is that color is then interpolated across the face. This can cause some less than favorable effects. There is another way to accomplish this same lighting effect, but with improved accuracy. We can move the calculation to the fragment shader instead. In the fragment shader, instead of interpolating across the face, we interpolate normal and position and use these values to calculate at each fragment instead. This technique is often called **Phong interpolation**. The results of this techniques are much more accurate than when using a per-vertex implementation. However, since this per-fragment implementation evaluates each fragment, as opposed to just the vertices, this implementation will run slower than the per-vertex technique.

Let's start our look at the shader implementation by looking at the vertex shader for this example first:

```
#version 410
in vec3 vertexPosition_modelspace;
in vec2 vertexUV;
in vec3 vertexNormal;
out vec2 UV;
out vec3 Position;
out vec3 Normal;
uniform mat4 ModelViewMatrix;
uniform mat3 NormalMatrix;
uniform mat4 ProjectionMatrix;
uniform mat4 ModelViewProjection;
void main(){
    UV = vertexUV;
    Normal = normalize( NormalMatrix * vertexNormal);
    Position = vec3( ModelViewMatrix *
            vec4(vertexPosition_modelspace,1.0));
    gl_Position = ModelViewProjection *
            vec4(vertexPosition_modelspace,1.0);
}
```

Since this technique uses the fragment shader to perform the calculations, our vertex shader is considerably light. For the most part, we are doing a few simple equations to calculate the normal and the position, and then passing the values along to the next stage.

Next, we will look at the core of this technique's implementation in the fragment shader. Following is the complete fragment shader, and we will cover the differences from the previous examples:

```
#version 410
in vec3 Position;
in vec3 Normal;
in vec2 UV;
uniform sampler2D TextureSampler;
struct LightInfo {
  vec4 Position; // Light position in eye coords.
  vec3 Intensity; // A,D,S intensity
};
uniform LightInfo Light;
struct MaterialInfo {
  vec3 Ka; // Ambient reflectivity
  vec3 Kd; // Diffuse reflectivity
  vec3 Ks; // Specular reflectivity
  float Shininess; // Specular shininess factor
};
uniform MaterialInfo Material;
out vec3 color;
void phongModel( vec3 pos, vec3 norm, out vec3 ambAndDiff, out vec3
spec ) {
  vec3 s = normalize(vec3(Light.Position) - pos);
  vec3 v = normalize(-pos.xyz);
  vec3 r = reflect( -s, norm );
  vec3 ambient = Light.Intensity * Material.Ka;
  float sDotN = max( dot(s,norm), 0.0 );
  vec3 diffuse = Light.Intensity * Material.Kd * sDotN;
  spec = vec3(0.0);
  if( sDotN > 0.0 )
    spec = Light.Intensity * Material.Ks *
        pow( max( dot(r,v), 0.0 ), Material.Shininess );
        ambAndDiff = ambient + diffuse;
}
void main() {
  vec3 ambAndDiff, spec;
  vec3 texColor = texture( TextureSampler, UV ).rbg;
  phongModel( Position, Normal, ambAndDiff, spec );
  color = (vec3(ambAndDiff * texColor) + vec3(spec));
  }
```

This fragment shader should look very familiar, as this is nearly identical to the vertex shader from our previous examples. The big difference, besides the fact that this will run per fragment, not per vertex, is that we have cleaned up the shader by implementing a function to handle the Phong model calculation. We are also going to pass through a texture this time, to give our texture back to the gnome. The Phong model calculation is exactly the same as we have seen before, so I won't cover it again. The reason we moved it out into a function is mostly for readability, as it keeps the main function uncluttered. Creating a function in GLSL is nearly the same as in C++ and C. You have a return type, a function name followed by arguments, and a body. I highly recommend using functions in any shader more complex than a few lines.

To connect our shaders to the values from our game, we follow the same technique as before, where we set the needed attributes and uniform values. For this example, we must supply the values for Ka, Kd, Ks, Material Shininess, `LightPosition`, and `LightIntensity`. These values match up with the previously described ADS equation. We also need to pass in the usual matrices values. The full code can again be found in the `Chapter07` folder of the GitHub repository.

If we run the `Phong_Example` from the `Chapter07` solution, we will see the new shader in action, complete with texture and a more accurate reflection representation. The following is a screenshot of the output:

We will end our discussion on lighting techniques here, but I encourage you to continue your research on the topic. There are many interesting lighting effects that you can achieve with shaders, and we have only really begun to scratch the surface. In the next section, we will look at another common use for shaders: rendering effects.

Using Shaders to create effects

Shaders are not just limited to creating lighting effects. You can create many different visual effects using different shader techniques. In this section, we will cover a couple of interesting effects that you can achieve, including using the discard keyword to *throw away* pixels, and using shaders to create a simple particle effect system.

Discarding fragments

With the use of fragment shader tools, we are able to create some cool effects. One of these tools is the use of the discard keyword. The discard keyword, like its name suggests, removes or throws away fragments. When the discard keyword is used, the shader immediately stops its execution and skips the fragment, not writing any data to the output buffer. The created effect is holes in the polygon faces without using a blending effect. The discard keyword can also be combined with the use of alpha maps to allow textures to specify what fragments should be discarded. This can be a handy technique when modeling effects such as damage to an object.

For this example, we are going to create a fragment shader that will use the discard keyword to remove certain fragments based on the UV texture coordinates. The effect will be a lattice or perforated look for our gnome model.

Let's begin with looking at the vertex shader for this example:

```
#version 410
// Input vertex data, different for all executions of this shader.
in vec3 vertexPosition_modelspace;
in vec2 vertexUV;
in vec3 vertexNormal;
out vec3 FrontColor;
out vec3 BackColor;
out vec2 UV;
struct LightInfo {
vec4 Position; // Light position in eye coords.
vec3 La; // Ambient light intensity
vec3 Ld; // Diffuse light intensity
vec3 Ls; // Specular light intensity
};
uniform LightInfo Light;
struct MaterialInfo {vec3 Ka; // Ambient reflectivity
vec3 Kd; // Diffuse reflectivity
vec3 Ks; // Specular reflectivity
float Shininess; // Specular shininess factor
```

```
};
uniform MaterialInfo Material;
uniform mat4 ModelViewMatrix;
uniform mat3 NormalMatrix;
uniform mat4 ProjectionMatrix;
uniform mat4 ModelViewProjection;
void getCameraSpace( out vec3 norm, out vec4 position )
{
norm = normalize( NormalMatrix * vertexNormal);
position = ModelViewMatrix * vec4(vertexPosition_modelspace,1.0);
}
vec3 phongModel( vec4 position, vec3 norm )
{
...
//Same as previous examples
...}
void main()
{
vec3 cameraNorm;
vec4 cameraPosition;
UV = vertexUV;
// Get the position and normal in eye space
getCameraSpace(cameraNorm, cameraPosition);
FrontColor = phongModel( cameraPosition, cameraNorm );
BackColor = phongModel( cameraPosition, -cameraNorm );
gl_Position = ModelViewProjection *
vec4(vertexPosition_modelspace,1.0);
}
```

In this example, we are moving our lighting calculation back to the vertex shader. You may have noticed that this vertex shader is very similar to the previous example, with some slight changes. The first change to note is that we are using the UV texture coordinates in this example. We use the texture coordinates to determine the fragments to throw away, and we are not going to render the texture of the model this time. Since we are going to be discarding some fragments of the gnome model, we will be able to see through the model to the other and inside. This means we will need to calculate the lighting equation for both the front and back of the face. We accomplish this by calculating the Phong model for each side, changing the normal vector being passed in. We then store those values for each vertex in the FrontColor and BackColor variables to be passed along to the fragment shader. To again make our main class slightly easier to read, we also move the camera space transformation to a function.

Next, let's look at the fragment shader for this example:

```
#version 410
in vec3 FrontColor;
in vec3 BackColor;
in vec2 UV;
out vec4 FragColor;
void main() {
const float scale = 105.0;
bvec2 toDiscard = greaterThan( fract(UV * scale), vec2(0.2,0.2) );
if( all(toDiscard) )
discard;
else {
if( gl_FrontFacing )
FragColor = vec4(FrontColor, 1.0);
else
FragColor = vec4(BackColor, 1.0);
}
}
```

In our fragment shader, we are calculating which fragment to discard to give us the desired perforated effect. To accomplish this, we first scale the UV coordinate using our scaling factor. This scaling factor represents the number of perforated rectangles per texture coordinate. Next, we calculate the fractional part of the texture coordinate components by using the GLSL function `fract()`. We then compare each x and y component to the float value of 0.2 using another GLSL function, `greaterThan()`.

If both the x and y components of the vector in the `toDiscard` variable evaluate to true, this means the fragment lies within the perforated rectangle's frame, and we want to discard it. We can use the GLSL function to help us perform this check. The function call will return true if all of the components of the parameter vector are true. If the function returns true, we execute the `discard` statement to throw away that fragment.

Next, we have an `else` block where we color the fragment depending on whether it is a back-facing or front-facing polygon. To help us, we use the `gl_FronFacing()` function to return true or false based on the polygon's normal.

Just as we have in the previous examples, we must again make sure to set the attributes and uniform variables needed for the shader in our game program. To see the full implementation of the example, see the `Chapter07`, `DiscardExample`, project. If we run this example program, you will see our gnome model looking as if he was made of lattice. The following is a screenshot of the output:

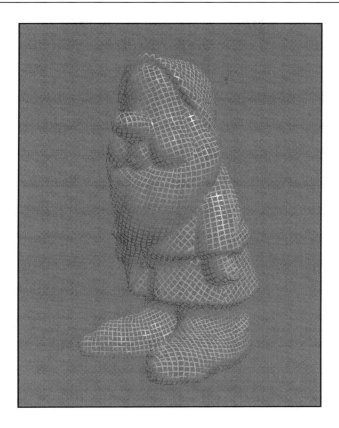

Generating particles

Another effect that you can achieve through the use of shaders is what is commonly referred to as particle effects. You can think of a particle system as a group of objects that are used in unison to create the visual appearance of smoke, fire, explosions, and so on. A single particle in the system is considered to be a point object with a position, but no size. To render these point objects, the GL_POINTS primitive is usually the most common method. You can, however, render particles just like any other object, using triangles or quads.

For our example, we are going to implement a simple particle system that will have a fountain appearance. Each particle in our system will follow these rules. It will have a limited lifetime, it will be created and animated based on defined criteria, and will then terminate. In some particle systems, you could then recycle the particle, but for simplicity's sake, our example here will not. The animation criteria for a particle is most often based on kinematic equations which define the movement of the particle based on gravitational acceleration, wind, friction, and other factors. Again, to keep our example simple, we will animate our particles using the standard kinematics calculation for objects under constant acceleration. The following equation describes the position of a particle at a given time t, where P_0 is the initial position, V_0t is the initial velocity, and a represents the acceleration:

$$P(t) = P_0 + V_0t + \tfrac{1}{2}at^2$$

In our example, we will define the initial position of the particles to be at the origin (0,0,0). The initial velocity will be calculated randomly within a range. Since each particle will be created at a different time interval in our equation, time will be relative to the creation time of that particle.

Since the initial position is the same for all particles, we won't need to provide it as an attribute to our shader. We will only have to provide two vertex attributes: the initial velocity and the start time for the particles. As mentioned previously, we will render each particle using GL_POINTS. The cool thing about using GL_POINTS is it is easy to apply a texture to a point sprite because OpenGL will automatically generate texture coordinates and pass them to the fragment shader via the GLSL variable gl_PointCoord. To give the appearance of the particle fading away, we will also increase the transparency of the point object linearly over the lifetime of the particle.

Let's begin with a look at the vertex shader for this example:

```
#version 410
in vec3 VertexInitVel; // Particle initial velocity
in float StartTime; // Particle "birth" time
out float Transp; // Transparency of the particle
uniform float Time; // Animation time
uniform vec3 Gravity = vec3(0.0,-0.05,0.0); // world coords
uniform float ParticleLifetime; // Max particle lifetime
uniform mat4 ModelViewProjection;
void main()
{
// Assume the initial position is (0,0,0).
vec3 pos = vec3(0.0);
Transp = 0.0;
// Particle dosen't exist until the start time
```

```
if( Time > StartTime ) {
float t = Time - StartTime;
if( t < ParticleLifetime ) {
pos = VertexInitVel * t + Gravity * t * t;
Transp = 1.0 - t / ParticleLifetime;
}
}
// Draw at the current position
gl_Position = ModelViewProjection * vec4(pos, 1.0);
}
```

Our shader begins with the two required input attributes, the initial velocity of the particle, VertexInitVel, and the start time of the particle, StartTime. We then have the output variable Transp which will hold the calculation of the particle's transparency to be passed to the next shader stage. Next, we have our uniform variables: time, the animation runtime, gravity, used to calculate the constant acceleration, and ParticleLifetime, which specifies the maximum amount of time a particle can stay active. In the main function, we first set the initial position of the particle to be the origin, in this case (0,0,0). We then set the transparency to 0. Next, we have a conditional that checks if the particle has been activated yet. If the current time is greater than the start time, the particle is active, or else the particle is not active. If the particle is not active, the position is left at the origin and the particle is rendered with full transparency. Then, if the particle is alive, we determine the current *age* of the particle by subtracting the start time from the current time, and we store the result in a float value t. We then check t against the ParticleLiftime value, and if t is greater than the lifetime value for the particle, the particle has already run through its lifetime animation and is then rendered fully transparent. If t is not greater than the lifetime value, the particle is in an active state and we animate the particle. We accomplish this animation using the equation we discussed previously. The transparency is determined by interpolation based on the runtime or *age* of the particle.

Now let's look at the fragment shader for this example:

```
#version 410
in float Transp;
uniform sampler2D ParticleTex;
out vec4 FragColor;
void main()
{
FragColor = texture(ParticleTex, gl_PointCoord);
FragColor.a *= Transp;
}
```

Our fragment shader for this example is pretty basic. Here, we are setting the color of the fragment based on its texture lookup value. As mentioned previously, because we are using the GL_POINT primitive, the texture coordinates are automatically calculated by OpenGL's gl_PointCoord variable. To wrap up, we multiply the alpha value of the fragment's final color by the Transp input variable. This will give us the fade away effect as our particle's runtime elapses.

In our game code, we need to create two buffers. The first buffer will store the initial velocity for each of the particles. The second buffer will store the start time for each particle. We will also have to set the uniform variables needed, including the ParticleTex for the particle texture, the Time variable for the amount of time that has elapsed since the animation beginning, the Gravity variable for representing the acceleration constant, and the ParticleLifetime variable for defining how long a particle will run its animation for. For brevity's sake, I will not go through the code here, but you can see the implementation of Chapter07 folder's particle example project.

Before testing our example, we also need to make sure that depth test is off and that enable alpha blending is on. You can do this with the following lines of code:

```
glDisable(GL_DEPTH_TEST);
glEnable(GL_BLEND);
glBlendFunc(GL_SRC_ALPHA, GL_ONE_MINUS_SRC_ALPHA);
```

You may also want to change the point object size to be a more reasonable value. You can set the value to 10 pixels using the following line of code:

```
glPointSize(10.0f);
```

If we now run our example project, we will see a particle effect similar to a fountain. A couple of captured frames can be seen as follows:

While this is a simple example, it has room for a lot of performance and flexibility increases, and it should provide you with a good starting point for implementing GPU based particle systems. Feel free to experiment with different input values, maybe even adding more factors to the particles animation calculation. Experimentation can lead to a lot of interesting outcomes.

Summary

In this chapter, we covered the basics of working with shaders. We learned how we can build a compiler and link abstraction layers to save us time. We gained knowledge about lighting technique theories and how we can implement them in shader language. Finally, we closed out the chapter by looking at other uses for shaders such as creating particle effects. In the next chapter, we will expand our example game framework further by creating advanced gameplay systems.

8
Advanced Gameplay Systems

Games are more than just simple mechanics and underlying engines. They are made up of complex gameplay systems that allow us to interact with the game world, making us feel included and immersed. These systems often take large amounts of time and developer expertise to implement. In this chapter, we will look at a couple of these advanced gameplay systems and how we can give ourselves a layer of help when implementing them in our own projects.

This chapter includes the following topics:

- Implementing a scripting language
- Building a dialog system
- Scripting quests

Implementing a scripting language

As mentioned previously, implementing an advanced gameplay system can often take many coding hours and could require the developer to have expertise in that specific system. We can, however, make this a little easier on ourselves and others working on the project by including support for a scripting language.

Why a scripting language

You may be wondering why we are spending time talking about scripting languages when this is a book about C++ after all. Why incorporate a scripting language? Couldn't we just build the whole engine and game in C++? Yes, we could! However, once you start to work on larger and larger projects, you will quickly notice the amount of time lost to compiling and re-compiling every time you need to make a change. While there are some ways to get around this, like breaking the game and engine into smaller modules and loading them dynamically, or using a JSON or XML descriptive file system, techniques like these cannot provide all the benefits of implementing a scripting system.

So, what are the benefits of adding a scripting language to your game engine? Well, first, most scripting languages you will use are interpreted languages, meaning unlike C++, you do not have to compile the code. Instead, your code is loaded and executed at runtime. The big advantage to this is you can make changes to a script file and quickly see the results without having to recompile the entire game. In fact, you could reload the script on the fly while the game is running and see the changes immediately. Another possible benefit of using a scripting language is the perceived ease of use when compared to a language like C++. Most scripting languages are dynamically typed, with a simplified syntax and structure. This can open up opportunities for the creative side of the team, such as artists and designers, to be able to make small changes to the project without the need to understand the complexity of a language like C++. Imagine a GUI designer being able to create, place, and modify GUI elements without the need to know how the IGUI framework is implemented. Adding scripting support also opens up a path to the community content support—think maps, levels, and items all designed by the players of the game. This is becoming a huge selling point for new games and provides some possible longevity to your title. On the topic of longevity, the implementation of DLC can be done through scripts. This allows for quicker development turnaround and can be dropped into the game without the need for a hefty patch.

Those are some of the benefits of using a scripting language, but they are not always the best solution in every situation. Scripting languages are notorious for running slower than native code, and as we know, performance matters when building games. So, when should you use a script instead of using C++? We will take a closer look at some system examples, but as a simple rule to follow, you should always use C++ for anything that can be considered CPU intensive. Program flow and other high-level logic are great candidates for a script. Let's take a look at where scripts can be used in our game engine components.

Let's start with the physics components. Of course, when we think of physics, we immediately think of heavy CPU usage. For the most part, this is true. The heart of the physics system should be constructed in C++, but there are opportunities to introduce scripting into this system as well. Take, for instance, the concept of physics materials. We can define the materials' properties in a script—things like mass, friction, viscosity, and so on. We can even modify these values from inside the script itself. Another potential use of scripts in the physics system would be defining the response to collisions. We could handle the generation of sounds, special effects, and other events, all from within the script.

How about the AI system? This is arguably one of the most common uses for a scripting language in game engines, and one we will look at deeper in the next chapter. A lot of the components of the AI system can be moved into scripts. These include things like complex behavior definitions, the specification of AI objectives, inter-AI communication, the definition of AI personalities and traits, plus much more. While the list is large, you should note that the examples given are not CPU intensive, and again the complex components of the AI system such as pathfinding, fuzzy logic, and other intensive algorithms should be handled in C++ code.

You can even add scripting to systems seemingly CPU and GPU heavy, such as the graphics engine. Scripts can handle the setting of lighting parameters, adjust effects like fog, and even add and remove gameplay elements from the screen. As you can see, there is very little in the engine that cannot be supplemented with some form of script abstraction.

So, what scripting language should you use? There are a lot of options out there, from game-specific languages such as GameMonkey (which appears to be defunct at the time of writing this book), to more general languages such as Python and JavaScript. The choice really depends on your specific needs. While languages like Python and JavaScript have some amazing features, they add more complexity to learning and execution to get those features. For our example in this book, we are going to use a language called Lua. Lua has been around for many years, and while its popularity has seen a decline in recent years, it has a very strong track record in the game development industry. In the next part of this chapter, we will get to know Lua a little better, and see how we can incorporate it into our existing engine systems.

Introducing LUA

Lua, pronounced LOO-ah, is a lightweight, embeddable scripting language. It supports modern programming methodologies such as object-oriented, data-driven, functional, and procedural programming. Lua is a portable language that is able to be built on almost every system that provides a standard C compiler. Lua runs on all flavors of Unix, Windows, and Mac. Lua can even be found on mobile devices running Android, iOS, Windows Phone, and Symbian. This makes it a great fit for most gaming titles and is one of the main reasons that companies including Blizzard Entertainment have used it for titles such as World of Warcraft. Lua is also free, is distributed under an MIT permissions license, and may be used for any commercial purpose with no cost incurred.

Lua is also a simple but powerful language. In Lua, there's just a single data structure referred to as a **table**. This table data structure can be used like a simple array, a key-value dictionary, and we can even implement a form of OOP by using tables as prototypes. This is very similar to doing OPP in other languages such as JavaScript.

While we won't go through the language in full detail, there are some great resources available for that, including the Lua documentation website. What we will do is skim over some of the key language concepts that we will see in action throughout the examples.

Let's start with variables and simple program flow. In Lua, all numbers are doubles. You assign a number with the following syntax:

```
number = 42
```

Notice the lack of a type identifier and a semicolon to denote the statement end.

Strings in Lua can be defined in a few ways. You can define them with single quotes, such as the following:

```
string = 'single quote string'
```

You can also use double quotes:

```
string = "double quotes string"
```

For a string that spans multiple lines, you can use double square brackets to denote the start and end of the string:

```
string = [[ multi-line
            string]]
```

Lua is a garbage collected language. You can remove a definition by setting the object to `nil`, the equivalent to *NULL* in C++:

```
string = nil
```

Statement blocks in Lua are denoted with language keywords such as `do` and `end`. A `while` loop block would look like the following:

```
while number < 100 do
    number = number + 1
end
```

You may notice we used number + 1 here, as there are no increment and decrement operators (++, --) in the Lua language.

An `if` condition code block would look something like the following:

```
if number > 100 then
    print('Number is over 100')
elseif number == 50 then
    print('Number is 50')
else
    print(number)
end
```

Functions in Lua are constructed in a similar fashion, using end to denote the completion of the functions code statement block. A simple function to calculate Fibonacci numbers would look similar to the following example:

```
function fib(number)
    if number < 2 then
        return 1
    end
    return fib(number - 2) + fib(number -1)
end
```

As mentioned, tables are the only compound data structure in the Lua language. They are considered associative array objects, very similar to JavaScript objects. Tables are hash lookup dictionaries that can also be treated as lists. Using a table as a map/dictionary would look like the following example:

```
table = { key1 = 'value1',
          key2 = 100,
          key3 = false }
```

You can also use the JavaScript-like dot notation when working with tables. For example:

```
print (table.key1)
Prints the text value1

table.key2 = nil
```

This removes `key2` from the table.

```
table.newKey = {}
```

This adds a new key/value pair to the table.

That concludes our very quick look at Lua language specifics; you will have the chance to learn more as we build out our examples. If you want to know more about Lua, I would again recommend reading through the documentation on the official website `http://www.lua.org/manual/5.3/`.

In the next section, we will look at the process of including Lua language support in our example game engine project.

Implementing LUA

In order for us to use Lua in our example engine, we need to take a few steps. First, we will need to obtain the Lua interpreter as a library that we can then include in our project. Next, we will have to obtain, or build our own, helper bridge to make the interaction between our C++ code and the Lua scripts easier. Finally, we will have to *expose* or *bind* functions, variables, and other objects that we wish to have access to our Lua scripts. While these steps might be slightly different for each implementation, this will provide us with a good starting point for our next examples.

To start with, we will need a copy of Lua as a library that we can use in our engine. For our examples, we are going to use Lua 5.3.4, which at the time of writing is the latest version of the language. I have opted to use a dynamic library in the examples. You can download both the dynamic and static version of the library, as well as the necessary include files, at the precompiled binaries page on the Lua project site (`http://luabinaries.sourceforge.net/`). Once you have the precompiled library downloaded, extract it and then include the necessary files in our project. I am not going to go through the process of including a library in our project again. If you do need a refresher, flip back to `Chapter 2`, *Understanding Libraries*, where we walked through the steps in detail.

As with other examples we have seen throughout the book, it is sometimes important to create helper classes and functions to allow easier interop between various libraries and components. This is again the case when we are working with Lua. To make the interaction easier for us as developers, we need to create a bridge class and functions to provide the functionality we need. We could build this bridge using the interface provided by Lua itself, which has great documentation, but there is also the option of using one of the numerous libraries available, which were created for this purpose. For the examples in this chapter and throughout the rest of the book, I have chosen to use the sol2 library (`https://github.com/ThePhD/sol2`), as this library is lightweight (a header only library), fast, and provides all the features we will need for our examples. Having this library in place will abstract a lot of the maintenance of the bridge and allow us to focus on implementation. To use the library in our project, all we have to do is copy the single header implementation into our `include` folder, and it will be ready to use.

Now that we have the Lua engine and the sol2 bridge library in place, we can move on to the last step, the implementation of the scripts. As mentioned, in order for us to use the underlying game engine components, they have to be exposed to Lua first. This is where the sol2 library fits in. To demonstrate how this can be accomplished in our example engine, I have created a little project called `Bind_Example`. You can find the full source code in the `Chapter08` folder in the code repository.

To get started, let's first look at the Lua script itself. In this case, I have called mine `BindExample.lua`, and have placed it in the `Scripts` folder of my example projects parent directory:

```lua
player = {
    name = "Bob",
    isSpawned = false
}

function fib(number)
    if number < 2 then
        return 1
    end
    return fib(number - 2) + fib(number -1)
end
```

In this example, our Lua script is quite basic. We have a table named `player` with two elements. An element with the key `name` and the value `Bob`, and an element with the key `isSpawned` and a value of `false`. Next, we have a simple Lua function named `fib`. This function will calculate all the numbers in the Fibonacci sequence up to the number passed in. I thought it would be fun to sneak a little math in for this example. I should note that this calculation can become quite processor intense the higher the sequence, so if you want it to process quickly, don't pass in a number larger than, say, 20.

This gives us some quick example Lua code to work with. Now we need to connect our program and its logic to this newly created script. For this example, we will add this connection code to our `GameplayScreen` class.

We start out by adding the necessary include for the `sol2` library:

```
#include <sol/sol.hpp>
```

Next, we will create the Lua state. A `state` in Lua can be considered analogous to an operation environment for your code. Think of it as a virtual machine. This `state` is where your code will be executed, and it is through this `state` that you will have access to the code running within:

```
sol::state lua;
```

We then open a few helper libraries that we will need for our Lua code interaction. These libraries can be thought of as the equivalent of `#include` in C++. The Lua philosophy is to keep the core small, and to offer more functionality through these libraries:

```
lua.open_libraries(sol::lib::base, sol::lib::package);
```

After we have opened the libraries, we can then move on to loading the actual Lua script file. We do this by calling the `script_file` method of the Lua `state` we created previously. This method takes one parameter: the location of the file as a string. When this method is executed, the file will be loaded and executed automatically:

```
lua.script_file("Scripts/PlayerTest.lua");
```

With the script now loaded, we can begin to interact with it. First, let's look at how we can pull data out of a variable (table) in Lua and use it in our C++ code:

```
std::string stringFromLua = lua["player"]["name"];
std::cout << stringFromLua << std::endl;
```

The process of retrieving data from the Lua script is quite simple. In this case, we are creating a string called stringFromLua and assigning it the value stored in the Lua table players' name element. The syntax looks similar to calling an array element, but here we are specifying the element with a string. If we wanted the isSpawned element values, we would use lua["player"]["isSpawned"], which in our case would currently return a Boolean value of false.

Calling a Lua function is just as easy and quite similar to retrieving values:

```
double numberFromLua = lua["fib"](20);
std::cout << numberFromLua << std::endl;
```

Here we are creating a variable of the type double, called numberFromLua, and assigning it the value of the return from the Lua function fib. Here, we specify the function name as a string, fib, and we then specify any parameters needed by that function. In this example, we are passing in the value of 20 to calculate the Fibonacci sequence up to the twentieth number.

If you run the Bind_Example project, you will see the following output in the engine's command window:

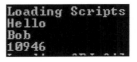

While this covers the basics of the interaction between our C++ code and the Lua scripting system, there is a lot more to be discovered. In the next few sections, we will look at ways to utilize this scripting structure to augment various advanced gameplay systems and provide us with a flexible way to expand our gaming projects.

Building a dialog system

One of the most common forms of interacting with the game world is through some form of dialog. Being able to communicate with NPC classes, getting information and quests, and of course, driving the story narrative through dialog is a must in most modern game titles. While you could easily hardcode interactions, this approach would leave us with very little flexibility. Each time we wanted to make a slight change to any dialog or interaction, we would have to open up the source code, dig through the project, make any necessary changes, and then recompile to see the effects. Obviously, this is a tedious process. Just think about how many games you have played where spelling, grammar, or other errors appeared. The good news is there is another approach we can take. Using a scripting language, such as Lua, we can drive our interactions in a dynamic way, which will allow us to make quick changes without the need for the tedious process described previously. In this section, we will look at the detailed process of building a dialog system that, at a high-level description, will load a script, attach it to an NPC, present dialog with choices to the player, and, finally, drive a dialog tree based on the returned player input.

Constructing the C++ infrastructure

To start, we will need to build the infrastructure in our example engine to support the scripting of the dialog system. There are quite literally thousands of different ways that you could approach this implementation. For our example, I am going to do my best to keep it simple. We are going to use some of the techniques and patterns we have learned throughout the previous chapters, including the state and update patterns, as well as the GUI system we built to handle interactions and display.

They say a picture is worth a thousand words, so to give you a general idea of how this system is going to be connected, let's take a look at a code map diagram that depicts the connections between all the classes:

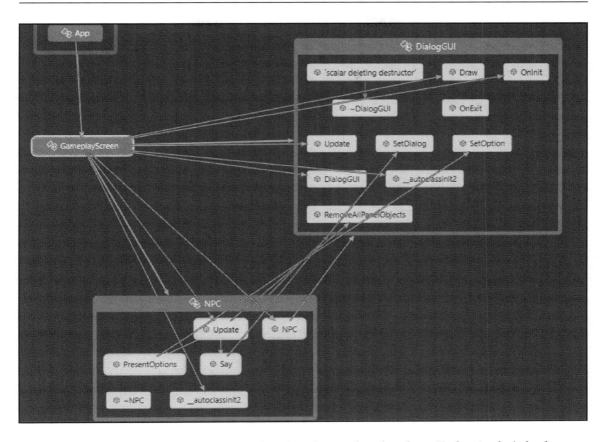

There is a bit going on here, so we will break it down class by class. To begin, let's look at the `DialogGUI` class. This class builds off of the IGUI example we built in a previous chapter. Since we have already gone through the design of the IGUI class in depth, we will only cover the specific aspects we are adding to provide the functionality we need for our dialog system.

First, we will need a few variables to hold the dialog and any choices that we want to provide the player with. In `DialogGUI.h`, we have the following: the vector of `IGUILabel` objects for the choices and a single `IGUILabel` for the dialog. For the implementation of the `IGUILabel` class, take a look at its source code:

```
std::vector<BookEngine::IGUILabel*> choices;
BookEngine::IGUILabel* m_dialog;
```

Next, we will need to add a few new functions to provide us with the needed interaction for our GUI and the data being provided from the scripts. To do this, we will add three methods to our `DialogGUI` class:

```
void SetDialog(std::string text);
void SetOption(std::string text, int choiceNumber);
void RemoveAllPanelElements();
```

The `SetDialog` function, as its name suggests, will handle the setting of the dialog text for each of the interaction screens. The function takes only one parameter, the text we want to place on the GUI for this interaction:

```
void DialogGUI::SetDialog(std::string text)
{
    m_dialog = new BookEngine::IGUILabel(glm::vec4(0, 110, 250, 30),
        glm::vec2(110, -10),
        text,
        new BookEngine::SpriteFont("Fonts/Impact_Regular.ttf", 72),
        glm::vec2(0.3f), m_panel);

    AddGUIElement(*m_dialog);
}
```

In the function body, we are assigning the `m_dialog` label variable to a new instance of an `IGUILabel` object. The constructor should look similar to the `IGUIButton` seen previously, where the text value is passed in. Finally, we add the label to the GUI panel by calling the `AddGUIElement` method.

The `SetOption` function, again as its name suggests, sets the text for each option on the current interaction screen. This function takes two parameters. The first is the text we want to set the `IGUILabel` to, and the second is the choice number, which is its number in the list of choice options being presented. We use this to see which option has been selected:

```
void DialogGUI::SetOption(std::string text, int choiceNumber)
{
    choices.resize(m_choices.size() + 1);
    choices[choiceNumber] =
new BookEngine::IGUILabel(glm::vec4(0, 110, 250, 20),
            glm::vec2(110, 10),
            text,
            new BookEngine::SpriteFont("Fonts/Impact_Regular.ttf", 72),
            glm::vec2(0.3f), m_panel);

    AddGUIObject(*choices[choiceNumber]);
}
```

In the function body, we are doing a very similar process to the `SetDialog` function. The difference here is we are going to be adding the `IGUILabel` instance to the choices vector. First, we perform a little trick to increase the size of the vector by one, and this will then allow us to assign the new label instance to the vector position at the choice number value passed in. Finally, we add the `IGUILabel` to the panel with the `AddGUIElement` method call.

The last function we add to the `DialogGUI` class is the `RemoveAllPanelElements`, which of course will handle removing all the elements we have added to the current dialog screen. We are removing the elements so we can reuse the panel and avoid recreating the panel each time we change interactions:

```
void DialogGUI::RemoveAllPanelElements()
{
    m_panel->RemoveAllGUIElements();
}
```

The `RemoveAllGUIElements` function in turn just calls the same method on the `m_panel` object. The `IGUIPanel` class' implementation simply calls the clear method on the vector, removing all of its elements:

```
void RemoveAllGUIObjects() { m_GUIObjectsList.clear(); };
```

That takes care of the GUI setup for our dialog system, so now we can move on to building the `NPC` class which will handle the majority of the script to engine bridging.

As I mentioned previously, we are going to be employing some of the patterns we learned in previous examples to help us build our dialog system. To help us control when we are constructing the GUI elements and when we are waiting for the player to make a choice, we are going to use a finite-state machine coupled with an update pattern. To start with, in the `NPC.h` file we have the `enum` that will define the states we will use. In this case, we have only two states, `Display` and `WaitingForInput`:

```
...
    enum InteractionState
    {
        Display,
        WaitingForInput,
    };
...
```

Of course, we will also need a way to track the states, so we have an `InteractionState` variable called `currentState` that we will set to the state we are currently in. Later, we will see the completion of this state machine in the `Update` function:

```
InteractionState currentState;
```

We also need a variable for holding our Lua state, which we saw in the previous section of this chapter:

```
sol::state lua;
```

You might recall from the code map diagram shown earlier that our `NPC` will have an instance of a `DialogGUI` for handling the displaying of the dialog content and interaction with the player, so we will also need a variable to hold it:

```
DialogGUI* m_gui;
```

Moving on to the implementation of the `NPC` class, we first will look at the constructor for the class in the `NPC.cpp` file:

```
NPC::NPC(DialogGUI& gui) : m_gui(&gui)
{
    std::cout << "Loading Scripts n";
    lua.open_libraries(sol::lib::base, sol::lib::package, sol::lib::table);
    lua.script_file("Scripts/NPC.lua");
    currentState = InteractionState::Display;
}
```

The constructor takes a single parameter, a reference to the dialog instance we will be using for our interaction. We set this reference to the member variable `m_gui` for later use. We then handle the loading of the Lua script we will use. Finally, we set the current state of our internal state machine to the `Display` state.

Let's revisit our code map to see the different connections we need to implement for passing the `NPC` class' loaded script information to the GUI instance we have attached to:

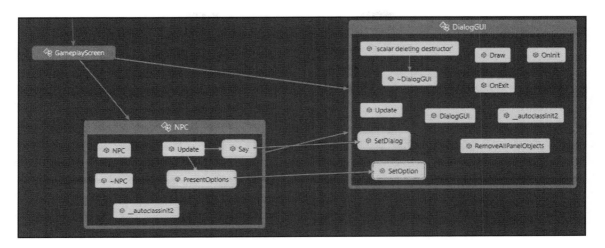

As we can see, we have two methods that are handling the connection. The Say function is the simplest of the two. Here, the NPC class is just calling the SetDialog method on the attached GUI, passing along a string containing the dialog to display:

```
void NPC::Say(std::string stringToSay)
{
    m_gui->SetDialog(stringToSay);
}
```

The PresentOptions function has slightly more to it. To start, the function retrieves a table from the Lua script that denotes the choices for this current interaction, and we will see how this is set up in the script shortly. Next, we are going to iterate through the table, if it is valid, and simply call the SetOption method on the attached GUI, passing along the choice text as a string and the choice number used for selection:

```
void NPC::PresentOptions()
{
    sol::table choices = lua["CurrentDialog"]["choices"];
    int i = 0;
    if (choices.valid())
    {
        choices.for_each([&](sol::object const& key, sol::object const&
value)
        {
            m_gui->SetOption(value.as<std::string>(), i);
            i++;
        });
    }
}
```

The last piece of our engine side of the dialog system we need to put in place is the Update method. This method, as we have seen many times, will drive the system forward. By connecting to the existing Update event system of the engine, our NPC class' Update method will be able to control what is happening with our dialog system on each frame:

```
void NPC::Update(float deltaTime)
{
    switch (currentState)
    {
    case InteractionState::Display:
        Say(lua["CurrentDialog"]["say"]);
        PresentOptions();
        currentState = InteractionState::WaitingForInput;
        break;
    case InteractionState::WaitingForInput:
        for (int i = 0; i < m_gui->choices.size(); i++)
        {
            if (m_gui->choices[i]->GetClickedStatus() == true)
            {
                lua["CurrentDialog"]["onSelection"](m_gui->
choices[i]->GetLabelText());
                currentState = InteractionState::Display;
                m_gui->choices.clear();
                m_gui->RemoveAllPanelElements ();
            }
        }
        break;
    }
}
```

As with our previous finite-state machine implementation, we are going to use a switch case to determine what code should be run based on the current state we are in. For this example, our Display state is where we are going to call our connecting methods Say and PresentOptions. Here, the Say call is passing, alone, the text it is pulling from the script file that has been loaded. We will see how this works in the script next. If, in this example, we are in the WaitingForInput state, we are going to iterate through each of the choices we have loaded and see if the player has selected any of them yet. If one is found, we are going to call back to the script and tell it which choice has been selected. We are then going to switch our state to the Display state, which will kick off the loading of the next dialog screen. Then, we will clear our choices vector in the attached DisplayGUI, allowing it to be then loaded with the next set of choices, and finally calling the RemoveAllPanelElements method to clean up our GUI for reuse.

With the `Update` method in place, we now have all the framework set up to handle the loading, displaying, and input handling needed for our NPC interaction scripts. Next, we will look at how we can construct one of these scripts to use with our engine's newly created dialog system.

Creating a dialog tree script

A dialog or conversation tree can be thought of as the determined flow of an interaction. In essence, it works by first providing a statement, then, based on a selection of presented responses, the interaction can branch off into different paths. A visual representation of how our example dialog flow is determined is pictured in the following diagram:

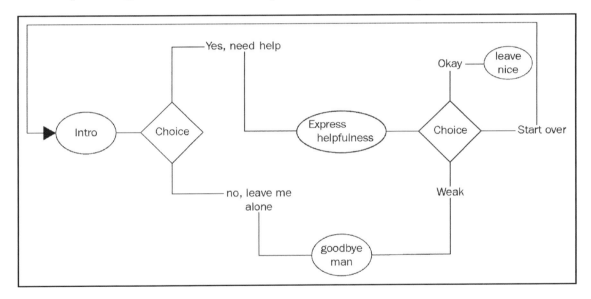

Here, we are beginning the dialog tree with an intro. The user is then presented with two choices: **Yes, need help** and **No, leave me alone**. If the user selects the **Yes** path, then we move on to the **Express helpfulness** dialog. If the user selects **No**, we move to the **Goodbye man** dialog. From the **Express helpfulness** dialog, we present three choices: **Okay**, **Start over**, and **Weak**. Based on the choice, we then move again to the next stage of the dialog tree. **Okay** leads to the **leave nice** dialog. **Weak** leads to the **Goodbye man** dialog, and **Start over**, well, starts over. This is a basic example, but it demonstrates the overall concept of how dialog trees work.

Now let's take a look at how we can implement this example tree in our Lua scripting engine. The following is the full script, and we will dive into the details next:

```lua
intro = {
    say = 'Hello I am the Helper NPC, can I help you?',
    choices = {
                choice1 = "Yes! I need help",
                choice2 = "No!! Leave me alone"
    },
    onSelection = function (choice)
        if choice == CurrentDialog["choices"]["choice1"] then CurrentDialog
= getHelp end
        if choice  == CurrentDialog["choices"]["choice2"] then
CurrentDialog = goodbye_mean end
    end
}

getHelp = {
    say = 'Ok I am still working on my helpfulness',
    choices = {
                choice1 = "That's okay! Thank you!",
                choice2 = "That's weak, what a waste!",
                choice3 = "Start over please."
        },
    onSelection = function (choice)
        if choice  == CurrentDialog["choices"]["choice1"] then
CurrentDialog = goodbye
        elseif choice  == CurrentDialog["choices"]["choice2"] then
CurrentDialog = goodbye_mean
        elseif choice  == CurrentDialog["choices"]["choice3"] then
CurrentDialog = intro end
    end

}

goodbye = {
    say = "See you soon, goodbye!"
}

goodbye_mean = {
    say = "Wow that is mean, goodbye!"
}

CurrentDialog = intro
```

As you can see, the whole script is not that long. We have a few concepts that make this script work. First is a very simple version of a state machine. We have a variable called `CurrentDialog`, and this variable will point to the active dialog. At the very end of our script we are initially setting this to the `intro` dialog object, which will kick off the dialog tree upon the loading of the script. The next important concept we have in our script design is the concept of every interaction screen being described as a table object. Let's take a look at the intro dialog table as an example:

```
intro = {
    say = 'Hello I am the Helper NPC, can I help you?',
    choices = {
            choice1 = "Yes! I need help",
            choice2 = "No!! Leave me alone"
    },
    onSelection = function (choice)
        if choice == CurrentDialog["choices"]["choice1"] then CurrentDialog
= getHelp end
        if choice  == CurrentDialog["choices"]["choice2"] then
CurrentDialog = goodbye_mean end
    end
}
```

Each dialog table object has a `Say` element, and this element is the text that will be displayed when the `Say` function asks the script for its dialog content. Next, we have two optional elements, but that are required if you want to have an interaction with the player. The first is a nested table called `choices`, which has elements that house the choices that will be presented to the player when requested by the dialog system. The second option element is actually a function. This function is called when the user selects a choice, and is comprised of some `if` statements. These `if` statements will test which choice has been selected, and based on that choice, will set the `CurrentDialog` object to the next dialog on the path of the dialog tree.

That's really it. The greatest bonus of designing our dialog tree system this way is that, with very little guidance, even a non-programmer could design a simple script like the one previously shown.

If you go ahead and run the `Dialog_Example` project using the `Chapter08` solution, you will see this script in action and will be able to interact with it. Following are a few screenshots showing what the output would look like:

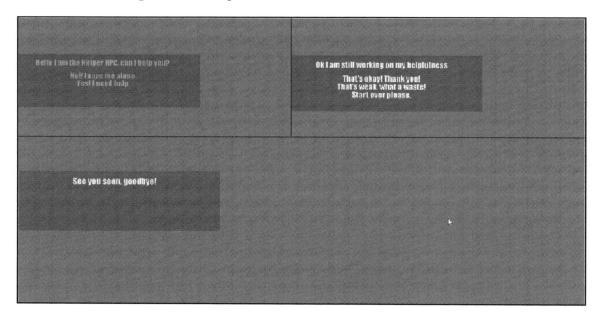

Although this is a simple system implementation, it is very flexible. It should be noted again that these scripts do not need to be recompiled to make changes. Try it for yourself. Make some changes to the `NPC.lua` file, rerun the example program, and you will see your changes appear.

In the next section, we will see how we can take the inclusion of a scripting system even further by implementing a quest system driven by Lua scripts.

Scripting quests

Another very common advanced gameplay system is the quest system. While more commonly seen in role-playing games, quests can appear in other genres as well. Often, these other genres will disguise a quest system by referring to it as a different name. For example, some games have challenges, which in essence are really the same as quests.

A quest can be simply thought of as an attempt to achieve a specific outcome. Typically, a quest will involve a certain number of steps that must be conducted before the quest will be considered complete. Some types of common quests include kill quests, where players typically will have to kill a specific number of enemies, commonly referred to as **grinding**, and **delivery** quests, where a player will have to play the role of courier and often has to travel to new locations in the game world to deliver goods. This, of course, is a great way to get the player to travel to the next desired location without forcing them. In gathering quests, a player will have to collect a certain amount of a specific item. In escort quests, often dreaded by players because of historically bad implementations, players often have to accompany an NPC to a new location while protecting them from harm. Lastly, hybrid quests are often a mix of the mentioned types, and are more typically longer quests.

Another common part of a quest system is the support for what is referred to as a quest chain or quest line. In a quest chain, the completion of each quest is a prerequisite for beginning the next quest in the sequence. These quests often involve more and more complex quests as the player progresses through the chain. These quests are a great way to reveal a plotline gradually.

That explains what quests are. In the next section, we will discuss a few different ways we can add support for quests in our game projects. However, before we look at the specifics of implementation, it is useful for us to define what we expect each quest object to require.

For the sake of our simple examples, we will assume that quest objects will be comprised of the following:

- **A quest name**: The name of the quest
- **Objectives**: The actions that must be taken to complete the quest
- **Reward(s)**: What the player will receive for completing the task
- **Description**: A little information about the quest, maybe some backstory as to why the player is undertaking the task
- **Quest giver**: The NPC that gave the quest

With these simple elements, we can construct our basic quest system.

As we have seen in previous gameplay system examples, there are many different ways we could approach the implementation of our quest system in the example engine. Let's now take a brief look at a few and discuss their merits and pitfalls.

In engine support

One way we could go about supporting a quest system would to be to build it into the game engine itself. The entire system would be designed close to the engine code and in the native engine language, in our case C++. We would create an infrastructure to support the quest using techniques we have seen numerous times. Using inheritance, we could expose the basic functions and variables needed and let the developer build this construct. A simple, high-level quest class might then look similar to the following:

```
class Quest
{
public:
    Quest(std::string name,
    std::vector<GameObjects> rewards,
    std::string description,
    NPC questGiver);
    ~Quest();
    Accept(); //accept the quest
    TurnIn(); //complete the quest
private:
    std::string m_questName;
        std::vector<GameObjects> m_rewards;
        std::string m_questDescription;
        NPC m_questGiver;
    Bool isActive;
};
```

Of course, this is just meant to be a simple demonstration, and in this case, we will skip the implementation.

The pros of this implementation approach are that it is writing in native code, meaning it will run fast, and it's close to the engine, meaning it will have greater access to the underlying systems without the need of interface layers or other libraries.

The cons of this implementation approach include that as it's part of the game engine or game code itself, and this means that any changes that are made will need to be recompiled. This also makes it harder for non-coders to add their own ideas for quests or to handle the expansion of the quest system after release.

While this approach does work, it's more suited to smaller projects where you will not have to, or want to, make changes to the quests or system once it is in place.

Engine/script bridge

This approach is the same approach we took to implement our NPC dialog system earlier. In this design, we create an interface class that handles the loading of the scripts and the passing of data to and from the quest scripts. Since we have seen a similar implementation before, I will skip the example code here and instead move on to the pros and cons of this approach.

The pros of this implementation approach include flexibility when compared to the engine only implementation. If we want to make any changes, we simply need to load up the script in an editor, make the changes, and reload the game. This again also makes it far more accessible for non-coders to create their own quests.

The cons of this implementation approach include that it is still partially tied to the engine itself. The scripts can only have access to elements and functions exposed by the engines interface. If you wanted to add more functionality to a quest, you would have to build that into the engine side before any scripts could make use of it.

This approach is better suited to larger projects, but as noted, still has its drawbacks.

Script-based system

Another approach we can take is to build the entire system within our scripting language, with only generic methods exposed from the engine. These generic methods would likely be good candidates for template functions. In this approach, the quests system internals and quest scripts alike would be written in the scripting language. Each quest written in a script would include a reference to the quest system script that would handle the management. This approach is very similar to the engine only approach; it's just been moved out of the engine and into the scripting system.

Let's take a look at a simple version of the quest system script. Some pieces are omitted for brevity's sake:

```
local questsys = {}
questsys.quest = {}

function questsys.new(questname, objectives, reward, description, location,
level, questgiver)
for keys, value in ipairs(objectives) do
    value.value = 0
  end
  questsys.quest[#questsys.quest+1] = {
    questname = questname,
```

```
      objectives = objectives,
      reward = reward,
      description = description,
      questgiver = questgiver,
      accepted = false,
      completed = false,
      isAccepted = function(self) return self.accepted end,
      isCompleted = function(self) return self.completed end
   }
end

function questsys.accept(questname)
   for key, value in ipairs(questsys.quest) do
      if value.questname == questname then
         if not value.accepted then
            value.accepted = true
         end
      end
   end
end


...


function questsys.turnin(questname)
   rejectMsg = "You have not completed the quest."
   for key, value in ipairs(questsys.quest) do
      if value.questname == questname then
         for i, j in ipairs(questsys.quest[key].objectives) do
            if j.value == j.maxValue then
               value.completed = true
               value.reward()
            else return rejectMsg end
         end
      end
   end
end


...


questsys.get(questname, getinfo)
   for key, value in ipairs(questsys.quest) do
      if value.questname == questname then
         if getinfo == "accepted" then return value:isAccepted() end
         if getinfo == "completed" then return value:isCompleted() end
         if getinfo == "questname" then return value.questname end
         if getInfo == "description" then return value.description end
         if getInfo == "location" then return value.location end
         if getInfo == "level" then return value.level end
         if getInfo == "questgiver" then return value.questgiver end
      else error("No such quest name!")
```

```
      end
   end

   return questsys
```

Again, I have omitted a few functions to save space, but the core components needed to understand the system are here. First, we have a function that creates a new quest, taking in the name, objective, description, and quest giver. We then have the accept function that sets the quest to active. Notice how we are using the key/pair lookup method to iterate through our tables—we will do this a lot. Then we have a function to turn in the quest, and finally a simple function that returns all the quest information. The functions not depicted here are for getting and setting the various objective values for the quest. For the full implementation, take a look at the Quest_Example project in the Chapter08 folder of the code repository.

Now, with the quest system script in place, we have a few options. First, we could just add this system to other scripts by using the Lua build in the require system which would allow us to use the script in other scripts. The syntax for this looks like the following:

```
local questsys = require('questsys')
```

Or we could simply load the script in our game engine and use an interface, like we did in the previous example, and interact with our quest system that way. With this flexibility, the choice is up to the developer and situation.

The pros of this implementation approach include great flexibility. In this approach, changes not only to the quest but the quest system itself can be modified on the fly without the need to rebuild the game or engine. This is often a method that is used to include downloadable content (DLC), game modifications (mods), and other extra content after a product's release.

The cons of this implementation include, although it is very flexible, the addition of an extra layer of complexity. It can also be slower because the system is writing in a scripting language that is interpreted, and performance can take a hit. It also requires developers to have greater knowledge of the scripting language and can require more learning time.

Like the other approaches, this one, too, has its place and time. While I tend to lean towards a system like this in larger projects, if the team is not prepared, this approach could add more overhead then ease of use.

Summary

In this chapter, we covered a great deal when it comes to implementing advanced gameplay systems. We dove deep into how you can include a scripting language like Lua in your game projects. Then we built on that knowledge to examine ways of implementing dialog and quest systems into our example engine. While we did discuss a lot, we have barely scratched the surface of this topic. In the next chapter, we will continue to build on this newfound knowledge to construct some artificial intelligence for our games.

9
Artificial Intelligence

Most games are built on the concept of competing to win. This form of competition can take many forms. Since the earliest video games, players have found themselves competing against the machine. The inclusion of thinking, reacting, and challenging computer opponents makes games feel alive and connected to the player. In this chapter, we are going to learn how to add thinking to our games with the inclusion of artificial intelligence.

The following is covered in this chapter:

- What is game AI?
- Making decisions
- Motion and pathfinding techniques

What is game AI?

Often misunderstood, defining what game artificial intelligence is and, for that matter, what game AI is not is a very challenging endeavor. With such an encompassing field as AI, it would be very easy to fill many volumes of books on the subject. Given we only have a chapter to discuss the concept and implementation, in this section we are going to do our best to develop a reasonable definition of what game AI is and what it is not.

Defining game AI

As mentioned, defining exactly what game AI is can be a difficult task, but I am going to do my best to describe what I feel is a concise interpretation when it comes to electronic video games. When a designer creates a game world, they do so by sculpting a vision and defining some common rules for interaction in that world. Typically, players will experience this world through the observation of the world's elements. Interactions, such as with the world's NPCs, opponents, and environments, and through narrative aspects, give the player a sense of immersion in the game's world. These interactions can take many shapes and forms. In games, players constantly have some interaction with the world through inanimate objects, but it's the interactions with other people that really stands out. It's what makes the game feel more immersive, more tangible, and more alive.

The sensation of something in the game world feeling alive generally comes through the observations of the game world and objects, such as an NPC making decisions. This is a great flag in the search to find a definition for game AI. In a broader sense, AI can be thought of as the application of this perceived decision-making. Commonly, this perception of decision-making comes in the form of an autonomous AI agent, for example, the common NPC. These decisions might include anything from movement, dialog choices, or even changes to the environment that might convey the experience the developer is attempting to create. This again is another flag for me when defining game AI. In essence, it is about the experience the developer is trying to create. To that end, game AI is more about an approximation of getting a desired effect, not necessarily a perfect scientific interpretation.

It is important that when developers are setting out to create an AI experience, they do it with the key aspects of the player's fun and immersion in mind. No one wants to play against the perfect opponent. We want to perceive intelligence on the other end of the interaction, we just don't want it to be smarter. This is where developing game AI and the field of general AI development starts to become at odds. We will dive deeper into this diversion in the next section, but for now, let's look at some uses of AI in game development.

Conversations

Games that have some sort of interaction through dialog tend to give a sense of immersion in a world through how the characters' connect with the player and how the player becomes invested in their story. This, however, has been a challenge, and is often implemented, as we looked at in the last chapter, through dialog trees. This dialog tree approach, while solid in some situations, can easily grow in complexity.

Another issue with completely scripted conversations is, as the conversation continues over time, the player is quickly taken out of the illusion that this is an intelligent interaction. It makes the interaction feel constrained and in turn makes the world also feel constraining. One way to battle this issue is to introduce AI into the conversations. You could have scripted interactions augmented with decision-making algorithms to give a feeling of deeper intelligence in the responses. On the extreme side of this concept, you could employ a method of parsing player input and custom generating responses on the fly. An approach such as this would likely include what is referred to as **Natural Language Processing (NLP)**. By utilizing something akin to a chatbot, designers and engineers can create worlds populated by agents that think when responding to user interactions. While this might sound extremely tempting, the field of Natural Language Processing is still considered to be in its infancy. With APIs powered by cloud computing, such as Microsoft's Cognitive Services APIs, the processes of creating the infrastructure to support NLP is getting easier. However, proper implementation and training of the language models can be quite time-consuming.

Competitive opponents

A lot of games include the concept of enemies or competitive opponents for players to interact with. I would, in fact, say this is what most folks would think of as an example of game AI. How these opponents interact with the player, their environment, and other AI-controlled opponents is all part of their AI design. Often, this AI design will include concepts of decision-making, such as behavior trees, feedback loops, states, and other patterns. They will also often include other AI components such as motion algorithms and pathfinding techniques, both of which we will cover in more depth later in the chapter. Creating fun yet challenging opponents is not an easy task. As I stated earlier, no one wants to play a game where they feel they have no chance of winning. Having an AI that is constantly quicker and smarter than the player should not be the goal of designing an opponent AI; you should instead focus on giving the user a competitive AI that could potentially scale to meet the growing skill of the player. It's in this light where advanced techniques, such as using machine learning to build adaptive AI, are starting to gain traction. Although these techniques are still in their exploratory phases, the day of tailored AI opponents could soon be near.

Motion and pathfinding

Arguably, just as common as using AI for opponents is the concept of utilizing AI for motion and pathfinding. Using AI in motion includes the implementation of algorithms to handle the autonomous movement of game elements. Ideas such as steering, pursuit, and avoid are all concepts you can express in AI algorithms. Motion AI is also commonly implemented to handle simple collision avoidance. Pathfinding is the concept of using AI to find the most efficient or effective route when moving a game object from one location to the next. Algorithms such as **Dijkstra** and **A*** have been around since the sixties and have provided a staple for pathfinding AI development. We will dive deeper into motion and pathfinding algorithms and techniques later in this chapter.

What game AI is not

Artificial intelligence, as a field of study, is very large, and really does include a lot more than what games use. As of late, discussions around AI in the developer space have become more expansive, with more and more developers looking for ways to leverage AI technologies lies in their projects. For this reason, I thought it would be important to touch on some of the more commonly known use cases for AI outside of the realms of game development.

One of the hottest areas for AI outside of the game development is machine learning. **Machine learning** (**ML**) is probably best described by Arthur Lee Samuel, when he coined the term machine learning: *A computers ability to learn how to achieve an outcome or prediction without being explicitly programmed to do so.* Within the field of data analytics, machine learning is used as a method to devise complex models and algorithms that help forecast outcomes for a given problem. This is also known as predictive analytics. These analytical models allow researchers and data scientists to create reliable, repeatable computations and results and discover other insights through historical relationships and trends in the data. As mentioned in the previous section, the idea of tailored AI that learns from your play style and adapts is a very appealing concept. However, it can be a slippery slope; if the AI becomes too smart, then the game's fun level can and will quickly drop. A good example of how ML is being used in gameplay is in the Forza racing game series. Here, racing AI avatars are processed in a cloud computing powered machine learning implementation to tailor the competitive level of the AI racers you encounter to your current ability level.

Another growing use for AI outside of game development field is its implementation in data mining scenarios. While this area of AI is still in its early stages, its use in understanding user and customer data is extremely appealing to a lot of business sectors. The boundaries of this AI use case and its potential overlap with game development concepts have yet to be defined. However, some of the core components of data mining for understanding how players interact with a game and its various components can easily be seen as beneficial to game developers. Knowing exactly how players interact with elements such as the game GUI will allow developers to create better experiences for each user.

The last use case for AI outside of game development that I want to address is probably one of the most recognized uses when the average person thinks of AI, and that's the use of AI in the study of cognitive processing. In academic interpretations of AI, cognitive processing is the process of developing scientifically provable models for these processes. This can basically be summarized as the modeling of human intelligence in AI processes. While this approach is very important for scientific research, the current use cases for game development are still too far abstracted to be considered useful. That being said, the use of bots and NLP is starting to creep its way into game development, as mentioned.

Often, the specific goals of academic and research AI differ completely from game AI goals. This is because of inherent differences, such as the implementations and techniques used in each being completely different. More often, game AI solutions will favor a simplistic approach, allowing easy changes and tuning, whereas the research approach will more than likely opt for the most scientifically complete implementation. In the next sections, we will look at a few of these simpler game development implementations and discuss their use cases and theory.

Making decisions

More often, the goal of AI is to give the appearance of human intelligence. One of the key aspects to the perception of intelligence is the idea that the AI agent is making decisions. Having choice over certain actions, even if scripted, gives the player a feeling of a thinking world, populated by thinking entities. In the next section, we will cover some of the more well-known decision-making techniques in game AI.

AI state machines

If you have been following through the book chapter by chapter, you may have noticed the use of the state pattern more than a few times. This pattern is a very powerful pattern, hence its common use throughout our various component designs. In the realm of artificial intelligence, the state pattern is again a shining star. The use of the state machine, specifically the **FSM (finite-state machine)**, allows for the detailed representation of the code's execution flow. It is a perfect fit for the implementation of AI in games, allowing the design of powerful interactions without complex code.

I am not going to spend much time on the concept and theory of finite-state machine implementation, since we have covered it ad nauseam. Instead, we are going to look at an example of its implementation in an AI script. If you do need a refresher on the pattern, review the `Chapter 5`, *Building Gameplay Systems*, section on understanding states.

The following is a diagram depicting the simple brain of an enemy. In this example, each state represents an action, such as search or attack:

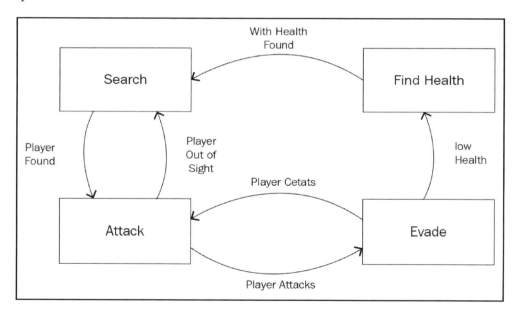

While this is a simple example, it does provide useful AI for many situations. We can implement this inside a game project using C++, as we have seen in the *Screen* example and elsewhere. However, if you have read through the previous chapter, you would have seen how we can implement logic such as this in a script. This, of course, allows us the flexibility of scripting, such as not having to rebuild the project to adjust the elements of the code. This is very beneficial for AI, so in this chapter I will be showing the example code using Lua scripts that can be implemented using the steps described in the previous chapter.

A possible implementation of this AI design in a Lua script could look something similar to the following:

```
Search = function ()
{
    //Do search actions..
    if playerFound == true then currentState = Attack end
}
Attack = function()
{
    //Do attack actions
    if playerAttacks == true then currentState = Evade
    elseif playerOutOfSight == true then currentState = Search end
}
Evade = function()
{
    //Do evade actions
    If healthIsLow == true then currentState = FindHealth
    Elseif playerRetreats == true then currentState == Attack end
}
FindHealth = function()
{
    //Do finding health actions
    If healthFound == true then currentState = Search end
}
currentState = Search
```

This should look familiar to the NPC dialog example from the last chapter. Here, to complete the system, we would first load the script into an instance of an AI agent or NPC, and then call the `currentState` variable's currently-assigned function in the `Update` loop of the game code itself. With this code implementation, we have an effective way of building basic AI interactions. This technique has been around since the early days of game development. In fact, this would be a very similar implementation to the ghost opponents AI in the arcade classic, PAC-MAN.

We can also expand on this simple FSM implementation and add a stack-based FSM into the solution. This is, again, much the same as the implementation example we saw in Chapter 5, *Building Gameplay Systems*, so I am not going to go through all the details about the theory of stack-based FSM. The basic principle of the stack-based FSM is that we can add to and remove our objects from the stack in a first in, last out order. The term commonly used for adding items to a stack is called pushing, and the removal of an object from the stack is called popping. So, for a state example, the stack would look something like the following diagram during the different functions:

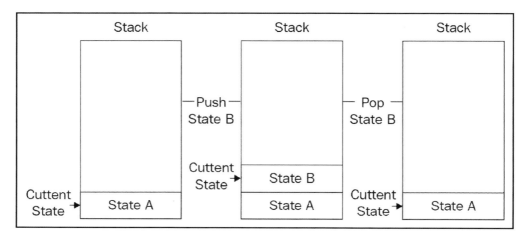

One of the major advantages of using a stack-based FSM is that you can now use the stack to control the current state. Each state can pop itself from the stack, allowing the execution of the next state. We can also implement the concept of *on entry* and *on exit*, allowing us to have states within states. We can do things such as set up and clean up in each state, giving us much more flexibility in our AI state system.

Implementing our states for a stack-based FSM in a Lua script might look something similar to the following:

```
StateA =
{
    Update = function ()
    {
        //Do state update actions
}
OnEnter = function()
{
    //Do actions for first load
}
```

```
OnExit = function()
{
    //Do action for last call for this state
}
}
```

Then, in our C++ code, we would add the rest of the architecture needed to power the state-based FSM. Here, we would create a vector or array object that would hold pointers to the state objects loaded in from the Lua script. We would then call the functions for OnEnter, OnExit, and Update for the state object currently occupying the last element in the array. As seen before, we could handle this by simply creating an enum and switching cases to handle the state flow. We could also go the route of creating a StateList class that would implement the required functions to wrap up the FSM. This StateList class, for our example, could look like the following:

```
class StateList {
    public:
        StateList ();
        ~ StateList ();

        LuaState * GoToNext();
        LuaState * GoToPrevious();

        void SetCurrentState(int nextState);
        void AddState(State * newState);

        void Destroy();

        LuaState* GetCurrent();

    protected:
        std::vector< LuaState*> m_states;
        int m_currentStateIndex = -1;
    };
}
```

Whichever way you choose to implement the state-based FSM, you will still get the added benefit of having the stack control in place. As you can see, the state pattern, when used in AI development, gives us a great, flexible starting point for creating AI interactions. Next, we will look at some other techniques to introduce decision-making into your AI design.

Decision trees

A decision tree is a flowchart-like structure comprised of branches and leaves. Each branch of the tree is a conditional, where a decision is made. Each leaf is the action for the choice made in the conditional. At the farthest extents of the tree, the leaves are the actual commands that control the AI agent. Using a decision tree structure allows for easier design and understanding of the flow of the AI implementation. A simple AI brain implemented in a decision tree would look something similar to the following diagram:

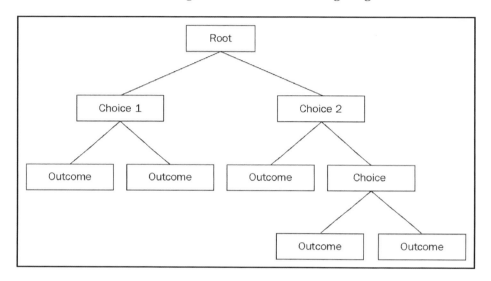

You might be thinking to yourself that this looks and sounds very much like the dialog trees we implemented in Chapter 8, *Advanced Gameplay Systems*. That is because they are! Just like in the case of working with dialog and choices, using a tree structure is a great way to script out the flow of an AI interaction. The decision trees can be extremely deep, with branches and nodes calling sub-trees which perform particular functions. This gives the designer the ability to use an extensive library of different decisions that can be chained together to provide a convincing depth of AI interaction. You can even go as far as developing branches that can be ordered by their overall desirability based on the current task, which could then fall back to other decisions, should the desired one fail. This resiliency and flexibility is where tree structures really stand out.

Those familiar with data structures in C++ are probably already thinking about how this tree structure can be implemented in code. Maybe Lists are coming to mind. There are many different ways to implement a decision tree. We could define the tree in an external format, such as XML. We could implement it along with the structure and architecture with a mix of C++ and a scripting language such as Lua, but since I really want to drill home the understanding of the tree design, we are going put the entire implementation in Lua. A great example of how this can be accomplished is demonstrated by David Young in the book *Learning Game AI Programming with Lua*, so we are going to base our simple example on David's more detailed example.

To start with, let's look at the structure of the tree object. In the `DecisionTree.lua` file, we could have something like the following code:

```lua
DecisionTree = {};

function DecisionTree.SetBranch(self, branch)
self.branch_ = branch;
end

function DecisionTree.Update(self, deltaTime)
-- Skip execution if the tree hasn't been setup yet.
if (self.branch_ == nil) then
        return;
    end
    -- Search the tree for an Action to run if not currently
    -- executing an Action.
    if (self.currentAction_ == nil) then
        self.currentAction_ = self.branch_:Evaluate();
        self.currentAction_:Initialize();
    end
        local status = self.currentAction_:Update(deltaTime);
end
function DecisionTree.new()
    local decisionTree = {};
        -- The DecisionTree's data members.
    decisionTree.branch_ = nil;
    decisionTree.currentAction_ = nil;
        -- The DecisionTree's accessor functions.
    decisionTree.SetBranch = decisionTree.SetBranch;
    decisionTree.Update = decisionTree.Update;
        return decisionTree;
end
```

Here, in our tree structure, we implement an update loop, which evaluates the root branch within the tree and processes the resulting action. Once the action has been created, processed, and finished, the decision tree will reevaluate itself starting again from the root branch to determine the next action to be executed.

Next up is the branch object. In our implementation, the branches will consist of a conditional that will determine which element will be executed next. It is the responsibility of the conditional evaluation to return a value that ranges from one to the maximum number of children in the branch. This will denote which element should be executed next. Our decision branch Lua class object will have basic functions for adding additional children as well as setting the conditional function used during the branch's calculation. In the `DecisionBranch.lua` file, we could have an implementation that looks similar to the following:

```lua
DecisionBranch = {}
DecisionBranch.Type = " DecisionBranch ";
function DecisionBranch.new()
    local branch = {};
    -- The DecisionBranch data members.
    branch.children_ = {};
    branch.conditional_ = nil;
    branch.type_ = DecisionBranch.Type;
    -- The DecisionBranch accessor functions.
    branch.AddChild = DecisionBranch.AddChild;
    branch.Evaluate = DecisionBranch.Evaluate;
    branch. SetConditional = DecisionBranch. SetConditional;
    return branch;
end
function DecisionBranch.AddChild(self, child, index)
    -- Add the child at the specified index, or as the last child.
    index = index or (#self.children_ + 1);
        table.insert(self.children_, index, child);
end
function DecisionBranch.SetConditional (self, conditional)
    self. conditional _ = conditional;
end
```

As pointed out by David in his example, since leaves are simply actions, we can include each leaf action in the branches themselves. This allows us to get the needed functionality without the need for an additional structure in the code. With the use of the `type_` `variable`, we can determine whether a child of the branch is another branch or an action that needs to be executed.

For the evaluation of the branch itself, we execute the conditional and then use the returned value to determine the next step in the tree. It should be noted that every branch within the tree must eventually end with an action. If the tree has any leaves that do not end in actions, the tree is malformed and will not evaluate properly.

Staying in the `DecisionBranch.lua` file, the code to evaluate the branch would look something like the following:

```
function DecisionBranch.Evaluate(self)
    -- Execute the branch's evaluator function, this will return a
    -- numeric value which indicates what child should execute.
    local conditional = self. conditional _();
    local choice = self.children_[conditional];
    if (choice.type_ == DecisionBranch.Type) then
        -- Recursively evaluate children to see if they are decision
branches.
        return choice:Evaluate();
    else
        -- Return the leaf action.
        return choice;
    end
end
```

Now that we have the tree data structure in place, we can go ahead and build one for use. To do this, we first create a new instance of the decision tree, create each branch needed in the tree, connect the conditional branches, and finally add the action leaves. In the `AILogic.lua` file, we could have something similar to the following:

```
function AILogic_DecisionTree()
    --Create a new instance of the tree
    local tree = DecisionTree.new();
    --Add branches
local moveBranch = DecisionBranch.new();
    local shootBranch = DecisionBranch.new();
    --Connect the conditional branches and action leaves
...
moveBranch:AddChild(MoveAction());
        moveBranch:AddChild(randomBranch);
        moveRandomBranch:SetConditional(
            function()
```

```
            if Conditional_HasMovePosition() then
                return 1;
            end
            return 2;
        end);
...
    --Set initial branch
    tree:SetBranch(moveBranch);
return tree;
end
```

With the decision tree in place, we could now call this script and load the tree into an AI agent object. We could make changes on the fly, add more decisions and actions, and even add in other AI techniques to augment the decisions. While a decision tree allows developers and designers to create easy to understand and read AI structures, it does have its drawbacks. One of the most notable drawbacks is its modeling of complicated logical conditions, where you need to account for each possible outcome of the condition. Also, with the larger number of branch possibilities, a tree will also start to have the need to be balanced. If this balancing does not occur, parts of the tree will need to be replicated, quickly increasing the complexity of the tree structure and leading to more bug-prone code.

Feedback loops

The last topic in AI decision-making I want to briefly touch on is the concept of feedback loops. A feedback loop is a situation where a certain output value of a system is fed or given back to the system which, in turn, influences the state of the system, affecting its subsequent value. Ideally, in video games, especially in AI interactions, every loop should be a stable feedback loop. A simple definition of a stable feedback loop is a situation where the output of the system is used to reverse the circumstances that caused the feedback value in the first place, making the feedback system move to the convergence of a stable state. This keeps your AI feedback from causing a runaway effect with a negative or positive feedback loop taking place.

To help you understand what a feedback loop really is, let's take an example most commonly seen in video games, stamina. Stamina is seen in many scenarios such as a character's ability to sprint or run, or a character's ability to climb. In our example, we will look at the example of a boxing match. The following is a diagram showing the feedback loop we want to implement:

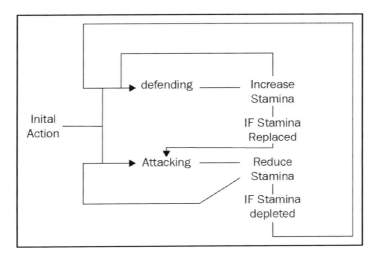

As stated previously, we need to make sure the stamina feedback loop for our boxing example is stable. This means that when we reach a predefined low level of stamina, we need to switch the loop to defending, allowing us to recover stamina. If we reach a predefined replenished level, we do the opposite and switch to attacking to reduce the stamina level. This switching allows us to keep the loop stable and is referred to as an oscillating feedback loop.

To implement this in code is surprisingly simple:

```
void Update(float deltaTime)
{
    if(currentState == attacking)
    {
        ReduceStamina();
    if(player.stamina <= depleted)
{
        currentState = defending;
}
}
}
else if (currentState == defending)
{
    IncreaseStamina();
```

```
        if(stamina >= replenished)
        {
            currentState = attacking;
        }
    }
}
```

That is it, honestly. It is not complicated to code the implementation of this technique. We did skip over a few things, like how to handle reducing and increasing stamina. Considering this is in an AI system, we want it to appear more realistic, so it wouldn't be great to just increase these values statically. Finding a good random value to put in place here could give it a more realistic feel. Ultimately, this is an easy to implement technique which provides a nice way to vary outcomes and provides a more unique interaction with AI components.

Motion and pathfinding techniques

AI agents and other non-player characters quite often need to move around the game world. Implementing this movement so that it appears in a lifelike fashion is a challenging process. In the next section, we will look at how we can implement algorithms and techniques to add AI agent movement and pathfinding to our game development projects.

Motion algorithms and techniques

Using motion algorithms to control an AI agent's movements throughout a level or game world is a very common use case for AI algorithms in video games. These algorithms can implement behaviors to give the impression of a thinking and reacting AI agent, and they can also perform other tasks such as simple object avoidance. In the next section, we are going to look at a few of these motion techniques.

Steering behaviors

Steering behaviors are a subset of motion algorithms comprised of various techniques for controlling the movement of the AI agent based on external and internal variables. In our example engine, we have already incorporated a 3D physics calculation library—refer back to `Chapter 5`, *Building Gameplay Systems*, for a refresher—and we already have a concept for an NPC class to act as our AI agent. This means we have a large part of the needed framework to create a Newtonian physics-based steering system, also known as a steering-based locomotion system. The steering-based locomotion system is comprised of a few different classifications for adding forces to an AI agent. These include the classifications of seeking, fleeing, evasion, wandering, pursuit, and a few more. The completely detailed implementations of these algorithms would take up chapters on their own, so instead we will focus on the high-level concepts and use cases for each algorithm. To help you out on the implementation side, I have included the `OpenSteer` library in the example engine. `OpenSteer` will handle the details of the calculations, making it easier for our engine and our AI Lua scripts to easily use these algorithms to control the agents' movements.

Following is a screenshot of an `OpenSteer` library program running a seek and evade algorithm:

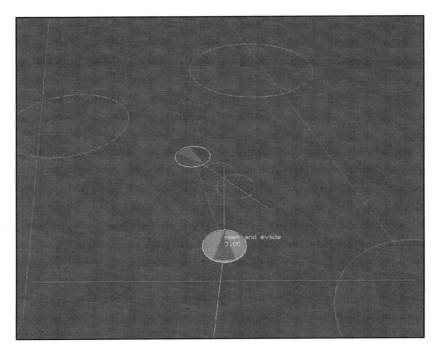

Seek

Let's start with the seek algorithm. The seek algorithm's goal is to steer the AI agent towards a specific position in the game space. This behavior applies force so that the current heading and the desired heading will align towards the target destination point. The following diagram describes this process:

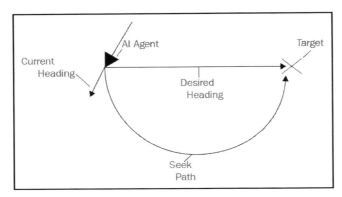

The **Desired Heading** is really a vector in the direction from the character to the target. The length of the **Desired Heading** could be set as a value, such as the character's current speed. The steering vector or **Seek Path** is the difference between this desired heading and the character's current heading. The equation for this can be simplified to something like the following:

```
desiredHeading = normalize (position - target) * characterSpeed
steeringPath = desiredHeading - velocity
```

An interesting side effect of the seek algorithm is that if an AI agent continues to seek, it will eventually pass through the target, and then flip its direction to approach the target again. This produces a motion path that looks a bit like a moth buzzing around a light bulb. To use OpenSteer to calculate the steering force, you call the steerForSeek function, passing a 3-point vector to describe the target's position:

```
Vec3 steerForSeek (const Vec3& target);
```

Flee

The flee steering behavior is simply the inverse of seek. Instead of working to align the heading to a specific target, the flee algorithm steers the AI agent's heading to be aligned away from the target point. The desired heading, as such, points in the opposite direction. The following diagram shows this process:

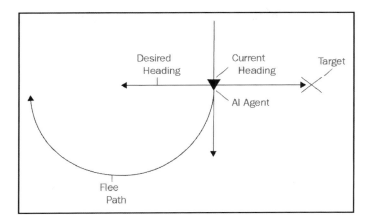

To use `OpenSteer` to calculate the steering force for a fleeing AI agent, you call the `steerForFlee` function, passing a 3-point vector to describe the target's position:

```
Vec3 steerForFlee (const Vec3& target);
```

Pursuit

The pursuit steering behavior is very similar to the seek behavior, but the difference here is that the target point is actually a moving object or player. The following diagram illustrates this behavior:

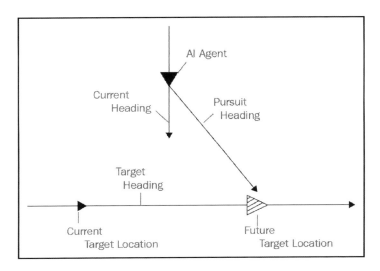

In order to create effective pursuit behavior, we will need to do some predicting when it comes to the target's future position. One approach that we can take is to use a prediction method that we can revaluate in each update loop. In our simple predictor, we are going to make the assumption that our target will not turn during this update loop. While this assumption will more often be wrong, the predictor result will only be used for a fraction of a second (1/30). Which means that if a target does veer away, a quick correction based on the target changing direction will be calculated in the next simulation step. Also with this assumption, the position of a target that is X units of time in the future can be calculated by scaling its velocity by X and adding that offset to its current position. Then it is literally a matter of applying the seek steering behavior to the predicted target location to achieve the pursuit behavior.

To use `OpenSteer` to calculate the steering force for a pursuing AI agent, you call the `steerForPursuit` function, passing an object to use as the target we are pursuing:

```
Vec3 steerForPursuit (const TargetObject& target);
```

Evasion

Much like flee is the opposite of seek, evasion is the opposite of pursuit. This means that instead of steering the AI agent toward the target's calculated future position, we are instead fleeing from the target's current position. The following diagram illustrates this behavior:

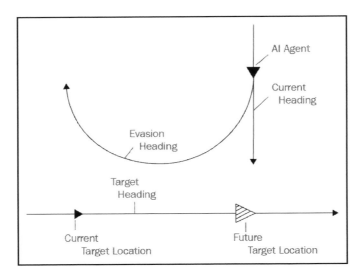

When using evasion steering behavior, the AI agent will head away from the predicted point of interception. This can often result in a less than natural behavior, as most truly fleeing entities will likely have a random evasion pattern. One way to achieve a more natural effect would be to modify the force applied with another behavior, such as the wandering behavior we will touch on next.

To use `OpenSteer` to calculate the steering force for an evading AI agent, you call the `steerforEvasion` function, passing an object to use as the target we are evading, as well as a float value to specify the maximum amount of time in the future to use when calculating the force to apply:

```
Vec3 steerForEvasion (const AbstractVehicle& menace,
                      const float maxPredictionTime);
```

Wandering

As I mentioned previously, sometimes it's better to have some fluctuation in a behavior by adding another behavior to modify the force. The wandering behavior is a great example of a modifying behavior. The wandering behavior basically returns a tangent steering force in relation to the agent's forward vector. It should be noted that, since the wandering behavior is meant to add some deviation to an agent's movement, it should not be used as a steering force all by itself.

To use `OpenSteer` to calculate a wandering steering force for an AI agent, you call the `steerForWander` function, passing a float value to specify the time step between wanders. The time step value allows the wander rate to be consistent when frame times vary:

```
Vec3 steerForWander (float dt);
```

While that is all the time we can dedicate to AI steering behaviors in this book, we have only really begun to scratch the surface of what is available. Concepts like flocking and simple object avoidance are unfortunately outside of the scope of this chapter, but are fully supported by the `OpenSteer` library. If you are interested in learning more about these behaviors, I highly recommend reading through the `OpenSteer` documentation.

Search algorithms and pathfinding techniques

In a lot of cases in games, we often need to find a path from one location to the next. Another very common need for AI in game development, and the last one we will touch on in this chapter, is the use of search algorithms to find optimal paths for moving around AI agents.

For example, here we are going to focus on graph search algorithms. Graph search algorithms, as their name suggests, work with graphs as their source of data input. In our example of a map, the graph is a set of locations and the connections between them. These are often referred to as nodes and edges respectively. The following is an example of what very basic graph data might look like:

The output from these graph search algorithms can be used to develop the path needed to be taken by the AI agent. This path is made up of the graph's nodes and edges. It should be noted that the algorithms will tell your AI where to move, but it won't provide the how. These algorithms are not like the steer-force algorithms from earlier in the chapter, as they won't move the AI agent. However, combined with the steering algorithms, these pathfinding algorithms will create great overall AI behavior.

Now that we have a basic understanding of how graphs represent the map and the points we want to find paths between, let's look at some of the most common algorithms used.

Breadth first

The breadth first search is the simplest of search algorithms. It explores all directions equally. So how does it explore? Well, in all of these search algorithms, the key idea is to keep track of an expanding area, referred to as the frontier. The breadth first algorithm expands this frontier by moving out from the starting point and checking its neighbors first, then its neighbor's neighbors, and so on. The following is a diagram showing how this expansion takes place on a grid. The numbers denote the order the grid square was visited:

A simple example of how we can implement this in C++ follows. I have left out a few sections of code for the sake of space in the book. The full implementation can be found in the Chapter09 example project, in the source code repository:

```cpp
void SearchGraph::BreadthFirst(int s)
{
    // Mark all the vertices as not visited
    bool *visited = new bool[V];
    for(int i = 0; i < V; i++)
        visited[i] = false;
    // Create a queue for BFS
    list<int> queue;
    // Mark the current node as visited and enqueue it
    visited[s] = true;
    queue.push_back(s);
    // 'i' will be used to get all adjacent vertices of a vertex
    list<int>::iterator i;
    while(!queue.empty())
    {
        // Dequeue a vertex from queue and print it
        s = queue.front();
        cout << s << " ";
        queue.pop_front();
        // Get all adjacent vertices of the dequeued vertex s
        // If a adjacent has not been visited, then mark it visited
        // and enqueue it
        for(i = adj[s].begin(); i != adj[s].end(); ++i)
        {
            if(!visited[*i])
            {
                visited[*i] = true;
                queue.push_back(*i);
            }
        }
    }
}
```

As you may have noticed from the source code, one trick with this algorithm is we need to avoid doubling back and processing a node more than once. In this simple example, we implement an array of Boolean values of visited nodes. If we don't mark visited vertices in this example, we create an endless loop process.

This is an incredibly useful algorithm, not only for regular pathfinding but also for procedural map generation, flow field pathfinding, distance maps, and other types of map analysis.

Dijkstra's algorithm

In some cases, we will need to find the shortest path when each step can have different costs associated. For example, in the *Civilization* game series, moving through different land types requires different amounts of turns per movement. In cases like this, we can implement the Dijkstra's algorithm, also known as a **Uniform Cost Search**. This algorithm lets us prioritize which paths to explore. Instead of exploring all possible paths equally, it favors the lower cost paths. In order to accomplish the prioritization of paths, we need to track movement costs. In essence, we want to take the movement costs into account when deciding how to evaluate each location. In this algorithm, we are going to need what is known as a priority queue or heap. Using a heap instead of a regular queue changes the way the frontier expands. The following is an excerpt of the example code that demonstrates the Dijkstra's algorithm in C++, and I have again skipped over a few pieces for the sake of space. You can find the full Dijkstra example in the `Chapter09` folder of the source repository:

```cpp
// Prints shortest paths from src to all other vertices
void SearchGraph:: Dijkstra(int src)
{
    // Create a priority queue to store vertices that are being
preprocessed
    priority_queue< iPair, vector <iPair> , greater<iPair> > pq;
    // Create a vector for distances and initialize all distances as
infinite (INF)
    vector<int> dist(V, INF);
    // Insert source itself in priority queue and initialize its distance
as 0.
    pq.push(make_pair(0, src));
    dist[src] = 0;
    /* Looping till priority queue becomes empty (or all
      distances are not finalized) */
    while (!pq.empty())
    {
        int u = pq.top().second;
        pq.pop();
        // 'i' is used to get all adjacent vertices of a vertex
        list< pair<int, int> >::iterator i;
        for (i = adj[u].begin(); i != adj[u].end(); ++i)
        {
            // Get vertex label and weight of current adjacent of u.
```

```
            int v = (*i).first;
            int weight = (*i).second;
            // If there is shorted path to v through u.
            if (dist[v] > dist[u] + weight)
            {
                // Updating distance of v
                dist[v] = dist[u] + weight;
                pq.push(make_pair(dist[v], v));
            }
        }
    }
    // Print shortest distances stored in dist[]
    printf("Vertex    Distance from Sourcen");
    for (int i = 0; i < V; ++i)
        printf("%d tt %dn", i, dist[i]);
}
```

This algorithm is great when finding the shortest path using different costs, but it does waste time exploring in all directions. Next, we will look at another algorithm that lets us find the shortest path to a single destination.

A*

Arguably one of the best and most popular techniques used in pathfinding is the **A***
algorithm. A* is a modification of Dijkstra's algorithm that is optimized for a single destination. Where Dijkstra's algorithm can find paths to all locations, A* finds paths to one location. It prioritizes paths that seem to be leading closer to the goal. The implementation is very similar to the Dijkstra implementation, but the difference is in the use of a heuristic search function to augment the algorithm. This heuristic search is used to estimate the distance to the goal. What this amounts to is that A* uses the sum of a Dijkstra search and a heuristic search to calculate the fastest path to a certain point.

The following is a great example of a pseudo-code implementation explaining the A*
algorithm's process, courtesy of Wikipedia (https://en.wikipedia.org/wiki/A*_search_
algorithm):

```
function A*(start, goal)
    // The set of nodes already evaluated
    closedSet := {}

    // The set of currently discovered nodes that are not evaluated yet.
    // Initially, only the start node is known.
    openSet := {start}
```

```
    // For each node, which node it can most efficiently be reached from.
    // If a node can be reached from many nodes, cameFrom will eventually
contain the
    // most efficient previous step.
    cameFrom := the empty map

    // For each node, the cost of getting from the start node to that node.
    gScore := map with default value of Infinity

    // The cost of going from start to start is zero.
    gScore[start] := 0

    // For each node, the total cost of getting from the start node to the
goal
    // by passing by that node. That value is partly known, partly
heuristic.
    fScore := map with default value of Infinity

    // For the first node, that value is completely heuristic.
    fScore[start] := heuristic_cost_estimate(start, goal)

    while openSet is not empty
        current := the node in openSet having the lowest fScore[] value
        if current = goal
            return reconstruct_path(cameFrom, current)

        openSet.Remove(current)
        closedSet.Add(current)

        for each neighbor of current
            if neighbor in closedSet
                continue          // Ignore the neighbor which is already
evaluated.

            if neighbor not in openSet    // Discover a new node
                openSet.Add(neighbor)
            // The distance from start to a neighbor
            tentative_gScore := gScore[current] + dist_between(current,
neighbor)
            if tentative_gScore >= gScore[neighbor]
                continue          // This is not a better path.

            // This path is the best until now. Record it!
            cameFrom[neighbor] := current
            gScore[neighbor] := tentative_gScore
            fScore[neighbor] := gScore[neighbor] +
heuristic_cost_estimate(neighbor, goal)
```

```
        return failure

function reconstruct_path(cameFrom, current)
    total_path := [current]
    while current in cameFrom.Keys:
        current := cameFrom[current]
        total_path.append(current)
    return total_path
```

That wraps up our quick look at some of the more common pathfinding techniques. While we did see some implementation in this section, if you are looking for a great starting point for your production games, I would highly recommend looking at some of the open source libraries available. These are extremely valuable learning resources and provide proven implementation techniques you can build on.

Summary

In this chapter, we covered a large field of study in a short period of time. We developed a base definition of what game AI really is and, for that matter, what it is not. In this chapter, we also looked at expanding the decision-making functions with the inclusion of AI techniques. We covered how an AI agents' movements can be controlled through the use of steering forces and behavior. Finally, we capped off the chapter by looking at the use of pathfinding algorithms to create paths from point to point for our AI agents. While we did cover a fair amount in this chapter, there is still much more to be uncovered in the world of game AI. I implore you to continue your journey. In the next chapter, we will look at how we can add multiplayer and other network functionalities to our example game engine.

10
Multiplayer

Since my earliest gaming adventures, I have found that sharing the experience always made it more memorable. Back in those days, the concept of multiplayer revolved around playing with friends on the couch or getting together with other game fans for an epic **LAN (local area network**) party. Things have changed dramatically since then, with online, worldwide, shared gaming experiences the new norm. In this chapter, we will cover the concept of adding multiplayer support to your game project, specifically focusing on networked multiplayer. As I have said before, the topic of computer networking is a very large and diverse topic and would require more time and space than we have to cover in full. Instead, we will focus on the high-level overview and go deep where required. In this chapter, we will cover the following topics:

- Introduction to multiplayer in games
- Network design and protocol development
- Creating a client/server

Introduction to multiplayer in games

To boil it down to its simplest terms, a multiplayer game is a type of video game where more than one person can play simultaneously. While single-player video games are usually geared around one player competing with AI opponents and achieving predefined goals, multiplayer games are designed around interaction with other human players. These interactions can be in the form of competition, partnership, or simply social engagement. How these multiple player interactions are implemented can vary depending on factors such as location and genre, from fighter games with same screen multiplayer to online multiplayer role-playing games, with users sharing a common environment. In this next section, we will look at some of the various ways multiplayer interactions can be included in video games.

Local multiplayer

The idea of multiplayer in games first appeared in the form of local multiplayer. Very early on a lot of games had two-player modes. Some games would implement a two-player mode known as turn-based multiplayer, where players could take turns playing the game. While this but even early on developers saw the benefit of shared experiences. Even the earliest games such as *Spacewar!* (1962) and *PONG* (1972) pitted players against each other. The rise of the arcade gaming scene helped push local multiplayer games, with games such as *Gauntlet* (1985) offering up to four player co-operative gaming experience.

Most local multiplayer games can be placed into one of a few categories, turn-based, shared single-screen, or split-screen multiplayer.

Turn-based, as its name suggests, is a multiplayer mode where the players take turns playing the game using a single screen. A good example of a turn-based multiplayer game would be the original *Super Mario Bros*, for **Nintendo Entertainment System** (**NES**). In this game, if the two-player mode is selected, the first player plays as the Mario character; when the player dies, the second player has their turn and plays as the other brother, Luigi.

Shared single-screen multiplayer is a common local multiplayer mode where each player's character is on the same screen. Each player has control of their character/avatar simultaneously. This mode is very well-suited to versus gameplay such as sports and fighter games, as well as co-operative gameplay such as platformers and puzzle solvers. This mode continues to be very popular today, with a great example being the recently released Cuphead title.

Single-screen multiplayer

Split-screen multiplayer is another popular local multiplayer mode where each player has a portion of the entire local screen as their gameplay view. Each player controls their character/avatar simultaneously. This mode is very well-suited to versus games such as shooter titles. Although most games choosing to implement a split-screen mode are two-player games, some titles supported as many as four local players, with the local screen being split vertically and horizontally into quarters. A great example of a game that implements split-screen multiplayer is the first person shooter, *Halo*.

Local area network

With the proliferation of personal computers in the early 1990s' the idea of connecting computers together to share information soon developed into a core need for most computer users. One early way of connecting multiple computers together was through a LAN. A LAN allows computers in a limited area, such as a university, office, school, or even a personal residence. LAN's are not by default connectable unless you are in that limited area in which the LAN is located. While the business computing world had already adopted the idea of LAN computing, the gaming industry really started using the technology for multiplayer with the release of *DOOM* in 1993.

The popularity of LAN-based multiplayer games has weaned since the wide adoption of the internet. That being said, LAN is still the way multiplayer games are played at competitions such as the e-sport leagues of today. The idea of LAN-based multiplayer gaming also spawned a phenomenon known as the **LAN party**. LAN parties are getting where players of games come together in the same physical location and connect all their computers together in order to play with each other. These events usually spanned multiple days, with players traveling large distances to take part. LAN parties were a staple of the gaming landscape in the early to late 1990's, for any gamer that took part, it was a memorable way to connect with other gamers.

Online multiplayer

The popularity of the internet brought with it the ability for gamers around the world to connect and play together in a whole new way. Unlike the LAN parties of old, gamers could now play and compete with fellow gamers from all over the world without leaving the comfort of their own home. The history of online multiplayer can be traced all the way back to the early examples such as **MUD** (**Multi-User Dungeon**), where users could play the simple RPGs over the internet. Online multiplayer games span almost every genre of games today, from first-person shooters to real-time strategy games. Internet-based gameplay also spawned a new genre of games called **Massively Multiplayer Online** (**MMO**) games. In MMOs' massive amounts of players can all connect and interact in a single instance or world. One of the most popular MMO games to date is *World of Warcraft*.

Network design and protocol development

Two of the biggest considerations when designing and developing multiplayer games is deciding on the network topology and connection protocol to use. Each choice has a significant bearing on the implementation and gameplay itself. In this next part of the chapter, we will cover the different network topologies and protocols in use, and discuss their various effects and considerations.

Network topology

Simply put, network topology is the way computers on a network are connected to one another. For online gaming, the network topology will determine how the computers on the network are organized to allow users to receive updates to the game. How the computers are networked will determine many aspects of the overall multiplayer design and each type of topology has its own strengths and weakness. In this next section, we will cover the two most popular topologies used in game development, the client/server, and the peer-to-peer model.

Peer-to-peer

In a peer-to-peer network, each individual player is connected to every other player in the game instance:

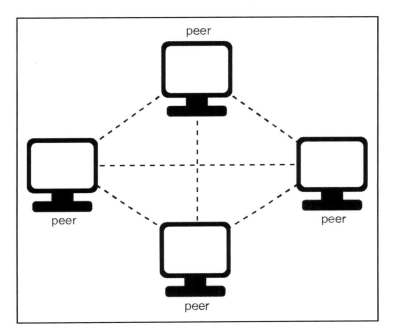

A peer-to-peer network is usually implemented in a non-authoritative design. This means that no single entity that controls game states, so every player must handle its own game state, and communicate any local changes to other players connected. This means as a consequence of this topology we have a few issues to think about. The first is bandwidth; as you have probably imagined, with this design there is a large amount of data that needs to be passed between players. In fact, the number of connections can be represented as a quadratic function where each player will have $O(n-1)$ connections, which means that there will be $O(2n)$ connections in total for this network topology. This network design is also symmetric, which means that every player will have to have the same available bandwidth for both upload and download streams. The other issue we need to consider is the concept of authority.

As I mentioned here, the most common approach to handling authority in a peer-to-peer network is to have all players share updates to every other player on the network. As a consequence of handling authority in this manner is that the player sees two situations accruing at the same time, the players own input updating the game state instantaneously and a simulation of the other player's movements. Since the updates from the other players have to traverse the network, the updates are not instantaneous. When the local player receives an update, to say move an opponent to (x, y, z), the chances of the opponent still being in that location at the time of receiving the update are low, that is why the updates from other players are simulated. The biggest issue with simulating updates is that as the latency increases, the simulation becomes more and more inaccurate. We will discuss techniques for handling this issue of update lag and simulation in the next section of this chapter.

Client/server

In a client-server topology, one instance is designated the server, and all of the other player instances connect to it. Each of the player instances (the client) will only ever communicates with the server. The server, in turn, is responsible for communicating all updates of the players to the other clients connected on the network. The following image demonstrates this network topology:

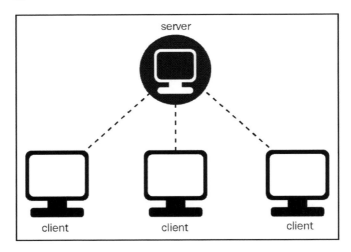

While not the only method, a client-server network commonly implements an authoritative design. This means, as a player performs an action, such as moving their character to another place, that information is sent in the form of an update to the server. The server checks whether the update is considered correct, and if it is, the server then relays this update information to the other players connected on the network. If there is ever a situation where the client and server disagree on the update information, the server is considered the correct version. Just like the peer-to-peer topology, there are some things to consider when implementing. When it comes to bandwidth, in theory, the bandwidth requirement for each player will not change depending on the number of players connected. If we looked at this in the form of a quadratic formula, given n players the total of connections would be O(2n). However, unlike the peer-to-peer topology, client-server topology is asymmetric, meaning the server will have only O(n) connections, or one to one per client. This means that as the number of players connected increases, the bandwidth required to support the connections will increase linearly. That said, in practice, as more players join, more objects need to be simulated, which might cause slight increases to bandwidth requirements for both client and server.

 An authoritative design is considered more secure against cheating. This is because the server fully controls the game states and update. If a suspicious update is passed from a player, the server can ignore it and provide the correct update information to the other clients instead.

Understanding the protocols

Before diving into implementing multiplayer, it is important to understand how things are handled under the hood so to speak. One of the most important aspects is how the data is being exchanged between two computers. This is where protocols come in. Although there are many different ways to exchange data on networks, in this section, we are going to look at the **Transmission Control Protocol/Internet Protocol (TCP/IP)** model with a focus on the host-to-host layer protocols.

TCP/IP model

The TCP/IP model is a description of a protocol suite, which is a collection of protocols that are designed to work together to transfer data from one computer to another. It is named after two of the main protocols (TCP and IP). TCP/IP is considered the de-facto standard protocol today and has replaced older protocol suites, such as IPX and SPX. The TCP/IP protocol suite can be broken down into a 4-layer model shown in the following image:

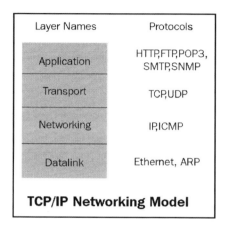

Most modern networking courses teach the 7-layer OSI model. The OSI model is an idealized networking model and, as of yet, not a practical implementation.

The four layers are broken down into the application layer, the transport layer, the networking layer, and the datalink layer. The application is the layer that represents the data to the user and handles the encoding and dialog control. A commonly known application layer protocol is the **Hyper Text Transfer Protocol (HTTP)**, which is the protocol that powers the websites we all use daily. The transport layer, also known as the host-to-host layer, is the layer that supports the lower level communications between various devices and networks, independent of the hardware being used. We will dive deeper into this layer next. The networking layer is the layer that determines the best path for the data through the network and handles addressing. The most common protocol in this layer is **Internet Protocol (IP)**. There are two versions of IP: the IPv4 standard, and the IPv6 standard. The fourth and final layer is the datalink or network access layer. The datalink layer specifies the hardware devices and media that make up the network. Common datalink protocols are Ethernet and Wi-Fi.

Now that we have a general understanding of the layers, let's take a closer look at the two most commonly used networking layer protocols in game development: TCP and UDP.

UDP – User Datagram Protocol

To begin with, let's look at the **User Datagram Protocol** (**UDP**). UDP is a very lightweight protocol that can be used to pass data from a specified port on one host to another specified port on another host. A grouping of data being sent in one instance is referred to as a datagram. The datagram consists of an 8-byte header followed by the data to be passed, referred to as the payload. A UDP header is depicted in the following table:

Bit#	0	16
0-31	Source Port	Destination Port
32-63	Length	Checksum

UDP header

To break it down bits by bits:

- **Source port**: (16 bits) This identifies the port from which the data being passed is originating from.
- **Destination port:** (16 bits) This is the target port of the data being passed.
- **Length**: (16 bits) This is the total length of the UDP header and the data payload combined.
- **Checksum**: (16 bits, optional) This is a checksum calculated based on the UDP header, payload, and certain fields of the IP header. By default, this field is set to all zeros.

Because UDP is such a simple protocol, it gives up a few features to keep it lightweight. One missing feature is a shared state between the two hosts. This means that no effort is made to ensure the complete passage of the datagram. There is no guarantee that the data will be in the right order when it arrives, if it arrives at all. This is very different to the next protocol we will look at, the TCP protocol.

TCP – Transmission Control Protocol

Unlike UDP, where a single datagram is passed, the TCP protocol, as its name suggests, creates a constant connection for transmission between two hosts. This allows a reliable stream of data to be passed back and forth between the hosts. TCP also attempts to ensure all data that is sent is actually received and in the proper order. With these added features, comes some added overhead. The header of a TCP connection is much larger than that of UDP. A depiction of a TCP header in a table format is as follows:

Bit#	0	4	7	16
0 - 31	Source Port			Destination Port
32 - 63	Sequence Number			
64 - 95	Acknowledgment Number			
96 - 127	Data Offset	Reserved	Control Bits	Receive Window
128 - 159	Checksum			Urgent Pointer
160 - ...	Options			

TCP header

For a TCP connection, a unit of data transmission is referred to as a segment. A segment consists of the TCP header and then the data that is being passed in that single segment.

Let's break it down bit by bit as follows:

- **Source port**: (16 bits) This identifies the port from which the data being passed is originating from.
- **Destination port**: (16 bits) This is the target port of the data being passed.
- **Sequence number**: (32-bits) This is a unique identifier number. Since TCP attempts to have the recipient receive the data in the order it was sent, each byte transferred through TCP receives a sequence number. These numbers allow the recipient and sender to ensure the order by following the sequence of these numbers.
- **Acknowledgment number**: (32-bits) This is the sequence number of the next byte of data that the sender is passing. This, in essence, acts as an acknowledgment for all data with sequence numbers lower than this number.
- **Data offset**: (4 bits) This specifies the length of the header in 32-bit words. It allows the addition of custom header components, if needed.

- **Control bits**: (9 bits) This holds metadata about the header.
- **Receive window**: (16 bits) This conveys the amount of remaining buffer space the sender has for incoming data. This is important when trying to maintaining flow control.
- **Urgent pointer**: (16 bits) This is the delta value between the first byte of data in this segment and the first byte of urgent data. This is optional and only relevant if the URG flag is set in the metadata of the header.

Introducing sockets

In the OSI model, there are a few different types of sockets that determine the structure of the transport layer. The two most common types are stream sockets and datagram sockets. In this section, we will briefly cover them and how they differ.

Stream sockets

A stream socket is used for the reliable two-way communication between different hosts. You can think of a stream socket as being similar to making a telephone call. When one host calls, other's connection is initiated; once the connection is made, both parties can communicate back and forth. The connection is constant like a stream.

An example of the use of stream sockets can be seen in the Transmission Control Protocol, which we discussed earlier in this chapter. Using TCP allows the data to be sent in sequences or packets. As mentioned before, TCP maintains state and provides a way to ensure that data arrives and that it is in the same order as it was sent. This is important for many types of applications including communications between web servers, mail servers, and their client applications.

In a later section, we will look at how you can implement your own stream sockets using the Transmission Control Protocol.

Datagram sockets

As opposed to stream sockets, datagram sockets are less like making a phone call and more akin to sending a letter in the mail. A datagram socket connection is a one-way only and is an unreliable connection. Unreliable in the sense that you can not be sure when or even if datagram socket data will arrive at the receiver. There is no way to guarantee the order in which the data arrives.

User Datagram Protocol, as described in the previous section, uses datagram sockets. Although UDP and datagram sockets are more lightweight, they provide a great choice when you just need to send data. The overhead of creating stream sockets, establishing and then maintaining that socket connection can overkill in many cases.

Datagram sockets and UDP are commonly used in networked games and streaming media. UDP is typically a good choice when a client needs to make a short query to a server, and it expects to receive a single response. To provide this send and receive service, we would need to use the UDP specific function calls, `sendto()` and `recvfrom()`, instead of `read()` and `write()` seen in the socket implementation.

Creating a simple TCP server

In this section, we will look at the process of implementing a simple TCP server example using the sockets technique discussed in the preceding sections. This example can then be expanded to support various gameplay needs and features.

Since the process of creating a server is slightly different for each platform, I have broken the examples into two different versions.

Windows

To begin with let's look at how we can use the WinSock libraries on the Windows platform to create a simple socket server that will listen for connections and print out a simple debug message when a connection is made. For the full implementation, check out the `Chapter10` directory of the code repository:

```
...
#include <stdio.h>
#include <windows.h>
#include <winsock2.h>
#include <ws2tcpip.h>

#define PORT "44000" /* Port to listen on */

...
```

First, we have our includes. This gives us access to the libraries that we need to create our sockets (this is different for other platforms).

```
...
if ((iResult = WSAStartup(wVersion, &wsaData)) != 0) {
    printf("WSAStartup failed: %d\n", iResult);
    return 1;
}
```

Jumping to the main method, we begin with initializing the underlying libraries. In this case, we are using the WinSock libraries.

```
ZeroMemory(&hints, sizeof hints);
hints.ai_family = AF_INET;
hints.ai_socktype = SOCK_STREAM;
if (getaddrinfo(NULL, PORT, &hints, &res) != 0) {
    perror("getaddrinfo");
    return 1;
}
```

Next, we set up our addressing information for the socket.

```
sock = socket(res->ai_family, res->ai_socktype, res->ai_protocol);
if (sock == INVALID_SOCKET) {
    perror("socket");
    WSACleanup();
    return 1;
}
```

We then create our socket, passing in the elements we created in the addressing stage.

```
    /* Enable the socket to reuse the address */
    if (setsockopt(sock, SOL_SOCKET, SO_REUSEADDR, (const char
*)&reuseaddr,
        sizeof(int)) == SOCKET_ERROR) {
        perror("setsockopt");
        WSACleanup();
        return 1;
    }
```

After we create our socket, it is good to setup our socket to be able to reuse the address we defined on a closer or reset.

```
    if (bind(sock, res->ai_addr, res->ai_addrlen) == SOCKET_ERROR) {
        perror("bind");
        WSACleanup();
        return 1;
    }
```

```
    if (listen(sock, 1) == SOCKET_ERROR) {
        perror("listen");
        WSACleanup();
        return 1;
    }
```

Now we can bind our address and finally listen for connections.

```
    ...
    while(1) {
        size_t size = sizeof(struct sockaddr);
        struct sockaddr_in their_addr;
        SOCKET newsock;
        ZeroMemory(&their_addr, sizeof (struct sockaddr));
        newsock = accept(sock, (struct sockaddr*)&their_addr, &size);
        if (newsock == INVALID_SOCKET) {
            perror("accept\n");
        }
        else {
            printf("Got a connection from %s on port %d\n",
                inet_ntoa(their_addr.sin_addr),
    ntohs(their_addr.sin_port));
      ...
        }
    }
```

In our main loop, we check for new connections, on receiving a valid one we print a simple debug message to the console.

```
    /* Clean up */
    closesocket(sock);
    WSACleanup();
    return 0;
}
```

Finally, we have to clean up after ourselves. We close the socket and call the WSACleanup function to initialize clean up of the WinSock library.

And, that's it. We now have a simple server that will listen for an incoming connection on the port we specified, 44000 in this example.

macOS

For macOS (and other *nix-based operating systems) the process is very similar to the Windows example, however, we need to use different libraries to help support us.

```c
#include <stdio.h>
#include <string.h> /* memset() */
#include <sys/socket.h>
#include <netinet/in.h>
#include <arpa/inet.h>
#include <unistd.h>
#include <netdb.h>
#define PORT    "44000"
...
```

First, we have the include, here we are using the system sockets, which on *nix systems is based on the BSD implementation.

```c
int main(void)
{
    int sock;
    struct addrinfo hints, *res;
    int reuseaddr = 1; /* True */
    /* Get the address info */
    memset(&hints, 0, sizeof hints);
    hints.ai_family = AF_INET;
    hints.ai_socktype = SOCK_STREAM;
    if (getaddrinfo(NULL, PORT, &hints, &res) != 0) {
        perror("getaddrinfo");
        return 1;
    }
```

In our main function, we begin by setting the addressing information.

```c
    /* Create the socket */
    sock = socket(res->ai_family, res->ai_socktype, res->ai_protocol);
    if (sock == -1) {
        perror("socket");
        return 1;
    }
```

We then create our socket, passing in the elements we created in the addressing stage.

```
    /* Enable the socket to reuse the address */
    if (setsockopt(sock, SOL_SOCKET, SO_REUSEADDR, &reuseaddr, sizeof(int))
== -1) {
        perror("setsockopt");
        return 1;
    }
```

After we create our socket, it is good to set up our socket to be able to reuse the address we defined on a closer or reset.

```
    if (bind(sock, res->ai_addr, res->ai_addrlen) == -1) {
        perror("bind");
        return 1;
    }
    if (listen(sock, 1) == -1) {
        perror("listen");
        return 1;
    }
```

Now we can bind our address and finally listen for connections.

```
    while (1) {
        socklen_t size = sizeof(struct sockaddr_in);
        struct sockaddr_in their_addr;
        int newsock = accept(sock, (struct sockaddr*)&their_addr, &size);
        if (newsock == -1) {
            perror("accept");
        }
        else {
            printf("Got a connection from %s on port %d\n",
                    inet_ntoa(their_addr.sin_addr),
htons(their_addr.sin_port));
            handle(newsock);
        }
    }
```

In our main loop, we check for new connections, on receiving a valid one we print a simple debug message to the console.

```
    close(sock);
    return 0;
}
```

Finally, we have to clean up after ourselves. In this case, we just have to close the socket.

And, that's it. We now have a simple server that will listen for an incoming connection on the port we specified, `44000` in this example.

To test our example, we can either use an existing program such as **putty** to connect to our server. Or we could create a simple client, which I will leave to you as a takeaway project. While just a simple server, this creates a starting point for building up your own implementations.

Summary

In this chapter, we took big steps to understand how multiplayer is implemented at a lower level. You learned about the TCP/IP stack and the different network topologies in use for game development. We looked at using UDP and TCP protocols in order to pass data to and from a client-server setup. Finally, we looked at some of the issues faced by developers when they start to implement multiplayer features. In the next chapter, we will look at how we can take our games to a new realm—virtual reality.

11
Virtual Reality

Virtual Reality (VR) is a very popular topic in game development these days. In this chapter, we will take a look at how the power of C++ can be leveraged to create an immersive VR experience. It should be noted that while the SDK used for the example integration is available for macOS, the hardware and example code presented in this chapter has not been tested on macOS and is not guaranteed to be supported. It should also be noted that you will need a VR headset and a significantly powerful PC and graphics card to run this chapter's closing example. It is recommend that you have a CPU that matches or exceeds an Intel i5-4590 or AMD FX 8350, and a GPU that matches or exceeds an NVIDIA GeForce GTX 960 or AMD Radeon R9 290. In this chapter, we will cover the following topics:

- Current VR hardware
- VR rendering concepts
- Headset SDKs
- Implementing VR support

Quick VR overview

VR is a computer technology that uses various forms of hardware to generate a simulation of the user's physical presence in a reconstructed or imaginary environment through the use of realistic imagery, sounds, and other sensations. A user that is in a VR environment is able to look around the artificial world, and with new advances in VR technology, move around in it and interact with virtual items or objects. While VR technology can date back to the 1950s, with recent advancements in computer graphics, processing, and power, VR has seen a resurgence. Well-known technology giants such as Facebook, Sony, Google, and Microsoft have bet big on virtual and augmented reality technologies. Not since the invention of the mouse has the way users interact with computers had such potential for innovation. Use cases for VR stretch beyond just game development. Many other fields are looking to VR technologies as a way to expand their own unique interactions. Healthcare, education, training, engineering, social sciences, marketing, and of course cinema and entertainment all hold promising opportunities for developers that possess the skill sets learned throughout this book and in game development in general. I often recommend that game developers looking for a change of pace, or a new challenge, look to the emerging VR development scene as an alternative use for their knowledge and skills base.

Current VR hardware

As developers, we are in a very fortunate time period of VR hardware development. There are many different options when it comes to VR hardware, including projected systems such as the **Cave Automatic Virtual Environment (CAVE)**, **head-mounted displays (HMDs)**, and even mobile phone based systems such as the Google Daydream and Cardboard. Here we will focus on immersive PC and console driven HMDs. Most of the technologies behind these HMDs are very similar. Each of the HMDs listed here have at least **six degrees of freedom (6DOF)** in terms of movement, head tracking in 3D space, and some even have basic spatial awareness, often referred to as *room sense*. Development for each of these headsets can, at a high level, be approached in much the same way, but it is good to have a general understanding of each of these different devices. Next, we will take a quick look at some of the most common headsets currently available to the consumer.

Oculus Rift CV1

Originally starting out as a crowd funded project, the Oculus Rift has become one of the most popular headsets currently available. The Oculus Rift has seen a few iterations. The first and second hardware releases were geared towards developers (the DK1 and DK2). Upon purchase of the Oculus startup by Facebook, the social media giant released the first commercial version of the hardware known as the **Consumer Version 1 (CV1)**. While supported on the **Steam** gaming platform, the Oculus is very much tied to its own launcher and software platform. The headset currently only supports PC development:

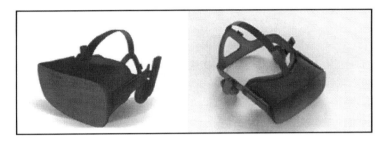

The following are the features of Oculus Rift CV1:

- **Screen type**: AMOLED
- **Resolution**: 1080 x 1200 per eye
- **Field of view**: ~110^0
- **Head tracking**: IMU (compass, accelerometer, gyroscope), IR optical tracing

The minimum recommended PC specifications are as follows:

- **GPU**: NVIDIA GeForce GTX 970 or AMD Radeon R9 290
- **CPU**: Intel i5-4590 or AMD FX 8350
- **RAM**: 8 GB
- **OS**: Windows 7

HTC Vive

Arguably the most popular headset currently available, the HTC Vive was created by HTC (a smartphone and tablet manufacturer) and the Valve corporation (a gaming company, best known for the Steam game platform). Often compared directly to the Oculus Rift, the HTC Vive does share many similarities in design, with slight differences that, in many developers' minds, make the HTC Vive the superior piece of hardware:

The following are the features of HTC Vive:

- **Screen type**: AMOLED
- **Resolution**: 1080 x 1200 per eye
- **Field of view**: 110^0
- **Head tracking**: IMU (compass, accelerometer, gyroscope), 2 IR base stations

The minimum recommended PC specifications are as follows:

- **GPU**: NVIDIA GeForce GTX 970 or AMD Radeon R9 290
- **CPU**: Intel i5-4590 or AMD FX 8350
- **RAM**: 4 GB
- **OS**: Windows 7, Linux

Open Source Virtual Reality (OSVR) development kit

Another very interesting hardware option is the OSVR kit, developed by Razer and Sensics. What makes the OSVR unique is that it is an open licensed, non-proprietary hardware platform and ecosystem. This gives developers lots of freedom when designing their AR/VR experiences. OSVR is also a software framework, which we will cover shortly. The framework, like the hardware, is open licence and designed to be cross-platform:

The following are the features of OSVR:

- **Screen type**: AMOLED
- **Resolution**: 960 x 1080 per eye
- **Field of view**: 100^0
- **Head tracking**: IMU (compass, accelerometer, gyroscope), IR optical tracing

The minimum recommended PC specifications are as follows:

- **GPU**: NVIDIA GeForce GTX 970 or AMD Radeon R9 290
- **CPU**: Intel i5-4590 or AMD FX 8350
- **RAM**: 4 GB
- **OS**: Cross-platform support

Sony PlayStation VR

Originally referred to as **Project Morpheus**, the Sony PlayStation VR is the Sony corporation's entry to the VR space. Unlike the other headsets in this list, the Sony PlayStation VR headset is not driven by a PC, but instead connects to the Sony PlayStation 4 gaming console. While not the highest fidelity or most technically advanced, by using the PS4 as its platform, the Sony PlayStation VR headset has a 30 million plus console base available:

The following are the features of Sony PlayStation VR:

- **Screen type**: AMOLED
- **Resolution**: 960 x 1080 per eye
- **Field of view**: ~100^{0}
- **Head tracking**: IMU (compass, accelerometer, gyroscope), IR optical tracing
- **Console hardware**: Sony PlayStation 4

Windows Mixed Reality headsets

One of the newest entries into the VR hardware space is the Windows Mixed Reality enabled group of headsets. While not a single headset design, Windows Mixed Reality has a set of specifications and software support that enables VR from the Windows 10 desktop. Referred to as **Mixed Reality (MR)**, the unique feature of these headsets is their built-in spatial awareness or room sense. Other headsets, such as the Oculus Rift and the HTC Vive, support similar features, but unlike the Windows MR devices, they require extra hardware to support tracking. This lack of extra hardware means that the Windows MR headsets should be simpler to set up and have the potential to make PC-powered VR experiences more portable:

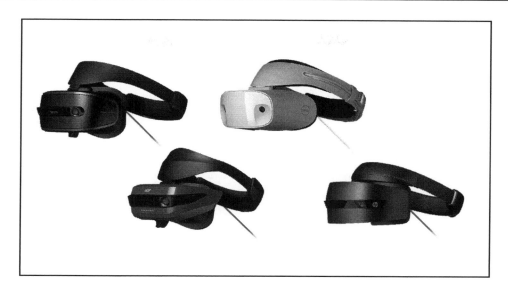

The following are the features of Windows MR headsets:

- **Screen type**: Various
- **Resolution**: Various
- **Field of view**: Various
- **Head tracking**: 9DoF inside out headset-based tracking system

The minimum recommended PC specifications are as follows:

- **GPU**: NVIDIA GeForce GTX 960, AMD Radeon RX 460 or integrated Intel HD Graphics 620
- **CPU**: Intel i5-4590 or AMD FX 8350
- **RAM**: 8 GB
- **OS**: Windows 10

VR rendering concepts

Looking at VR from a rendering point of view, it quickly becomes apparent that VR poses some unique challenges. This is due in part to some necessary performance benchmarks that need to be achieved and the current limitations of rendering hardware. When rendering VR content, it is necessary to render at a higher resolution than standard high definition, often twice or more. The rendering also needs to be extremely quick, with frame rates of 90 fps or higher per eye being the benchmark. This, combined with the use of anti-aliasing and sampling techniques, means that rendering a VR scene requires upwards of five times the computation power of a standard game running at 1080p with 60 fps. In the upcoming sections, we will cover some of the key differences when rendering VR content, and touch on some concepts that you can implement to retain performance.

Working with frusta

The biggest difference when developing a VR ready engine is understanding how to build a proper, clipped, view frustum when dealing with more than one viewpoint. In a typical non-VR game, you have a single view point (camera), from which you create a view frustum. Refer back to earlier in the book if you need a complete refresher, but this view frustum determines what will be rendered and ultimately displayed on screen to the user. The following is a diagram depicting a typical view frustum:

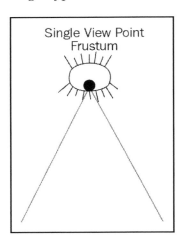

When rendering in VR, you have at least one frustum per eye, commonly displaying to single HMD in stereoscopic, meaning there are a pair of images displayed on a single screen, allowing for the illusion of depth. Often these images are depicting the left and right eye view of the scene. What this means is that we must take into consideration the position of both *eye* frusta and produce a final view frustum for rendering by combining them both. The following is a diagram depiction of these view frusta:

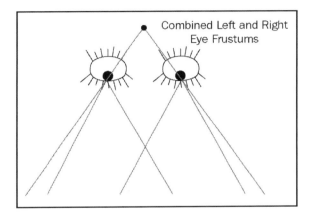

When it comes to the creation of a single frustum that combines both the left and right eye frusta, it is actually quite easy. As depicted in the following diagram, you need to place the vertex of the new frustum between both of the eyes and slightly behind them. You then move the near clipping plane position so that it is aligned with either of the eye frustum's clipping planes. This is important for the final display **frustum culling**:

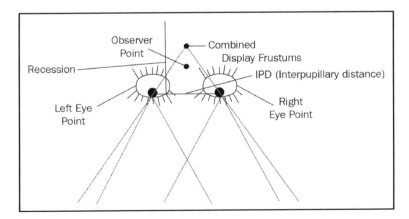

You can calculate this frustum with some simple math using the **interpupillary distance (IPD)**, as demonstrated perfectly in the following diagram by Cass Everitt from the Oculus Rift team:

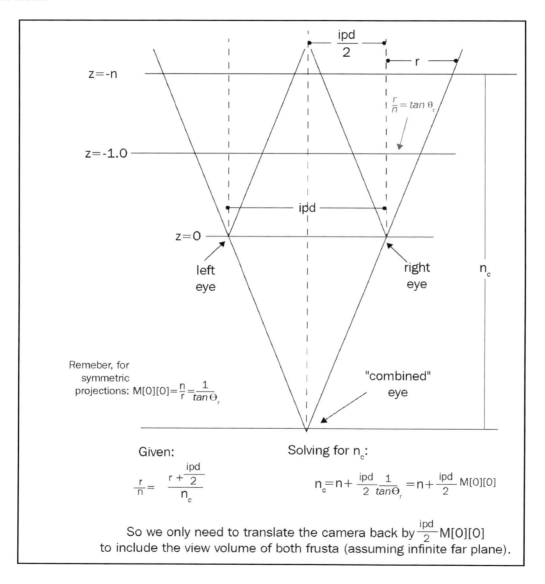

We could also simplify this procedure by simply culling against the shared eye frusta top and bottom planes. While not technically forming a perfect frustum, using a culling algorithm that tests a single plane at a given time will produce the desired effect.

The good news is most of this can be abstracted away, and in many headset SDKs there are methods to help you. It is, however, important to understand the difference between how frusta is used when compared to standard non-VR scene rendering.

Increasing rendering performance

When working with a single camera and view point, as with most non-VR games, we can simply treat the rendering process as one step within our engine. When working with multiple view points, this is different. We could, of course, just treat each view point as a single rendering task, processing one after the other, but this is would result in a slow-performing renderer.

As shown in the previous section, there is quite an overlap between what each *eye* sees. This provides us with the perfect opportunity to optimize our rendering process by sharing and reusing data. To do this, we can implement the concept of **data context**. Using this concept, we can classify which elements exist uniquely for a single eye, and which elements can be shared. Let's take a look at these data contexts and how we can use them to speed up our rendering:

- **Frame context**: Simply put, the frame context is used for any element that needs to be rendered and is view-orientation independent. This would include elements such as skyboxes, global reflections, water textures, and so on. Anything that can be shared across view points can be placed in this context.
- **Eye context**: This is the context for elements that cannot be shared between view points. This would include any element that needs stereo disparity when rendering. It is also in this context that we could store per eye data that would be used in our shader computations.

Using this simple separation of data into different contexts, we could then reorganize our rendering process to look similar to the following:

```
RenderScene(Frame f)
{
  ProcessFrame(f); //Handle any needed globally shared calculations
  RenderFrame(f); //Render any globally shared elements
  for(int i=0; i<numview points; i++) //numview points would be 2 for
stereo
    {
      ProcessEye(i, f); //Handle any per eye needed calculations
      RenderEye(i, f); //Render any per eye elements
    }
}
```

While this appears on the surface to be basic, it is a very powerful concept. By separating the rendering in this manner and sharing what we can, we are greatly increasing the performance of our renderer overall. This is one of the simplest optimizations with one of the biggest returns. We can also carry this over to how we set up our shader uniforms, breaking them into context pieces:

```
layout (binding = 0) uniform FrameContext
{
  Mat4x4 location; //modelview
  Mat4x4 projection;
  Vec3 viewerPosition;
  Vec3 position;
}frame;
layout (binding = 1) uniform EyeContext
{
  Mat4x4 location; //modelview
  Mat4x4 projection;
  Vec3 position;
}eye;
```

This division of data works great from a conceptual point of view, and each of these data pieces can be updated at different times, providing more performance overall.

That basically describes, at a high level, the performant way to handle the rendering of multiple view points for VR. As mentioned before, a large amount of the setup involved with getting the hardware and pipeline connected is abstracted away for us in the SDKs being developed. In the next section, we will look at some of these SDKs, and close out the chapter by looking at the implementation of an SDK in our example engine.

Headset SDKs

There are many SDKs available for implementing the various headsets and supporting hardware, with most manufactures supplying their own in some form. In the upcoming sections, we will quickly look at three of the most commonly used SDKs when developing PC driven HMD VR experiences:

- **Oculus PC SDK** (`https://developer.oculus.com/downloads/package/oculus-sdk-for-windows/`): This SDK was specifically created for use when developing Oculus Rift HMD experiences and games in C++. The core SDK supplies everything developers need to gain access to rendering, tracking, input, and other core hardware functionalities. The core SDK is sublimated by other supporting SDKs for audio, platform, and avatar.

- **OpenVR** (`https://github.com/ValveSoftware/openvr`): This is the SDK provided by the Valve corporation as the default API and runtime for the SteamVR platform. This is also the default SDK for HTC Vive HMD development, but is designed to have multiple vendor support. This means you have the ability to target multiple HMDs without having to know exactly which HMD is connected. This will be the SDK we implement for our example engine.

- **OSVR** (`http://osvr.github.io/`): The OSVR SDK, like its name states, is an open source SDK designed to work with multiple hardware vendors. This SDK is the default SDK for the HMD of the same name, the OSVR headset. The project is spearheaded by Razer and Sensics, with many large gaming partners signing on. The OSVR SDK is available for Microsoft Windows, Linux, Android, and macOS.

Implementing VR support

As with many other systems we have looked at throughout the book, implementing VR support from scratch can be a very challenging and time-consuming process. However, much like those other systems, libraries and SDKs exist to help ease and simplify the process. In the next section, we will cover how we can add VR rendering support to our example engine using the OpenVR SDK provided by the Valve corporation. We will cover only the main points in full. To see a more complete overview of each method, refer to the comments in the example code, and visit the OpenVR SDK Wiki for more SDK-specific information (`https://github.com/ValveSoftware/openvr/wiki`).

Verifying HMD

To start out, we need to do a few things to set up our hardware and environment. We need to first test if a headset is attached to the computer. Then we need check if the OpenVR runtime has been installed. We can then initialize the hardware and finally ask it a few questions about its capability. To do this, we will add some code to our GameplayScreen class; for brevity's sake we will skip over some sections. The full code can be found in the example project in the Chapter11 folder of the code repository.

Let's begin by checking to see if a VR headset has been attached to the computer and if the OpenVR (SteamVR) runtime has been installed. To do this, we will add the following to the Build() method:

```
void GameplayScreen::Build()
{
  if (!vr::VR_IsHmdPresent())
  {
    throw BookEngine::Exception("No HMD attached to the system");
  }
  if (!vr::VR_IsRuntimeInstalled())
  {
    throw BookEngine::Exception("OpenVR Runtime not found");
  }
}
```

Here, we throw an exception to be handled and logged if either of these checks fail. Now that we know we have some hardware and the required software, we can initialize the framework. To do this, we call the InitVR function:

```
InitVR();
```

The InitVR function's main purpose is to, in turn, call the VR_Init method of the OpenVR SDK. In order to do that, it needs to first create and set up an error handler. It will also require us to define what type of application this will be. In our case, we are stating that this will be a scene application, vr::VRApplication_Scene. This means we are creating a 3D application that will be drawing an environment. There are other options, such as creating a utility or overlay only applications. Finally, once we have the HMD initialized, with no errors, we ask the headset to tell us a little about itself. We do this using the GetTrackedDeviceString method that we will look at shortly. The whole InitVR method then looks like the following:

```
void GameplayScreen::InitVR()
{
  vr::EVRInitError err = vr::VRInitError_None;
```

```
m_hmd = vr::VR_Init(&err, vr::VRApplication_Scene);
if (err != vr::VRInitError_None)
{
  HandleVRError(err);
}
std::cout << GetTrackedDeviceString(m_hmd,
vr::k_unTrackedDeviceIndex_Hmd,vr::Prop_TrackingSystemName_String)
<< std::endl;
std::clog << GetTrackedDeviceString(m_hmd,
vr::k_unTrackedDeviceIndex_Hmd, vr::Prop_SerialNumber_String)<<
std::endl;
}
```

The `HandleVRError` method is just a simple helper method that takes the error passed in and throws an error to be handled and logged while providing an English translation of the error being thrown. The following is the method in its entirety:

```
void GameplayScreen::HandleVRError(vr::EVRInitError err)
{
  throw
BookEngine::Exception(vr::VR_GetVRInitErrorAsEnglishDescription(err));
}
```

The other method that the `InitVR` function calls is the `GetTrackedDeviceString` function. This is a function provided as part of the OpenVR example code, which allows us to return some information about the attached device. In our case, we are asking for the system name and the serial number properties, if available, for the attached device:

```
std::string GameplayScreen::GetTrackedDeviceString(vr::IVRSystem * pHmd,
vr::TrackedDeviceIndex_t unDevice, vr::TrackedDeviceProperty prop,
vr::TrackedPropertyError * peError)
{
  uint32_t unRequiredBufferLen = pHmd-
>GetStringTrackedDeviceProperty(unDevice, prop, NULL, 0, peError);
    if (unRequiredBufferLen == 0)
      return "";

  char *pchBuffer = new char[unRequiredBufferLen];
    unRequiredBufferLen = pHmd->GetStringTrackedDeviceProperty(unDevice,
prop, pchBuffer, unRequiredBufferLen, peError);
    std::string sResult = pchBuffer;
    delete[] pchBuffer;
    return sResult;
}
```

Finally, back in our `Build` method, now that we have completed the initialization steps, we can check that all went well by asking the system if the `VRCompositor` function is set to a value other than NULL. If it is, that means everything is ready to go and we can then ask our HMD what it would like our rendering target size to be and display that as a string output in our console window:

```
if (!vr::VRCompositor())
  {
    throw BookEngine::Exception("Unable to initialize VR compositor!\n ");
  }
m_hmd->GetRecommendedRenderTargetSize(&m_VRWidth, &m_VRHeight);

std::cout << "Initialized HMD with suggested render target size : " <<
m_VRWidth << "x" << m_VRHeight << std::endl;
}
```

The last thing we need to do is make sure we clean up on our program's completion. Here, in the `Destroy` method of the `GamplayScreen`, we are first checking to see if the HMD was initialized; if it was we call the `VR_Shutdown` method and set the `m_hmd` variable to NULL. It is very important to call the `VR_Shutdown` on application closing, as if you do not, the OpenVR/SteamVR may hang and could require a reboot before it is operational again:

```
void GameplayScreen::Destroy()
{
    if (m_hmd)
    {
        vr::VR_Shutdown();
        m_hmd = NULL;
    }
}
```

Now if we go ahead and run this example, in the console window you should see something similar to the following:

Rendering

Now that we have the HMD set up and talking with our engine, the next step is to render to it. The process is actually not that complicated; as mentioned before, a great deal is handled for us by the SDK. To keep things as simple as possible, this example is just a simple rendering example. We are not handling head tracking or input, we are simply just going to display a different color in each eye. As with the previous example, in order to save time and space, we are only going to cover the important elements for you to grasp the concept. The full code can be found in the example project in the `Chapter11` folder of the code repository.

As we discussed before, when rendering in stereoscopic, you are often rendering a single display that has been divided in half. We then pass the appropriate data to the half, depending on what is viewable in that eye. Look back to the *Working with frusta* section for a refresher on why this is. What this boils down to is that we need to create a framebuffer for each eye. To do this, we have a `RenderTarget` class that creates the framebuffer, attaches the texture, and finally creates the needed viewport (which is half of the total display width). To save space, I won't print out the `RenderTarget` class; it is fairly straightforward and nothing we haven't seen before. Instead, let's move on to setup and the actual functions that will handle the displaying of the scene in the HMD. To start with, we need to connect our `RenderTarget` to our texture, and for proper implementation clear and set the buffers. To do this we add the following to our `OnEntry` method of `GameplayScreen`:

```
BasicRenderTarget leftRT(1, vrApp.rtWidth, vrApp.rtHeight);
BasicRenderTarget rightRT(1, vrApp.rtWidth, vrApp.rtHeight);

leftRT.Init(leftEyeTexture.name);
rightRT.Init(rightEyeTexture.name);

glClearColor(1.0f, 0.0f, 0.0f, 1.0f);
leftRT.fbo.Bind(GL_FRAMEBUFFER);
glClear(GL_COLOR_BUFFER_BIT | GL_DEPTH_BUFFER_BIT);

if (glCheckFramebufferStatus(GL_FRAMEBUFFER) != GL_FRAMEBUFFER_COMPLETE)
  {
    throw std::runtime_error("left rt incomplete");
  }
glClearColor(0.0f, 1.0f, 0.0f, 1.0f);
rightRT.fbo.Bind(GL_FRAMEBUFFER);
glClear(GL_COLOR_BUFFER_BIT | GL_DEPTH_BUFFER_BIT);
if (glCheckFramebufferStatus(GL_FRAMEBUFFER) != GL_FRAMEBUFFER_COMPLETE)
  {
    throw std::runtime_error("right rt incomplete");
  }
```

```
glBindFramebuffer(GL_FRAMEBUFFER, 0);

glClearColor (0.0f, 0.0f, 1.0f, 1.0f);
```

I will not go through the previous code line by line since we have seen all this done before. Now, with our buffers and textures set, we can move onto adding the drawing call.

The OpenVR SDK provides the needed methods to handle the complex pieces of displaying VR scenes. The majority of this complex work is done by the compositor system. As stated by Valve, *"The compositor simplifies the process of displaying images to the user by taking care of distortion, prediction, synchronization, and other subtle issues that can be a challenge to get operating properly for a solid VR experience."*

To connect to the compositor subsystem, we have created a simple method called SubmitFrames. This method takes three arguments—a texture for each eye and a Boolean value to specify whether the color space should be linear. At the time of writing, we always want to specify that the color space should be Gamma for OpenGL. Inside the method, we get the device we wish to render to, set the color space, convert the texture, and then submit these textures to the VRCompositor, which then, under the hood, handles the displaying of the textures to the correct eye. The entire method looks like the following:

```
void GameplayScreen::SubmitFrames(GLint leftEyeTex, GLint rightEyeTex, bool
linear = false)
{
 if (!m_hmd)
  {
    throw std::runtime_error("Error : presenting frames when VR system
handle is NULL");
  }
  vr::TrackedDevicePose_t trackedDevicePose[vr::k_unMaxTrackedDeviceCount];
  vr::VRCompositor()->WaitGetPoses(trackedDevicePose,
vr::k_unMaxTrackedDeviceCount, nullptr, 0);

  vr::EColorSpace colorSpace = linear ? vr::ColorSpace_Linear :
vr::ColorSpace_Gamma;

  vr::Texture_t leftEyeTexture = { (void*)leftEyeTex,
vr::TextureType_OpenGL, colorSpace };
  vr::Texture_t rightEyeTexture = { (void*)rightEyeTex,
vr::TextureType_OpenGL, colorSpace };

  vr::VRCompositor()->Submit(vr::Eye_Left, &leftEyeTexture);
  vr::VRCompositor()->Submit(vr::Eye_Right, &rightEyeTexture);

  vr::VRCompositor()->PostPresentHandoff();
}
```

With our `SubmitFrames` function in place, we can then call the method form inside of the GameplayScreen update, right after the `glClear` function call:

```
...
glClear(GL_COLOR_BUFFER_BIT);
SubmitFrames(leftEyeTexture.id, rightEyeTexture.id);
```

If you now run the example project, provided you have the necessary SteamVR framework installed, you should see different colors being shown in each eye of the headset.

Summary

While this was a quick introduction to the world of VR development, it should provide you with a great testing bed for your experience ideas. We learned how to handle multiple view frusta, learned about various hardware options, and finally looked at how we could add VR support to our example engine using the OpenVR SDK. As advancements in hardware progress, VR will continue to gain momentum and will continue to push into new fields. Understanding how VR rendering works as a whole provides a new level of depth to your development knowledge pool.

Other Books You May Enjoy

If you enjoyed this book, you may be interested in these other books by Packt:

Beginning C++ Game Programming
John Horton

ISBN: 978-1-78646-619-8

- Get to know C++ from scratch while simultaneously learning game building
- Learn the basics of C++, such as variables, loops, and functions to animate game objects, respond to collisions, keep score, play sound effects, and build your first playable game.
- Use more advanced C++ topics such as classes, inheritance, and references to spawn and control thousands of enemies, shoot with a rapid fire machine gun, and realize random scrolling game-worlds
- Stretch your C++ knowledge beyond the beginner level and use concepts such as pointers, references, and the Standard Template Library to add features like split-screen coop, immersive directional sound, and custom levels loaded from level-design files
- Get ready to go and build your own unique games!

C++ Game Development Cookbook
Druhin Mukherjee

ISBN: 978-1-78588-272-2

- Explore the basics of game development to build great and effective features for your game
- Develop your first text-based game using the various concepts of object-oriented programming
- Use algorithms when developing games with various sorting and searching techniques
- Exploit data structures in a game's development for data storage
- Create your first 2D game using GDI library and sprite sheet.
- Build your first advanced 2D game of space invaders using patterns such as observer, fly-weight, abstract factory, command, state, and more

Leave a review - let other readers know what you think

Please share your thoughts on this book with others by leaving a review on the site that you bought it from. If you purchased the book from Amazon, please leave us an honest review on this book's Amazon page. This is vital so that other potential readers can see and use your unbiased opinion to make purchasing decisions, we can understand what our customers think about our products, and our authors can see your feedback on the title that they have worked with Packt to create. It will only take a few minutes of your time, but is valuable to other potential customers, our authors, and Packt. Thank you!

Index

loop
  working 34, 35, 36
Lua
  about 234, 235, 236
  implementing 236, 237, 238, 239
  reference link 236

M

machine learning (ML) 260
macOS 299
map 27
megabyte (mb) 107
memory construct 20
memory management 20, 21
memory virtualization 21
Mixed Reality (MR) 308
Model View Controller 38
models
  importing 120, 122, 123, 126, 127, 128, 130, 131, 132, 133, 134, 135
motion algorithms
  about 272
  evasion 276, 277
  flee 274
  pursuit 275, 276
  seek 274
  steering behaviors 273
  wandering 277
motion techniques 272
multiple inheritance 12

N

name collisions 9
namespaces
  working 9, 10
Natural Language Processing (NLP) 259
normalized device space 148

O

Oculus PC SDK
  reference link 315
Oculus Rift CV1
  about 305
  features 305

Open Source Virtual Reality (OSVR) development kit
  about 307
  features 307
OpenGL Architecture Review Board (OpenGL ARB) 194
OpenGL Mathematics (GLM) 88
OpenVR
  reference link 315
oriented bounding boxes (OBBs) 155
OSVR
  reference link 315
Overseer 38

P

parent hierarchy 11
pathfinding techniques 272, 277, 278
Per-fragment Phong interpolation 219, 220, 221
Per-vertex ambient 214, 215, 216, 218
Per-vertex diffuse 210, 211, 214, 215, 216, 218
Per-vertex specular 214, 215, 216, 218
Phong reflection model 214
physics
  Bullet physics library, implementing 158, 163
  point, in AABB 153
  sphere, to sphere 156
  working 153
point
  AABB, to AABB 154
  in AABB 153
pointers
  about 15, 16
  shared_ptr 16, 17
  unique_ptr 16, 17
polymorphism 10, 11, 12, 13
Portable Network Graphics (PNG) 116
positioning 166, 167, 169, 171, 172, 175
Project Morpheus 308

Q

quest objects
  description 251
  objectives 251
  quest giver 251

quest name 251
reward(s) 251
quest
engine support 252
engine/script bridge 253
script-based system 253
scripting 250, 251

R

referencing 15, 16
rendering 319
rendering performance
increasing 313, 314
resource manager 113
Run-time type information (RTTI) 39

S

scripting language
about 232, 233
implementing 231
search algorithm
A* algorithm 281
about 277, 278
search algorithms
breadth first 278, 279, 280
Dijkstra's algorithm 280
Seek Path 274
sequence containers 24
shader
about 193
C for graphics (Cg) 194
data, working 203, 204, 205, 207, 208
fragments, discarding 222, 224
High-Level Shading Language (HLSL) 194
languages 194
OpenGL Shading Language (GLSL) 194
particles, generating 225, 226, 228, 229
program infrastructure, building 194, 195, 196, 197, 198, 201, 203
used, for creating lighting effects 222
Single Instruction, Multiple Data (SIMD) 162
six degrees of freedom (6DOF) 304
Sony PlayStation VR
about 308

features 308
source libraries 54, 55
sphere
to sphere 156
Standard Template Library (STL) 24, 43
state machines 36, 37, 38
state pattern 36
states
about 138
cameras, working 143, 144, 146, 147, 149, 150, 151
statically linked libraries
about 45
on macOS X 47, 48
on Windows 45, 46, 47
Steam gaming platform 305
STL generic containers 24

T

TCP server
creating 296
macOS 299
Windows 296
templating
about 28
class templates 28, 29
function templates 30
variable templates 30
texture
about 114
resource manager 112
working 112
TextureCache 114
type interference
about 31, 32, 33, 34
using 31, 32, 33, 34
types
working 24

U

Uniform Cost Search 280

Printed in Great Britain
by Amazon